Praise for The Calling Journey

"You rocked my world—and nailed my middle age. This addresses the culmination of my journey— stepping up and risking my future on God's identity. [I must] give up my illusion of myself as still having enough game to run with the entrepreneurial crowd and risk who I am on God working through me as a coach/chair for Convene. I cannot find any convenient mental myths that allow me to dismiss the reality of taking the risk to do what God has called me to do. Thank you, friend!!"

Steve Tucker, Convene Chair

"I cried the first time I saw my life on The Calling Journey *timeline. The visual made it undeniable that God has orchestrated seasons and experiences to shape my life for others. It put events and seasons of life in perspective. What I'd thought was senseless suffering and failure was actually His way of making me the man I was born to be so that I could do the task I was born to do. Thank you!"*

Jeff Williams, Grace and Truth Relationship Education

"[The Calling Journey] gave me incredible insights into my life which allowed me to understand more of who God is and how He works. Thank you, Tony."

Lisa Schultz, Office of the Senate Chaplain

"[The timeline] has brought great encouragement to me that nothing is wasted in God's economy … It has inspired a new sense of hope to see the mighty hand of my loving heavenly Father through it all… I am thankful to Kathy and Tony for being there during a deep valley where nothing made sense. We came back out with a much different view and were even thankful for it all! I look forward to the next peak, and I'm not afraid of the journey it will take to get there."

Amy Heilman, Mother

"The timeline that Tony presents is amazing. It helped me to understand so many things and make sense of why the Lord takes us through the things He does."

Raeann Fitz, Certified Life Coach

"The Calling Journey timeline is a fantastic visual tool to use with people in helping them understand the season they are in. Tony makes it so easy for people to grasp where they are on their calling journey and thus respond in the best way possible."

Janine Mason, Dreamvesting

"As one who has often struggled to make sense of the many twists and turns of my life, The Calling Journey *helped me to see these events from the larger vantage point of God's purposes … one of the greatest truths that emerges is that, through all the ups and downs of our life, God's primary focus is on the shaping of who we are in preparation for what he has called us to do."*

David Smith, Businessman

Also by Tony Stoltzfus ...

A Leader's Life Purpose Workbook: Calling and Destiny Discovery Tools for Christian Leaders
Christian Life Coaching Handbook: Calling and Destiny Discovery Tools for Christian Life Coaching
Leadership Coaching: The Disciplines, Skills and Heart of a Christian Coach
Coaching Questions: A Coach's Guide to Powerful Asking Skills
Peer Coach Training Facilitator's Guide
Peer Coach Training Workbook

Available at www.Coach22.com

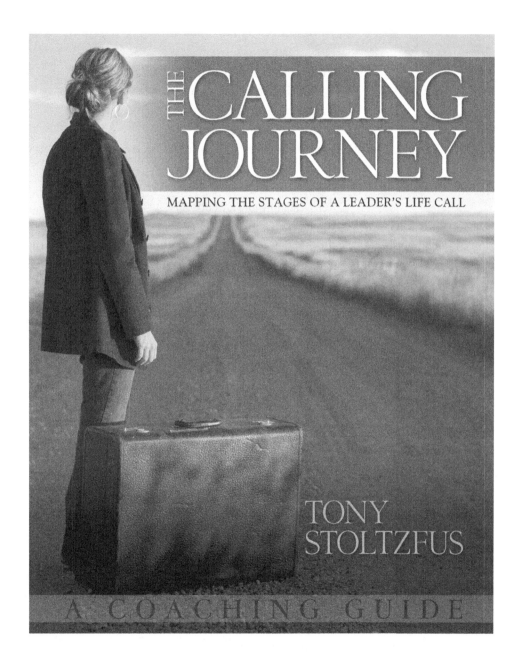

THE CALLING JOURNEY

MAPPING THE STAGES OF A LEADER'S LIFE CALL

TONY STOLTZFUS

A COACHING GUIDE

Cover Design by Mark Neubauer

Some of the anecdotal illustrations in this book are true to life, and are included with the permission of the persons involved. All other illustrations are composites where names and details have been changed. Any resemblance to persons living or dead is coincidental.

Unless otherwise identified, all Scripture quotations in this book are taken from the New American Standard Bible, Copyright © 1960, 1962, 1963, 1968, 1971, 1972, 1973, 1975, 1977, 1995 by The Lockman Foundation. Used by permission.

Scripture quotations denoted "RSV" are taken from the Revised Standard Version of the Bible, copyright 1952 [2nd edition, 1971] by the Division of Christian Education of the National Council of the Churches of Christ in the United States of America. Used by permission. All rights reserved.

Scripture quotations denoted as "MSG" are taken from *The Message*. Copyright 1993, 1994, 1995, 1996, 2000, 2001, 2002. Used by permission of NavPress Publishing Group.

To order copies of this book
and other coaching
materials, visit
www.Coach22.com
or phone 877-427-1645.

Table of Contents

INTRODUCTION

Out of all the several dozen leaders I interviewed for this book, Greg seemed to have travelled his calling journey exceptionally well. Raised in a dysfunctional home—he took out a life insurance policy on himself when he was 17, thinking he wouldn't live to see 20—Greg came to Christ in the midst of a drinking binge while throwing up in a toilet. Since then, he's been moving steadily onward through the calling stages toward God's big dream for him. I was particularly struck by how successfully Greg navigated the key transitions of his calling journey. He seemed to have gotten the lessons of those times with much less pain and dislocation than I (and others I studied) had experienced.

When asked to what he attributed his success as a journeyer, he replied:

> *"I always kept in touch with leaders that were farther along than me—at least ten years farther down the road—so I never went through these situations alone. When things got difficult I would go to them for help and insight."*

Greg had stumbled upon an important principle that sums up the purpose of this book: *Those who journey with the perspective of fellow travelers travel well.* My purpose in writing is to offer a perspective that will speed your journey and reduce the self-inflicted pain you might experience along the road.

While you cannot know exactly what life will bring, the future is not a complete mystery. God is in it, working out his plan to develop you as a leader. That plan includes predictable developmental stages all leaders walk through and surprisingly universal valley seasons when God focuses on claiming our hearts. While the specific details of each person's life are unique, the larger patterns are common to leaders who walk with God. In other words, God has you on a developmental timeline. And having perspective on this larger plan can be the difference between leaning into what God is doing in you or fighting against it.

The Value of a Timeline

It always makes me a little nervous to travel without a road map. Turn-by-turn directions don't do it for me: I want to visualize where I am going. Once I can see the route and where the important turns are in my mind, I am much more confident that I won't get lost.

This book shows you how to create a personalized map of the journey to your own calling: a Calling Timeline. By looking at the timelines of fellow travelers, you'll get a big-picture view of the road you are taking. Comparing your story to theirs will offer amazing insights into how different events in your life fit into God's plan for your development, in the same way that a road map lets you visualize the twists and turns on a cross-country trip.

The first thing you'll probably notice about the timeline is how bumpy and windy the road is. This map is very different from popular images of "following your call." The glamorous journey we imagine our heroes traveled—an ever-onward-and-upward path that, if we make the right choices, leads in a few short years to our full release—exists mostly in our imagination. The actual road is anything but straight, and it takes decades to walk it. Wilderness seasons, valleys, even being ejected from long-time roles are as much a part of the journey as great victories, golden opportunities and demonstrations of God's power.

This gap, between the road we expect and the one we eventually travel, is the source of a great deal of angst. Much of the pain and frustration of the calling journey is not so much from the actual heart surgery God does in us as it is from our fear of the operating table. We never imagined God would take us down such a path, and so we go kicking and screaming to the fulfilling of our call.

Last week I had a coaching session with a senior leader who was in the Valley of Identity[1]. God leverages this late-life wilderness season to help us fully embrace our calling identity, while at the same time teaching us to let our call go and find life in Him alone. It was a difficult time for this pastor: unable to find work for nearly a year, he was about to lose his home to foreclosure. Even more, he feared he'd lose the respect of his peers, become unemployable and literally end up on the street, homeless. He was asking himself painful questions: "Where is God in all this? Why hasn't he come through for me? What am I doing wrong?"

A few days after he shifted his focus from job-hunting to exploring what God was doing in his heart, God spoke to him about the control issues in his life (while he was counseling another person about her control issues!) and he had a significant breakthrough. My friend responded by placing his situation in God's hands, letting go of trying to make something happen and actively resting in where God had placed him. By the end of the week, he had a job and was able to renegotiate with the bank to save his house.

How you interpret this story depends on how you think God deals with us. Was my friend walking in disobedience for a year, only seeing his prayers answered when he finally repented and aligned with God's will? Was he just so hard of hearing on this issue that it took a year for God to get through to him?

---

1   Appendix A contains a glossary with definitions for the special terms used in *The Calling Journey*.

Or did God take him to the limit of losing everything just to "test his faith?"

That's not what this map shows us. The Calling Journey is not about how we fall short, but about the revelation of who our Father is to us. In our successes, he is revealed as the one who believes in us, treats us as partners and wants to tackle the job together with us. In our sufferings and failings, he makes himself known as the Great Redeemer. He is the only one who can take whatever life throws at us (including our mistakes and failures) and so completely transform it that even what seemed intended for evil is woven seamlessly into the flawless fabric of his good purposes.

In the Calling Journey, we don't interpret a story like this in terms of God's disfavor or our disobedience. Instead, we see God working to redeem the fallout of living in a broken world. He does not send financial distress or painful circumstances to his children, yet neither does he always save us out of them. Rather, he co-opts them, employing adversity to form us in ways that bring great good into our lives and the world. "Filling up the sufferings of Christ" refers to our participation in this redemptive process. The power of Jesus' resurrection invades this fallen world by redeeming our sufferings, bringing joy from sorrow, growth from pain and life from death. Adversity in a Christian's life is not the sign of God's anger, or our sin, or even our human frailty, but a giant advertisement of how the Great Redeemer turns mourning into dancing.

I've coached hundreds of senior ministry and business leaders, and time and again, seeing life in terms of this journey is one of the greatest gifts I have to give. Through this book I'd like to share that perspective with you. We'll get to know Jesus, the Great Redeemer and master developer of leaders. As you learn more about his ways, you'll find amazing parallels between your life story and the stories of others. You'll probably find that you are more in the center of God's will for your life than you ever realized or dared believe, and that the God you serve is so astonishingly prescient that he has already incorporated your failings and weaknesses into the plan.

Understanding the calling journey lets you take your hands off the wheel, knowing that in success or failure, expansion or demotion, dryness or overflow, Jesus is steering you through exactly the experiences you need to do what you were born to do. What a relief to paranoid travelers like me!

The Development of the Timeline Model

I began exploring the Calling Timeline model a decade ago through studying the life stories of biblical leaders. The first application I made was to my own life. It brought tremendous perspective to my wilderness years of Outside Preparation, and to the Releasing stage I was going through. Over the last ten years I've used it repeatedly with the ministry and business leaders I've coached and trained, often to great effect. Finally, during the writing of this book I undertook 40 in-depth interviews (and numerous informal ones) with contemporary leaders of all ages and vocations. For each of those leaders I constructed a timeline to help flesh out the model. While the research process has led to some significant additions to the model, the basic framework developed from the lives of Abraham, Joseph, Moses, David and Jesus remains at its core.

Because this is an attempt to create an ideal model of a calling timeline, I chose to interview people who seemed fairly on track in their call. I have not focused on the ways we can go awry, or examined cases where a person has fallen away from God, given up on a call or chosen not to follow it. Since this model starts with a Lordship decision to follow Christ, I have targeted individuals who made that commitment as interview subjects.

The timeline model addresses the developmental *process* of becoming who you are called to be. Figuring out what your calling actually is in the first place is covered in the companion volume, *A Leader's Life Purpose Workbook.* It contains over 60 discovery exercises you can use to identify your passions, dreams, values and strengths, discover who you are called to serve, develop a life mission statement and more.

If your interest lies in coaching or training others to find and follow their life call, a third book in the set, the *Christian Life Coaching Handbook,* provides sample dialogs, coaching questions, examples and techniques for coaching others to discover or clarify their call. If you are would like to offer calling discovery experiences for groups, the necessary workshop materials and PowerPoint presentations are also available through www.Coach22.com.

The Destiny Challenge

The thing that has most deeply impacted me through working with calling timelines is the amazing, unstoppable hand of God, moving his leaders toward their callings. I've listened to men and women who have contemplated suicide, had moral failures, shuttered businesses, endured divorces, shut down emotionally for years, run from God—about anything you can do to miss the mark. Still, their lives continue to move through the calling stages as Father's relentless gentleness overwhelms their failings to fulfill his purpose. Once you make Jesus Lord of your life, unless you tell him to stop, he *will* get you to your destination.

Hear a story of God's faithfulness in a leader's life, and it's a compelling tale. Hear 30 or 40 of them in a row, and a window opens onto the extraordinarily complex dance of God with the human will. No one but God could have pulled this off; none but him would think to walk in a way that is so mysterious and at the same time so manifest. It's pretty cool.

So as you read and work on your own timeline, tune into this mysterious, manifest God who gets a kick out of revealing himself in the most counter-intuitive ways. That's what the journey is about, really—the chance to travel together with Jesus and share your vocation with him. Enjoy the journey!

1: JOSEPH'S CALLING JOURNEY

Today, and every day, you are on a journey. God is moving you through a well-defined process to prepare you to be who you were made to be and do what you were born to do. Whether you are in business, politics, ministry, or any other vocation, the path is essentially the same.

The object of this book is to give you a map for the great adventure of living your God-given call. This map can help you understand the seasons and transitions of your life, why you go through them and how to meet God in them. Since this map was developed from the life stories of many leaders, the best way to introduce it is through a story.

We'll start with the tale of a fellow traveler—a business and political leader who journeyed well and left a legacy of insight into the ways of God for us all. Through his life story, we'll begin to discover the critical valleys and growth stages we go through on the road to our destiny.

The Calling Journey begins when we accept God's call and put him in charge of our lives.

Born in Palestine around 4000 years ago, Joseph is the second youngest in a fractured family torn by two wives battling for a husband and a dozen sons yearning for a father's attention most never receive. In spite of all that, Joseph is singled out as the favorite. He gets special clothes, special assignments and special attention—and his overlooked siblings despise him for it.

But more than that, he is the favored son in a family with a special generational calling. God had revealed to Joseph's great-grandfather that this family would become a great nation, his own covenant people. From a young age, Joseph knew that he was part of something big.

But the dreamer in him wanted to be more than merely an eleventh son in a culture where everyone assumed the eldest would be the heir. Joseph knew his father Jacob was younger than Esau, and yet had received the birthright and the blessing. His grandfather Isaac was the younger son, but God had preferred him over Ishmael. *"If God is in the habit of choosing a younger son for his promised line,"* Joseph thought, *"Why wouldn't he choose me?"*

Embracing the notion that he has a call during his teen years launches Joseph into the first stage of his calling journey, the season of *Natural Promotion*[2]. His father favors him, placing him in the position of reporting on his brothers and giving him a special multi-hued tunic. While his brothers are off herding the sheep, he gets to hang out with dad. In this time of growth and expansion, Joseph discovers he has a gift with prophetic dreams, and begins to practice functioning in it. That special talent offers a window into Joseph's God-given destiny.

*The journey's first stage is **Natural Promotion**, when God's grace on our natural gifts produces a rapid ascent.*

While this early season of favor and functioning is part of God's plan, it is also painfully evident that Joseph isn't ready. He has a prophetic gift from God, natural leadership ability and a call to lead, but he also has the petulant arrogance of a 17-year-old pretty boy whose dad thinks he can do no wrong. Lacking any ability to see the situation from his brothers' perspective, or the character to give them the honor they deserve, he blurts out his proud dreams of lording over them.

In Natural Promotion, we have the innate abilities for our call but not the character.

His brothers are livid. In a final blunder, Joseph has the hubris to stand before the whole family and claim his parents will bow to him, a cultural faux pas that earns him a public rebuke from his father. His brothers, emboldened by seeing dad finally stand up to the little tattle-tale, claim their revenge by faking Joseph's death and selling him into slavery. Like many of us at this point in life, Joseph's own arrogance is part of what leads him down off the mountain of Natural Promotion and into the wilderness with God.

Natural Promotion is followed by a valley season, where our lack of inner formation catches up to us.

Just as his upward ascent seemed to have him on the fast track to his call, Joseph's subsequent descent into the *Valley of Dependence* put him on a down-elevator to a brutal obscurity. Stripped of his special robe, his favored position, his rights and his future, Joseph is carried off to Egypt by Midianite traders. Several weeks later he is resold to Potiphar, an Egyptian captain of the guard. Thoughts of survival replace dreams of grandeur. Lost in a strange culture with strange gods and an unknown language, forced to do the dirty work he had always looked down on, Joseph has nothing to cling to but God.

*Sometimes our own hubris is what triggers our descent into the **Valley of Dependence.***

Through this first Valley we discover that even a divine calling, great abilities and a supernatural gift are not enough. There is a long journey ahead before

---

2   A list of each stage and its primary characteristics is found in Appendix B.

Joseph's dreams come true, and the once-clear road to his destiny is now hidden.

The Valley of Dependence teaches reliance on God instead of on natural abilities.

Down in the pit of the Valley of Dependence, the part of the human soul that craves self-sufficiency and having life under control is dealt a mortal blow. Up to this point Joseph is the one pulling the strings, playing the system and planning out his own future. But now there are no strings left to pull. Staring glumly at a once-bright future that lies dying in the Egyptian dirt, Joseph faces a universal choice: *Who do I trust for my future?* Do I grip tighter to my own abilities and believe that it depends on me to make my dreams happen? Do I let go and somehow trust God to do it all on his own, even though he seems absent and gives me no assurances? Or do I stop hoping at all to protect myself from disappointment, and reconcile myself to living an insignificant life?

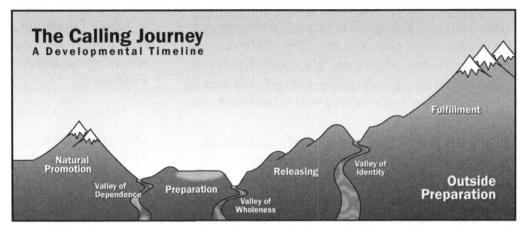

This map shows the Four Stages of calling (Natural Promotion, Preparation, Releasing and Fulfillment) and three critical Valleys leaders pass through on the calling journey.

Joseph did not give up hope (although there was probably a lot of sniveling and whining on that caravan trip to Egypt!). With the choice to cling to the God of his fathers, dependence on God replaces his previous posture of entitlement and self-sufficiency.

As Joseph learns to embrace his circumstances and let go of the life he once thought he deserved, God's favor and blessing launch a second period of upward promotion in his life. His years in this *Preparation* stage are a time where Joseph learns the practical disciplines of successful leadership. Eventually, his management abilities gain him a position over all of Potiphar's household. Finally, his life seems at least somewhat back on track.

*When we let go and allow God to lead us his way, he moves us into the next stage, **Preparation**.*

The Preparation stage is about developing the skills and experience needed for our call.

While his sphere of influence and responsibility is increasing, this period of Joseph's life is more about learning to lead than actually accomplishing his calling. Joseph develops skills that will someday be vital to his destiny role: managing a household, leading a staff, the culture and language, and how to do business with upper-class Egyptians. The formerly-pampered golden child is becoming a man of such utter dependability, trustworthiness and integrity that Potiphar doesn't feel any need to check up on him.

In the midst of all that was going well, Joseph still recalls his dreams. I imagine they were both a comfort and a sorrow to him. While the Preparation season is one of growth, Joseph probably does not experience it as a time of great significance and fulfillment. Like Joseph, leaders must learn to live in the tension of hope: maintaining the belief that a great dream awaits us, while often seeing little evidence that we are any closer to it than we were a year ago.

We live in tension in the Preparation stage, knowing that we are called but we are not yet released into that call.

Interestingly, the next test comes at a point of Joseph's strength. Potiphar's wife attempts to seduce Joseph, and then, spurned, accuses her husband's trusted right-hand man of attempting to rape her. Furious, Potiphar ships him off to prison.

·This second difficult season strips Joseph yet again. Once more, he must deal with betrayal—and by a master he had served flawlessly, whom God had blessed through the sweat of his own brow! The man's wife is his for the taking, but out of respect for God and his master Joseph refuses—and yet pays the penalty of disobedience all the same.

*Joseph is betrayed a second time. Unusual patterns of God's processing develop powerful **Life Messages** that form the core of our being call.*

Many things that look unjust or unfair from a human point of view become clearer when looking from God's perspective. In God's economy, getting Joseph back out of prison isn't a problem. In fact, the plan to do just that is already under way. The real question is, will Joseph himself be ready for what God wants to give him on the day he is released? We tend to focus on external circumstances that God has well in hand, while God concentrates on the real tipping point: our hearts.

At this point in the journey, *God is less concerned with where Joseph is and what job he is doing than with what type of man he is becoming.* He needs a man who can wield great power under Pharaoh and yet not be perceived as a threat or a potential rival. He is building a man who is utterly dependable, stellar in character, a skillful leader and manager. To fulfill his destiny, Joseph must be able to confidently take charge of the Egyptian economy, all the while knowing he is totally expendable. As a foreigner and former slave, he will certainly be Pharaoh's fall guy if things don't turn out as he has foretold. God is creating a man so secure in divine favor that he does not fear walking into a political dogfight with no power base, no influential friends, at the mercy of Pharaoh's whim—because he knows that no matter what happens, God is with him. Going to prison plays a vital part in making Joseph that man.

On the calling journey, we tend to focus on being in the right place at the right time, while God is concerned with the state of our heart.

By looking at how God is preparing us, we can predict how he will use us in the future.

But God's plan for Joseph's destiny reaches to a deeper, unforeseen level. Joseph's calling is not about success as a leader in Egypt, but healing and preservation for his estranged family. His story includes repeated loss and

*Joseph goes through the Preparation stage outside of his area of call, laboring in Potiphar's house and prison. This pattern is called "**Outside Preparation**".*

*Joseph has a **False Opportunity** to finagle his way out of prison. This disappointment leads him into the **Valley of Wholeness**.*

*The **Day of Release** is a sudden change God brings about to move leaders in Outside Preparation into their area of calling.*

elevation, betrayal and favor because reconciling with his family will require a great trust in a God who is bigger than betrayal and who works everything for good.

Although unjustly imprisoned, Joseph is soon back on the leadership track, doing for the prison warden what he had done for Potiphar: managing things so well the warden didn't have a care in the world. Joseph is learning that no matter where he goes, the favor and blessing of God go with him. But his Preparation season includes one more trying test before his release.

On a morning like any other in the bowels of a dirty prison, Pharaoh's disgraced butler and baker are disquieted by their dreams. Joseph's response tells a little of how far he has come: "Do not interpretations come from God? Tell it to me, please." The dream realm now belongs to God and not to Joseph.

But his self-will—the longing to be in charge of his own future—has one dying gasp left. "Please do me a kindness by mentioning me to Pharaoh and get me out of this house," Joseph plaintively requests (Gen. 40:14). The flame of that human desire to scheme our way into our calling instead of being content with the season God has ordained still flickers dimly. But God has a ready antidote. The butler promptly forgets, and two more years pass—two years in which the smoldering ember of Joseph's fleshly ambition is finally snuffed out.

Then, without warning, 13 years after he was sold into slavery, Joseph's *Day of Release* comes. A hurried summons, a quick shave and a haircut, and Joseph is brought to the palace to make sense of Pharaoh's enigmatic dream. Navigating this transition requires a huge risk on Joseph's part. After years of being hidden away in a small place of limited influence, Joseph must believe in what God has formed in him: that he has what it takes to function on a national scale.

He could have shrunk back from the risk and stayed in prison. Instead, Joseph takes up the challenges, interprets the dream, and so impresses Pharaoh with his wisdom and confidence that he is handed the reins to the Egyptian economy. Most astonishing, however, is that Pharaoh does not seem threatened or put off in the least by Joseph. What a contrast from the self-important son of Jacob we first met! Joseph is truly a different man.

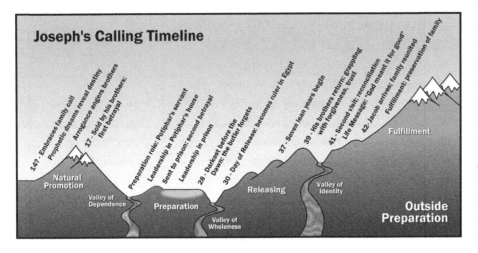

Interpreting the Original Dream

At 30 years old, after 13 years of Preparation, Joseph enters his *Releasing Stage*. God places him into large-sphere leadership over a nation, a position he seems to hold for the rest of his life. If calling is understood as an outward role to fill or a task to do, this day would be where Joseph 'moves into his calling.'

But that's not where the Calling Journey map leads. In this model, *the heart of the call is not doing a task or role, but being your Life Message through that role.* Joseph's vocation as a ruler in Egypt is only a vehicle for his true calling—a unique Message about the identity of God that is written on his heart by the life he has lived. In other words, Joseph's legacy has less to do with his accomplishments as an Egyptian leader than with how the story of his life reveals God to us. So although he has entered into a portion of his destiny role as a ruler of Egypt, that position will remain only an apprenticeship until the Message God is imprinting on his heart is fully formed.

Seeing our call in 'being' terms is sort of a fuzzy concept, so let's follow it through in Joseph's story. Joseph is out of prison. He is functioning in a role that fits his gifts and abilities, has the favor of the ruler, has great power and is doing significant work. He has returned to the role of favorite son (with Pharaoh), but this time without the arrogance that had so stirred up his brothers against him. He has a home, a wife and two sons, financial security, and the respect of his peers—especially when the famine starts and Joseph's foresight proves correct! At last, Joseph is really living the good life and enjoying God's favor.

The most poignant sign of his frame of mind is the names he bestows on his two boys. The first is named Manasseh ("Making to Forget"), because "God has made me forget all my troubles and all my father's household." The second he calls Ephraim ("Fruitfulness"), for "God has made me fruitful in the land of my affliction" (Gen. 42:51). These names show us how Joseph is dealing with the dissonance between his original dreams and his reality. At this point in life, Joseph sees his family background as something to forget. He seems to believe time will heal the wounds of his betrayal and suffering, and that what God has for him is favor and contentment outside the destiny of his family of origin.

But the call Joseph received as a teenager was not about Egypt: it was about Israel—his family. It would take a third major upheaval, the *Valley of Identity*, to fully form the Message God still speaks through Joseph's story 200 generations later. So in the fullness of time, nine years after his release from prison, 22 years after he was sold as a slave, out of the fog of forgetfulness, Joseph's brothers show up and throw his heart into chaos.

The Return of Joseph's Brothers

Joseph's harsh reaction to his siblings' reappearance reveals the wound still

*The **Releasing Stage** is an apprenticeship to your call, where you function in your calling but in a limited way.*

*The heart of calling is not **doing** a task, but **being** your Life Message through that task.*

As the years lengthen between calling and fulfillment, a temptation you may face is to lose hope that God will perform exactly what he has promised.

*The **Valley of Identity** is a third period of adversity where your Life Messages take mature form.*

buried inside. *"My brother Simeon, who threw me down a well, now wants* **my** *help? Judah, the one who would sell me off like cattle to salve his own conscience, wants* **my** *favor?"*

Now, at last, the tables are turned! Where once his brothers had the power of numbers, Joseph now wields the power of kings. One word and he can send them all to prison, just as they sent him. One word is all it would take to sell them as slaves, like they sold him. One word!

Then Joseph remembers his dreams: the almost-forgotten calling of his youth, where his family circled around and bowed to him. Imagine the inner turmoil as the door to his family, bolted and barricaded for all these years, finally cracks open. The pain of revisiting his past forces Joseph to re-evaluate the meaning of his life story. And rethinking your story means re-forming your identity.

"Who am I?" Joseph might have asked. *"Am I the slave of Egypt, who through the favor of God on my ability overcame every adversity and rose to be ruler of the nation? Is the meaning of my life that rags-to-riches story? Or is my story about what goes around comes around—that I can take vengeance and disown those who disowned me?"*

"Maybe instead I am still the favored younger son of Israel that I used to be, destined to rejoin my dysfunctional family and become dependent on dad's favor like before."

"Or is there something more? Am I a man of purpose, sent here to Egypt by God for… what? God, why am I really here? Is all this part of your plan? And if this is your will, how could you be working through something as horrible as betrayal, slavery and imprisonment?"

This inner identity struggle surfaces in the story of Joseph's reconciliation with his brothers (Gen. 42). At first, he reacts out of hurt, calling them liars and, when they do lie to him by claiming he was dead, throwing them all in prison. It seems as if the vengeance story line is getting the upper hand in Joseph's identity. But then God begins dealing with him. Three days later he releases his brothers from jail and gives them a chance to show that they'd really changed.

When Joseph overhears them discussing their guilt and God's judgment, he is reduced to tears. At that moment, Joseph first sees the possibility of real reconciliation, and the yearning to return to his family is rekindled. Entertaining the idea of coming home forces him to grapple with all the injustice he'd faced in a new light. *"If my story is about coming home, where is God in it? Is what I've gone through somehow a part of his purpose?"*

But even if God is in this, the matter of trust remains. Until the betrayal is addressed, a new relationship cannot flower. Joseph needs to hear that his half-brothers are truly repentant (and not just feeling bad about the consequences)

This valley is about identity: who you are and what your life story really means.

The **Life Message** *(the unique way you are called to incarnate Christ) that is the heart of your calling is most deeply formed in the identity struggles of the three valleys.*

for what they had done to him before he could risk opening his heart to them again.

He is also anxious about his blood brother Benjamin's fate. *"Where is he? Why isn't he here with the rest of his brothers? Did they do the same thing to him that they did to me?"* Trusting God to make use of a betrayal for his purposes is one thing: trusting the betrayers is another issue all together!

Fulfillment

The key that unlocks both the Releasing and Fulfillment stages tends to be taking a great risk for the sake of your call. Joseph's first great risk (launching his Releasing stage) is stepping up to interpret Pharaoh's dream. Re-opening the door to family is the second. The decision hangs in the balance for over a year. It is only when Judah (the same one who suggested selling Joseph to the traders) offers to give his own life in ransom for Benjamin's that the walls in Joseph's heart come crashing down and he re-embraces his family and his heritage. At this moment, Joseph reenters the family calling and fully takes on the mantle of his calling identity: to be the one who preserves the life of his family and heals the division between the sons of Rachael and Leah that threatens to tear it apart. It is at this point that his Valley of Identity comes to an end.

There is a brief *Interlude* while Jacob brings the whole clan to Israel, comes before Pharaoh, and settles in the land of Goshen. Then Joseph moves into his *Fulfillment* stage, where he functions in his convergent role as both a ruler in Egypt and a protector and provider for his family.

The Valley of Identity is what brings Joseph's Life Message to full fruit. He expresses it best years later when his father Jacob is near death. His brothers fear that once their father is gone, Joseph will turn on them and finally take his revenge. Hearing their pleas, Joseph is reduced again to tears, deeply grieved that they still do not know who he is nor understand the meaning of his life story. His reply rings down to us through the centuries, alive with the power of God: "Do not be afraid … You meant evil against me, but God meant it for good..."

*Entering the latter stages requires a **Big Risk** where you make a big bet on the reality of your call and your ability to fulfill it.*

*Sometimes those who go through Outside Preparation experience a brief **Interlude** between the Valley of Identity and Fulfillment.*

*When you enter into the **Fulfillment** of your call, you can honestly say, "Everything I've been through in life prepared me for this."*

God meant it for good. That's Joseph's calling: to incarnate this Message through his life story and pass it on to others. This verse is the core of God's unique revelation through Joseph's life.

Joseph did not simply complete a task by being reconciled to his family. In the middle of that struggle, he won an incredible revelation of the identity of God. Joseph got to know a God who redeems everything; who is so good and so sovereign that he can take the worst life throws at you and turn it into good. By

> **Joseph's Life Message**
> *"You meant evil against me, **but God meant it for good**… to preserve many people alive."*

internalizing that God-identity and living it out with his family, it became his Life Message. The outward role of ruler was not Joseph's call so much as it was the channel through which his calling Message was expressed.

That distinction is at the heart of our calling model: that your call is to *be* a Message *through* a role. Another way to look at this concept is through the lens of legacy. Joseph's primary legacy is not found in his leadership task (managing a famine in Egypt). He still impacts us 4000 years later by embodying that amazing part of God that makes all things in life turn out for good for those who love him and are called according to his purposes. We see that God in Joseph; and revealing *that* God is his call.

Joseph's life story demonstrates how our timeline unfolds. The Calling Journey is the well-defined path of stages and valleys leaders travel on the way to fulfilling their call. The diagram on the following page is our standard map[3] of the journey, with key points labeled to correspond with Joseph's life history. This timeline measures our sense at the time of whether we are moving toward or away from our calling. Let's briefly work through Joseph's story again to explain the timeline.

From early in life, Joseph embraced the destiny passed down through the generations of his family line. A timeline begins when a person fully embraces his or her place in the general calling to live as a part of God's Kingdom. For us, that means the starting point of the timeline is the **Lordship Decision** when we make Jesus master of our choices as well as Savior, and embrace his design for our destiny.

That commitment is followed by a season of **Natural Promotion**. Here Joseph experienced God's favor and anointing flowing through his natural character (or lack thereof!) and abilities. It's as if God gave him a taste of what walking in his call would be like when he reached maturity. Leaders who make a strong Lordship commitment tend to begin the journey with a season of being wild and radical for God, taking faith adventures and getting a taste of what God's power functioning through their natural talents and abilities can do.

Lordship Decision: *The one-time commitment to put Jesus in charge of all your decisions and your future.*

Natural Promotion: *The initial timeline stage where God's grace flows through your natural abilities to give you a taste of your call.*

---

3   This generic timeline shows the common elements of many life stories. Your life probably won't fit it exactly. Instead of trying to force your story into the model, see what the timeline model has to teach you about your story.

Valley of Dependence:
The first major season of adversity God uses to shape your Life Messages and build reliance on him.

The seeds of Joseph's descent into the **Valley of Dependence** are evident in the proud way he handles the favor of God and his dad. The character needed to support his call simply isn't there yet. Our need for character development is often what propels us into the Valley of Dependence (the downhill side of the Natural Promotion stage).

While this transition may be a direct result of our own arrogance and hubris, it is just as often triggered by external events beyond our control. Maybe our parents get a divorce, a relationship implodes, or we can't find a job and end up flipping burgers for a living. Life doesn't meet our lofty expectations. For the first time, God uses major adversity or failure to shape us, and we struggle and kick against those pricks to our ego.

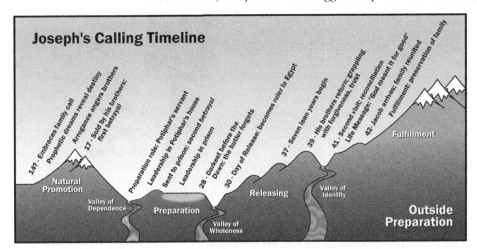

Preparation Stage:
A season after the Valley of Dependence focused on acquiring skills and experiences that prepare you for your call.

Inside/Outside Preparation: *Describes whether your primary role in the Preparation stage is inside or outside of your calling area.*

Valley of Wholeness:
A second season of adversity at the end of Preparation that God uses to shape your character.

Eventually, we discover how much we are depending on our own strength and how deeply we need God. Some learn this through a time of isolation that ignites an intense fellowship with God, while others get the same lesson through running away from him! The details of how it happens are unique to each person, but the valley experience is almost universal. In the Natural Promotion stage we discover that we can do anything *with* God; in the Valley of Dependence we learn we can't do anything *without* him.

As we discover how to let go of the wheel and let God steer (even if he steers us through difficulty instead of out of it), we move out into the **Preparation** stage. During this lengthy season we accumulate valuable skills and experience we'll need later in our calling journey.

While some go through this stage inside their area of call ("**Inside Preparation**") and experience it as a growing, fruitful time, God takes others (like Joseph) through **Outside Preparation**. Joseph's primary role in Preparation (as a prisoner and slave) is outside of his area of call. Like Joseph, we often feel we are living under restraint in this desert season, caught in the tension of yearning for God's release while hearing him say, "Not yet." This feeling tends to be most intense at the end of the stage. As the years lengthen, we wonder if we've missed it and God has passed us by.

Around the end of Preparation, God uses a second difficult **Valley of**

Wholeness (like Joseph's disappointment with the butler and the baker)[4] to free us from personal and relational patterns that threaten to torpedo our destiny later in life. This valley tends to be the shortest of the three, and commonly addresses issues unrelated to our vocation: marriage health, family, life balance, sexuality or secret sins.

After the Valley of Wholeness, leaders resume their upward movement toward the call throughout the **Releasing** stage, often filling a role that serves as an apprenticeship for their calling. For leaders in Outside Preparation (like Joseph), the onset of the Releasing stage has added significance. Often marked by a relocation or career change, this **Day of Release** catapults us into our sphere of call at a new level of favor and promotion. We experience the joy of finally being recruited into the kind of roles we were made for. Joseph's first nine years as Pharaoh's right-hand man comprise this season on his timeline.

> *The stages focus on accumulating skills and experience; the valley times are about inner renovation.*

But a third major transition remains. This late-life **Valley of Identity** (most commonly experienced in one's forties or fifties) transforms who we are—from one who is *being prepared* to one who actually *is prepared*. We must take on the full mantle of our calling identity, having the faith to see ourselves as the person we've always dreamed of becoming. God asks us to step up and risk our future on this identity—to act as if we are ready, he is really with us and we can do what he has called us to do. Taking that risk and crafting a convergent role move us into the **Fulfillment** stage, where we function with maximum impact.

In the Releasing stage, Joseph accomplishes great things outwardly in his Egyptian political role. However, his eternal impact and legacy are limited because his role is not effectively channeling his **Life Message**: revealing the God who turns what is meant for evil into good. Exemplifying that Message is the central purpose of his life. For Joseph's role and his Message to converge, he must come to terms with his past. God sends a Valley of Identity with the return of his brothers that compels him to let go of being betrayed and take on his calling identity as preserver of life for his family line. Like Joseph, we must embrace who we are made to be and take a big risk to channel the Message of our story through our role to move into our Fulfillment years.

To sum up, our map consists of four key stages focused on growth in our skills and vocational

Releasing Stage: *An apprenticeship to your call after the Valley of Wholeness which focuses on building Specific Skills for your calling role.*

Day of Release: *The sudden moment when leaders in Outside Preparation are recruited into their area of call.*

Valley of Identity: *A late-life transition where leaders take on the full mantle of their calling identity, move from doing to being and develop a healthy detachment from their call.*

Fulfillment Stage: *The culmination of the journey, where the leader's being and doing calls function together for maximum impact.*

---

4   Since the Bible does not give the age at which Joseph is sent to prison, there is some uncertainty on where to place this event on the timeline. Given his age and cultural naiveté when he went to Egypt, it seems most likely that it took Joseph a number of years to rise to leadership of Potiphar's house, and his imprisonment is later on in his Preparation years.

advancement (our doing): Natural Promotion, Preparation, Releasing, and Fulfillment. The stages are separated from one another by three valleys where the focus switches to shaping our inward being. The map as a whole depicts how we felt *at the time* about our progress toward our calling. Upward lines are

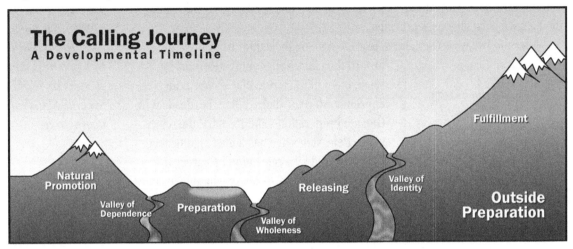

times when we felt we were moving toward our call, while downward slopes are when we felt we were moving away from it.

So we start by climbing the mountain peaks of Natural Promotion, where God gives us a taste of our calling. Our first descent leads us down into a difficult Valley of Dependence, where we unexpectedly find water as God meets us at the bottom. Then our journey leads into a season of Preparation, through a second valley and into the foothills of the Releasing stage. After a final valley season where God puts the finishing touches on our 'being' call and identity, we move up into the mountains again in the Fulfillment stage. The graphic above is a picture of how the individual stages and valleys fit together into a complete map of the journey: a Calling Timeline.

The Purpose of the Map

So what difference does it make to know where you are on the map? Last night I was talking to a young leader about her Valley of Dependence, which was triggered by a fiancé's betrayal. After pouring out her story of being emotionally undone by the situation, we had a great talk about what it all means. The situation has brought to the surface the walls around her heart and pushed her to trust God for her future instead of trying to control it. That's a good thing. While some around her are trying to protect her from being hurt, my contribution was simply to say, "This all sounds pretty normal to me." The idea that what she was going through was a common— even predictable—part of how God develops leaders was a great comfort and inspiration to her.

> *Knowing the timeline helps eliminate the unnecessary pain that comes from not understanding God's plan.*

I would have loved to hear those words in my mid-twenties when I was mired in my own Valley of Dependence. Everyone around me at that time was about my own age, so we had little experience with extended wilderness times or how God redeems times of suffering to transform us. I just knew that most of what was good in my life had come to an end, I was totally miserable, and therefore something must be wrong with *me*.

The assumption I was operating out of was that if God is with you, things will go good, and if bad things happen it is because you did something to upset him. Because my perspective on the situation was off, I asked the wrong questions and wasted energy looking for answers in the wrong places. I fought what God was attempting to do for two years before finally, at the end of all my reserves, I gave up trying to make my life and my belief system work and put any possibility that I might have a future in his hands. It was only when I reached the place of dependence (which was where God wanted me in the first place) that I experienced a breakthrough.

Paul's story is similar. During his conversion experience, he heard the voice of Jesus both rebuking and reaching out to him: "Saul, Saul, why are you persecuting me? It is hard for you to kick against the goads" (Acts 26:14). Goads (or "pricks") were pointed sticks used to prod a beast of burden and get it to go in a certain direction. Kicking back against those sharp sticks would be a painful experience for the animal, and would inevitably prove futile in the end. The master would certainly have his way.

Paul was quoting a Greek proverb of the time about the futility of resisting a deity. God was actively at work in Paul's life, moving him down a painful path of reevaluation that led to his destiny. Not understanding the plan, Paul found himself fighting against the very God he thought he was trying to serve, and hurting himself in the process.

Much of the pain we experience in times of adversity is not from the events themselves, but from our kicking back against the pricks life is making to our ego and our beliefs. Instead of meeting God in the event, we waste energy agonizing over the wrong questions. *Am I a failure? Has God passed me by? Is he even out there? Will my dreams ever come true? What is wrong with me?* When we don't have perspective on the journey, we fight, squirm and struggle to get out of the places God has us, so we can get to the completely different places that *we* think he wants us. Understanding what God has planned makes a huge difference.

> ### Are the Valleys Scary?
> *You might find yourself thinking, "You mean, I've got all these big, painful valley times to look forward to? That's scary!"*
>
> *However, the consistent testimony of those who navigate their valleys well is this: "That was a tough time, but I wouldn't trade it for anything in the world." The best of who you become—God's most precious gift to you, the thing that causes your greatest impact in the world—is usually produced in the valleys.*
>
> *Best of all, every valley season yields a quantum leap in intimacy with God and your ability to co-labor with him. By actively participating in redemptive suffering, you come to know a side of Jesus you would never see otherwise. The adversity of a valley is not even worth comparing to the glory that will be revealed in you through what God does there.*

The purpose of this book is to eliminate the unnecessary pain that comes from not understanding the plan. Perspective brings freedom—freedom from all the peripheral questions and the energy they require, so that you can focus in on what God is building within you. When you know where you are on the map, it's easier to engage God in a healthy way and avoid the distraction of the guilt, shame, fear and pride questions that lead nowhere.

Living out your call is a beautiful, peaceful, incredible thing. Here's how one senior leader I interviewed effusively described it:

> *"Now, we are working one-on-one with people to help them find inner peace, and I am so fulfilled. I'm in a role that is really exciting! [My wife and I] are dealing with people's problems at a level we rarely experienced before. The beautiful thing is, the lord meets these people at the point of their pain and speaks peace directly to them... and their minds are being renewed. Trusting the Holy Spirit to be the "wonderful Counselor" has been a form of death to self, because after praying I stop talking and trust God do the work. We are ministering with people who have been seeking peace for decades, and in one hour they find mind renewal."*

The Limitations of Models

The timeline model is an attempt to generalize a large number of life stories into a map that fits most people's lives most of the time. However, any model that tries to describe the infinite variation of human experience has built-in limitations. Statistician E.P. Box once famously remarked, "All models are wrong; but some are useful." What he's trying to say is that no model is a perfect fit for reality. Models describe general patterns, but no one individual fits them completely.

> **It's a Model, Not a Religion!**
> *"All models are wrong; but some are useful."*
> — *E.P. Box*

This model can give you great insight if you use it as intended: as a picture of the average, overall patterns of calling development. When you do your timeline, you'll discover places where your story fits the standard timeline to a tee. You'll probably also find places where your life doesn't seem to fit the model at all.

That's normal. *Don't so much try to fit your life to the timeline as allow the timeline to give you insights about your life.* You don't get brownie points for having a "good" timeline. Where it does fit your life, look for what the timeline can teach you about meeting God in your situation. There is great insight in the idea that your journey is common to humankind, because God works from a common developmental plan for every leader's life. As Joseph would say, God means it for good.

What is Calling?

What's it like to be called? In the past, the word "call" was applied almost exclusively to those who felt prompted to be pastors or missionaries. A light shone around you in the grove at 17, and in a nearly-audible voice God called you to the ministry. If you had a call from God on your life, it was to a spiritual occupation, not to business or politics or media. And it was supposed to come in a dramatic, one-time calling experience. Those without that experience often felt like second-class citizens of the Kingdom.

Thankfully, that mindset is changing. God calls each one of us, whether we are in ministry, business, health care, parenting or any other arena. But even so, most of us still think of calling as an occupation—as something we do. The next frontier in understanding call is grasping it as a Message, not an accomplishment. In the Calling Journey model, *your call is to embody a unique facet of Christ's character through the channel of your role or task.* The crux of your calling is to *be* Jesus in a unique way. Your life task or role—what you do—is a conduit for that incarnated Message of Christ to impact others. And the way you become Jesus is walking with him on the calling journey.

Think of it this way: every person has both a doing Call and a being Call. Joseph's doing call was to be a ruler in Egypt and a preserver of life for his family. That was his job. But his being call was to embody in his story the God he knew—the Great Redeemer who brought good even out of the worst evil. The insight that "God meant it for good" (Gen. 50:20) illustrated in Joseph's story has had far more impact on the world than anything he accomplished 4000 years ago as an Egyptian political leader.

Abraham is another great example. His doing call was to go to the land and father a great nation; his being call was to be a father of faith. Abraham was the first person in human history who really understood that God wanted people who believed in him instead of rule-followers. That revelation, and the life story that illustrates it, have literally shaped the lives of millions.

David's doing and being calls are summed up in one verse: "The Lord has sought out for himself *a man after his own heart*, and the Lord has appointed him as *ruler over his people*…" (I Sam. 13:14). David's doing call was a role as ruler of Judah and Israel. But his

	Doing Call (Task or Role)	Being Call (Life Message)
Joseph	Save family, rule in Egypt	"God meant it for good"
Moses	Deliverer, nation builder, law-giver	"Meekest man in all the earth;" total dependence on God
Paul	Apostle to the Gentiles	Salvation by grace through faith
David	Rule united Kingdom of Israel	"A man after God's own heart"
	Go to the land, be the father of many nations	The father of faith—being right with God by faith, not rules
Samuel	Prophet and judge for Israel	"Far be it from me to cease to pray for you:" God's representative in disobedience
Jesus	Redeem the world through his death	Incarnation; "He who has seen me has seen the Father"

being call was to live as a man after God's own heart—to embody bringing all that was in his heart, good and bad, before God. David is the Bible's exemplar of living naked before God, and the record of his communion captured in the Psalms has been read, sung and recited for 3000 years. The lasting legacy of his being call—the Psalms—has had far more impact on humanity than his role as a king.

However, that role was still vitally important. If David had not been king, his poetry would probably never have been preserved for us. But if David had *only* been king, and never had such an intimate dialog with God, he would be merely an obscure footnote in the history books.

So the calling timeline maps how God is shaping our Message—the being call within our hearts—

as well as our outward roles and accomplishments. The stages tend to focus on outward growth in our doing call, while the valleys are primary vehicles for developing the inward Message of our being call. In the Fulfillment stage, both being and doing calls function in partnership to yield a maximum impact.

The Power of Being

Looking at our calling as something to incarnate frees us from the great trap of trying to get the calling journey *right*. When we think we're called to do a task or fill a role, then hearing God on exactly what we are supposed to do is a life or death issue. If there is one right location, or right relationship, or right job I must get into to be in the center of God's will for me, then everything rests on hearing God right and making the right choices. No wonder we get so uptight about following our call!

But if your life purpose is to embody a certain facet of Jesus' character that's been forged in you through your story, suddenly the pressure is off. Your call is a function of how you've met God in your life story. You can let go of trying to social-engineer yourself into the right role, because everything you do already communicates the Christ-in-you that is the heart of your calling. Living your call is simply being yourself—being who you've become in Christ. What a relief!

A few months ago I met Joey, a foreman at a local utility company, while doing a destiny workshop. Our starting point for finding his calling wasn't his role: it was the Message of his life (his being call). Since Life Messages are most often formed in the crucible, the first step was identifying the times that had most molded who he is today. As his most important shaping event, Joey chose the experience of growing up as the youngest of a family of 12, born six years after his closest male sibling. He described it as being "born out of season"—never really feeling a part and never learning how to be a man. It had a tremendous impact on his life when God met him in that place of alienation and showed him how to live a life of excellence. Joey's Message was that Jesus meets those who are born out of season and shows them how to be men of excellence.

> ### Misconceptions about Call
>
> - *Calling is an event: a special moment where God gives me a life assignment.*
> - *My calling is about doing a task.*
> - *Once I figure out my calling, I'm supposed to start doing it immediately.*
> - *There is a prearranged route to my call, and if I miss a turn I won't get there.*
> - *My call is to one specific, preordained role or task.*

That Message quickly led Joey to identify the audience he was called to reach. It turned out that the place he had the best opportunities to touch the young men who needed his Message was through his job as a supervisor. From there, it was a simple matter to take the *Message* (his being call), combine it with his *Role* (his doing call) and his target *Audience* to create a great calling statement:

> *"To prove God as the source to young men born out of season by teaching them to live through excellence."*

Seeing such a dramatic connection between his Message and his job got Joey fired up. "See, at the power company, there's not always a lot of work to do," he joked, "So I have lots of time and opportunity to get into the lives of these young guys." Instead of being something unspiritual, Joey's job was a perfect channel for the Jesus-in-him to touch the people who most needed it.

Seeing call in being terms also protects us from the legalistic approach to destiny that ensnares so many Christians. In this doing-focused way of thinking, pursuing our call is like getting directions from MapQuest.com. We believe we are supposed to download every life decision from heaven, with each correct turn spelled out in detail. There is only one path to our destiny, and our job is to be attentive enough at all times that we hear and follow each direction.

Now, I am into hearing from God about our direction in life. But sometimes we go so far overboard closing our eyes to discern the "right" next turn that we end up rear-ending a parked car. It's as if we are on a journey with our great friend Jesus, driving through the most beautiful country on earth. We can choose to express our gratitude for who he is, fellowship together, share how we experience the incredible beauty all around us, make any request or ask about whatever we'd like to know. *The whole point of the journey is to do it together!* But we're so afraid of getting lost (with the mapmaker of the universe sitting right next to us!) that we fritter away the whole trip poring over the map, agonizing over each turn and trying not to "miss it." Ironically, our obsession with not making small mistakes becomes our biggest mistake of all.

What Does God's Call Look Like?

Sometimes, our expectations of what a call ought to sound like become an obstacle to hearing it. We tend to expect calling to be an unusual, supernatural experience early in life where God speaks to us directly, almost audibly telling us what to do with our lives. Examining the stories of biblical leaders offers a much more varied picture. Calling can come as a one-time event (as with David in I Samuel 16:13) or as a progressive unfolding of what one is to do and be (Abraham). Sometimes the task is revealed early on, while the heart of the being call is revealed much later (as with Joseph).

Calls also come through different channels. Some people are called through supernatural events where they hear directly from God about their future (like Paul). Others are called through a word from another leader (David), by being drawn to a need (Moses, when he went out and saw his people), through family inheritance (Isaac and Jacob), or by being recruited to a mission (the 12 apostles). A call can come in any of the myriad ways God speaks.

Awareness of call comes at all ages: to teenagers (David and Joseph), to the middle-aged (Moses) and to people who are well on in life (Abraham). Our calling may even be assigned before birth in answer to the prayers of others (Samuel). One thing is universal—a calling takes many years of preparation to come to fruition. The table below compares the calling circumstances of seven prominent biblical leaders[5].

Table: The Calling Circumstances of Biblical Leaders

	Calling Method	Age at Call	Inside/Outside Preparation	Time to Fulfillment
Joseph	Early functioning in prophetic dreams; progressive revelation of being call throughout life.	Teens	Outside Preparation: called to political leadership; prepared in prison, slavery.	20 years
Moses	Drawn to alleviate suffering he witnessed. His calling event at the burning bush came after his Preparation stage.	Mid-life	Outside Preparation: called as national leader, prepared as shepherd.	40+ years
Paul	Calling event: an audible voice at conversion announces his life mission. Confirmed by word of knowledge and his healing.	Mid-life	Outside Preparation? Called to ministry, probably a tent-maker during his Preparation years in Tarsus.	15 years
David	Called by another leader (anointed by Samuel).	Teens	Outside Preparation. Functioned as a leader in Preparation but outside sphere of call.	23 years until king of all Israel
Abraham	Progressive revelation over many years through multiple calling events.	Later in Life	Outside Preparation. Although he was a businessman all his life, he didn't become a father until his Releasing stage.	25 years until heir born; 500 years until nation inherits land
Samuel	Calling Event: prophetic word to mother before conception. Confirmed by early functioning in prophetic gifting.	Before birth	Inside Preparation. Called as a prophet, he grew up in the tabernacle and was a prophet all his life.	30 years?
Jesus	Prophecy before birth; miraculous signs at birth; confirmation at baptism by John.	Knew it at 12	Outside Preparation. Called to ministry, but worked as a carpenter.	21 years

Why Are We Called?

Have you ever wondered why you have a call in the first place? Why does God give us assignments to do things for him, knowing that we are such screw-ups that it will take infinitely more energy to work with us than it would to just do it himself?

An analogy might help. A farmer takes his eight-year-old boy out on the tractor with him to cultivate

---

5   Large-sphere leaders like these tend to receive a clearer picture of their call earlier in life than the norm. In these unusual biographies, the calling events also tend to be more dramatic than the norm.

his soybean crop. At that age, the boy isn't really contributing to the success of the farm—in fact, having him around and answering all his questions slows the work down. So why take him along in the first place?

One reason is to start teaching him how to farm. Dad is training him in a potential livelihood, so when he becomes a man he can succeed in the world. He may even join the business full time in his teen years. But that's still in the distant future. The real reason the farmer takes him out is just to be together with him. Up to this point, their relationship has been centered in the home. But taking him to the fields brings their relationship into dad's working life. By working together over the coming years, they'll have the opportunity to become much closer and share more of life than if they only interacted at meals and in the evening.

That's the main purpose of your call: it brings Jesus into your working life[6] and expands your relationship. Or maybe we should say it the other way around: Jesus calls *you* into *his* work, so your vocational life becomes

> ## When We First Receive a Call...
>
> - **We See It Dimly**
>   *God gives us an idea of where we are going, but not the particulars. The mental images we develop to describe our call are often something we later have to break free of.*
>
> - **It is Task-Focused**
>   *We see our call as something to do, not something to be.*
>
> - **We Miss the Message**
>   *It is rare for a person to grasp the heart of their call early in life. Fathering a nation made sense to Abraham, but being the first living person to grasp justification by faith took decades to understand.*
>
> - **What, Not When and How**
>   *God shows us what we are to do, but not the timing or how to get there. To find those, we have to meet him on the way.*
>
> - **We Don't See the Glory or the Cost**
>   *If we knew what it would cost, we'd never start. If we saw the glory of who we would become, our hearts would faint.*

a sacred, set-apart time to do things together with him. Without calling, your work would be about simple day-to-day provision. But stir in a mission—one that must be found, that connects with your deepest passions, that reveals God in ways you never saw before—and Jesus invades your work and makes it another part of your devotions. Calling transforms your working life into as much a part of the Kingdom as going to church on Sunday. Each day, it sends you on a journey to discover God's purpose in life and co-labor with him to accomplish it.

When you think of calling in being terms, staying on course with your call is less a matter of making all the right decisions than it is about hanging around with the right person—and becoming like him. It doesn't matter what wrong choices you've made in the past. It doesn't matter what opportunities you have or don't have, whether you are in the "right" job or if you have enough resources. Nothing can stop

---

6   Your calling role is not always synonymous with your day job.

you. Whether you abound or are abased, are free or imprisoned, in good health or disabled, well-known or unknown—you can walk in your call today, because your call is in you.

Clarifying Your Call

To travel the calling journey well, you need to steward what God has revealed to you so far about your destiny. Creating a formal calling statement is a great way to capture the essence of what God has revealed in memorable form. Joey's story (see page 26) illustrates a simple way to create such a statement using the Four Elements of Call:

- **Message**: The unique facet of Jesus' character you embody;
- **Audience**: The people you are called to touch or serve;
- **Impact**: The way your Message changes the lives of your audience;
- **Task/Role:** An efficient vehicle your Message flows through to your audience.

Your calling is *a Message to an Audience through a Task for an Impact*[7]. For an example, let's look at Dave, a businessman in his thirties.

Dave grew up in a dysfunctional home, living with three different fathers by age 13 and bearing the brunt of parental affairs, addictions, abandonment and more. After he surrendered his life to God, the redemptive power of Jesus' life began to work in those same areas, birthing in him a Message that revolves around restoration for broken people and broken relationships.

However, Dave has always been drawn to the business world. A born entrepreneur, at ten Dave sometimes brought home $400 a day selling roses on a street corner. By 14, he was lying about his age to work as a telemarketer. Combining these two seemingly-contradictory aspects of his call demonstrates the power of the four elements approach.

> **Four Elements Calling Statement**
> *Your call is a* Message *you embody to an* Audience *through a* Task or Role *for a specific* Impact.

A key part of his Audience is the sexually broken or those whose families have experienced the pain of adultery and sexual addictions. Dave has used his entrepreneurial skills to push the boundaries of how those individuals are served, launching a for-profit company to effectively channel his Message to that Audience for a significant Impact. He uses his *Role* as a business owner and entrepreneur (his doing call) to *Impact* the broken (his *Audience*) with a *Message* of restoration (his being call).

Another creative way Dave has combined his business role with his Life Message is through working to establish and run orphanages in Africa. Years ago, he and his wife were trying to adopt a child from an organization in East Africa. The orphanage was having so much trouble staying on track with the process that one day his wife said, "Dave, why don't you just fly over there and help them whip things

---

7   For an in-depth treatment of how to create a calling statement, see the companion book, *A Leader's Life Purpose Workbook*, by Tony Stoltzfus. It includes a set of self-study exercises to help you identify your Life Message, Audience, Impact and Task, and to roll them together into a formal calling statement.

into shape?" He's been doing hands-on work with orphanages ever since.

Dave's *Message* is restoration, his *Audience* is the sexually broken (whether his clients at work or in his ministry at the orphanage), and the different *Tasks and Roles* he has chosen as a channel for his Message create a great *Impact*. So a calling statement for him might be,

> *"I use entrepreneurial ventures [Task] to bring restoration [Message] to the sexually broken [Audience] so they can be set free [Impact]."*

Dave's story highlights the other-centered quality of calling. It's not about what you want—it comes from outside yourself, from God's heart, and it focuses on meeting others' needs, not your own. A call is never about attaining a wonderful life for yourself, or being your own boss, or becoming financially independent, or even doing work that gives meaning and significance to your life. All that stuff is about you. A calling is about serving God and others.

You have a commission from the one who bought your life with a price to do as he did: to lay down your life in service of the bigger Kingdom of God. Significance and joy and favor are the natural by-products of giving love and service, not an objective to be pursued. If the core desire that drives you is to be wealthy, or live the good life, or succeed in business, or to have a fulfilling life, your Lordship commitment is lacking. A call from God is a call to serve.

Summary of Key Learnings

- *There is a map for your journey, with predictable stages and transitions.*
- *Joseph's life is a good example of this timeline (see diagram page 20).*
- *You have a Doing Call (a task or role) and a Being Call (a Life Message).*
- *The Calling Timeline consists of four Stages that chart your growth in doing, and three Valleys that form your being.*
- *Your lasting legacy is generated primarily through your being call.*
- *To create a calling statement, lay out the Message you are called to embody to an Audience through a Task for an Impact.*

3: THE STORY OF MOTHER TERESA

Before we dive into creating a personal timeline, let's examine one more life story to enrich our understanding of the model. Biographies often record what a person did but little of what went on inside them in the process. In this case, we have the benefit of Mother Teresa's correspondence with her spiritual directors, which reveals an intimate picture of her internal struggles and triumphs. Her story (adapted from a calling biography by Dr. Myra Dingman) illustrates two major variations of the timeline model: *Inside Preparation* and *Descent before Lordship*.

Early experiences of watching her parents helping the poor directly shaped her calling.

Her **Valley of Dependence** *was triggered by a major negative event beyond her control.*

Mother Teresa[8] was born as Ganxhe Agnes Bojaxhiu in 1910 in Serbia as the youngest child of three. Her father, Nikola, was a politician and businessman who inherited a fortune from his mother's embroidery business and traveled often to buy and sell. Nikola had a profound influence on young Agnes as he sent home packages from his travels that included money and clothing marked for the poor. He reminded her, "My daughter, never take a morsel of food that you are not prepared to share with others." Likewise, Agnes' mother, Drana, was generous, provided for the poor and possessed a fervent Catholic faith. She taught her children, "When you give to the poor, you give directly to God."

Agnes' Valley of Dependence began at the age of nine when her father contracted an illness while traveling and died a few days later. It was a

---

8   All quotes from Mother Teresa's writings are taken from Brian Kolodiejchuk, *Mother Teresa: Come Be My Light* (New York: Doubleday Religion, 2007); or Sam Wellman, *Mother Teresa: Missionary of Charity* (Uhrichville, Barbour Publishing, 1997).

great blow to her and her family. They were thrown more than ever toward dependence on God. After Nikola's death, Agnes found out that her father's charity had been much more widespread than she had known. His funeral service was so packed the family could scarcely get into the church.

To the surprise of Agnes, her mother went into the textile business to provide for her young family. During this time, she began to take Agnes with her to visit the elderly and sick and made her comfortable among the "dirty and physically repellent," learning to "treat every person as a unique individual." They had guests at every meal. Drana modeled humility and taught, "When you do good, do it unobtrusively, as if you were tossing a pebble into the sea." Agnes' Life Messages of going to the poorest of the poor and the unique dignity of each individual took root in her heart during this first valley time.

At 11, a new priest came to her parish, and seeing the potential in her he soon had her functioning as an interpreter for priests who didn't know the local dialect. Before long she could have taught the catechism all by herself. At 12, Agnes first mentioned to her mother that she wanted to live a life of service in the church. After several years of weighing the issue and talking it through with those around her, by 16 she knew what she was supposed to do with her life. She accepted a divine call to serve God as a missionary, and submitted her life to "belong completely to God."

Meanwhile, a second new priest came to her church and began to pay more attention to the spiritual growth of the youth. Agnes joined a discipleship group for girls and threw herself into volunteering wherever she could. A born organizer, she often ended up leading the girl's activities. During this time her priest spoke to her about the church's need for missionaries, and encouraged Agnes to read their accounts in *Catholic Missions* magazine. These stories drew her heart more and more toward serving overseas, and she became particularly fascinated with India. Nothing gave her more joy than the thought of serving there.

But how could this dream ever be realized? As she began to look into how she could serve, she discovered that many of the letters from India that so inspired her were from an order called the Sisters of Loreto. They were headquartered in Ireland. So, she decided at the tender age of 18, to Ireland she must go, to become a nun.

When she told her mother of her intentions, Drana was stunned. Didn't she realize what this meant? She might never see her family again! Looking stricken, her mother fled into the bedroom and didn't emerge for an entire day. When she came out, she said sadly, "You may leave with my blessing. But please strive to live only for God and Christ."

Opposition also came from others. Well-meaning neighbors tried to talk her

Her life follows the **Descent before Lordship** *timeline, with the Valley of Dependence before Lordship and Natural Promotion.*

Life Messages *that form during early valley times often become the heart of our calling.*

Lordship *was a gradual process, culminating in submission to God's call at age 16.*

Natural Promotion *often sees doors open for us to function in our gifts and confirmation of call.*

Rapid Promotion *and being* **Wild and Radical** *for God were part of Agnes' Natural Promotion stage.*

Agnes faced a time of doubt and opposition to moving forward in her call.

out of it, wondering aloud how nuns could survive the terrible sacrifice of giving up pleasures and marriage for poverty and solitude. Her brother was especially upset. "Don't you know you are going to bury yourself alive in the middle of nowhere?" he wrote.

"Sometimes I doubted that I had a vocation at all," Agnes recalled, "But in the end I had the assurance that God really was calling me."

Her Life Message of serving with a big smile was driven more deeply into her heart in each succeeding valley.

Her response to this opposition was a defining moment for her calling. She determined that her life would be an example of the great joy of serving Christ. Years later, she expressed this Message of joy as, "Let us accept whatever He gives and give whatever He takes with a big smile." Her course was set.

*God took her on a **Faith Adventure** of believing he had called her and seeing him miraculously provide for her.*

But she still had to find a way to get to India. Agnes approached her priest for help in joining the Sisters of Loreto, because she had nowhere else to turn. After weeks of anxious waiting, she was accepted for an interview in Paris. Standing at the railway station saying goodbye to her family, her friends and everything familiar, the enormity of her decision came home to her. Her mother's parting words would serve as a purpose statement for Agnes for the rest of her life, "Only, all for God and Jesus." She would never see her mother again.

*Her **Preparation Stage** began when she entered into a **Preparation Role** as a nun.*

Preparation Stage

Accepted into the order as a postulant, Agnes was soon on a ship bound for Calcutta. The poverty she saw when they landed tore at her heart. Her first months there were spent in a convent, learning the language (she eventually mastered five) and training in the life of a sister. On becoming a novice, she changed her name to "Teresa" after St. Therese. For two more years Teresa studied the scriptures, the vows she would take and the rules of her order. She also began teaching children and serving at a medical station. In the same *Catholic Mission* magazine that inspired her to go to India, she inspired others with her description of the joy of serving:

Teresa began a time of intentional preparation for her ultimate call.

*Teresa learned **General Skills** like teaching and medical care that became an important part of her calling later on in life.*

"In the hospital pharmacy hangs a picture of the Redeemer surrounded by a throng of suffering people, on whose faces the torments of their lives have been engraved. Each morning, before I start work, I look at this picture. In it is concentrated everything I feel. I think, "Jesus, it is for you and for these souls!"

"Then I open the door. The tiny veranda is always full of the sick, the wretched and the miserable. All eyes are fixed, full of hope, on me. Mothers give me their sick children, their gestures mirroring those in the picture in the pharmacy. My heart beats in happiness: I can continue your work, dear Jesus. I can ease many sorrows. I console them and treat them, repeating the

words of the best friend of souls. Some of them I take to church…"

At 21, Teresa took the vows of the order of Loreto and became a nun. She returned to Calcutta, where she began teaching geography and history to both wealthy Bengali girls and orphans at the Convent of Entally in Calcutta. While the Sisters of Loreto had begun as an order devoted to working with the poorest of the poor, a papal decree centuries before had confined them to the convent, and they were only allowed to leave for travel or in emergencies.

Teresa excelled in her work and was very happy in the convent. But even

While her heart for the poor was already deep, it would be many years until she was released to fully function out of it.

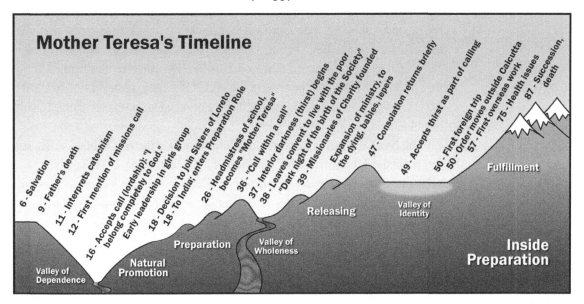

Mother Teresa's Timeline

6 - Salvation
9 - Father's death
11 - Interprets catechism
12 - First mention of missions call
16 - Accepts call (lordship): "I belong completely to God."
Early leadership in girls group
18 - Decision to join Sisters of Loreto
18 - To India; enters Preparation Role
26 - Headmistress of school, becomes "Mother Teresa"
36 - "Call within a call"
37 - Interior darkness (thirst) begins
38 - Leaves convent to live with the poor
"Dark night of the Society"
39 - Missionaries of Charity founded
Expansion of ministry; to the dying, babies, lepers
47 - Consolation returns briefly
49 - Accepts thirst as part of calling
50 - First foreign trip
50 - Order moves outside Calcutta
57 - First overseas work
75 - Health issues
87 - Succession, death

Valley of Dependence
Natural Promotion
Preparation
Valley of Wholeness
Releasing
Valley of Identity
Fulfillment
Inside Preparation

as she began moving up the ecclesiastical ladder and taking on new leadership tasks, her passion for the poorest of the poor that she saw outside the convent walls gnawed at her. She got permission on Sundays to walk from the convent walls to visit them in their squalid homes, and later to send her girl's group on service missions to the poor, although she could rarely go outside the convent to serve with them. In 1937, at 26, Teresa took her final vows, was placed in charge of the school at Entally and became Mother Teresa.

A few months later, she received a jarring letter from home. Instead of congratulating her on her promotion, her mother wrote, "Do not forget that you went out to India for the sake of the poor. Do you remember our File? [An elderly lady they had cared for together.] She was covered in sores, but what made her suffer much more was the knowledge that she was alone in this world. We did what we could for her. But the worst thing was not the sores; it was the fact that she had been forgotten by her family." The inner conflict in Mother Teresa, pitting obedience to her vows against her driving passion to serve the

*Teresa's Preparation took place inside her area of call, working in India as a mission-ary sister. This pattern is called **Inside Preparation.***

God began to stir up a discontent that would propel her toward her next stage.

poor, intensified.

The war years were a tumultuous time in India. Famine killed millions because all the boats that transported food had been requisitioned for the war effort. The Japanese invaded India, Muslims and Hindus bickered, Gandhi went on hunger strikes.

Soon after the war ended, the Muslim-Hindu feud erupted in violence. The Loreto compound sat on the border between Hindu and Muslim neighborhoods, and soon men began climbing the walls of the convent to seek refuge inside. After four days of killing and fire-bombing, thousands lay dead in the streets.

In the middle of this time of uncertainty, Mother Teresa left for her yearly retreat and rest in the mountains. On September 10, 1946, as the train wound through the rice paddies, she received the "Call within the Call" that would be celebrated as the Inspiration Day for her order. God said, "Go to the poor. Leave the convent. Live with the poorest of the poor." She later wrote: "I was to leave the Convent and help the poor while living among them. It was an order. To fail would have been to break the faith."

*This revelation launched Teresa into her **Valley of Wholeness.** Waiting and submitting were difficult assignments.*

But how? She had taken vows to be cloistered for the rest of her life. There was no manual, no process for this kind of thing to happen. In effect, she was asking to start a new order, an initiative to which the Vatican was quite resistant. But Teresa set out to try anyway. She spent her entire retreat praying, planning and sketching out what the rule of her new order would look like.

The Valley of Wholeness

She approached her archbishop, who directed her to work with the Daughters of Anne, a group of Bengali sisters. But after checking it out, Teresa realized her plan would not work there. The rules and ways of doing things they had in place were too rigid. She insisted on being able to start her own order. So the archbishop began the process of petitioning Rome, while Mother Teresa waited... and waited. It was a time of learning to leave her future up to God.

*During her Valley of Wholeness, Mother Teresa had a **False Opportunity** to work within the Daughters of Anne. This would have been an easier path but would have compromised her calling.*

Finally, two years after she first received her revelation, Mother Teresa received word that her request had been approved. She was 37. But that release had an important caveat: she had a year to prove herself, during which time she had to recruit ten novices to devote their lives to the poorest of the poor. It was not an easy task.

That year was also a time of deep inner struggle. Teresa was desperately lonely, afraid of failing, experiencing herself the pangs of hunger and the debilitation of poverty. "The poverty of the poor must be so hard for them," she wrote in her journal. "When I went around looking for a home, I walked and walked til my legs and arms ached. I thought how they must also ache in body and soul, looking for home, food, help. Then the temptation grew strong. The palace buildings of Loreto came rushing into my mind. All the beautiful things and comforts… 'You have only to say the word and all that will be yours again,' the tempter kept on saying… This is the dark night of the birth of the Society. My God, give me courage now, in this moment, to persevere in following your will."

The Releasing Stage

Teresa set aside her Catholic habit and donned the simple sari and plain sandals of the Indian poor. After several months of additional medical training, she began her work by going into a Muslim slum each day and visiting the children and their families. She had been given five rupees (roughly $15 in today's currency) to get started, and with them she bought a hut on Creek Street and began teaching the children, caring for the sick and cleaning houses. She lived as a beggar, asking for throw-away food at markets, petitioning doctors to visit the slums weekly and seeking money to provide for the children. She looked for opportunities and labored wherever she saw a need.

After months of working alone, a former pupil named Subhasini Das joined her full time to work in the slums, and became her first novice. Gradually more trickled in one by one. It wasn't an easy life. They were allowed two saris, a sleeping mat and a water jug as possessions. Often they had to walk a long way home because their streetcar fare had been given to the poor.

In the midst of it all, the sisters met Jesus in those they served. After one of her novices had ministered to a sick person in a particularly stomach-churning situation, Teresa would have them hold out a hand to her. She would fold their fingers back to their palm one by one, reciting, "You - did - it - unto - me."

By 1950, Teresa had recruited her ten novices, and the Missionaries of Charity became an official order of the Catholic Church in Calcutta. Over the next decade she expanded the order, instilled its values into her sisters and worked tirelessly with the poor. They moved into a new home known as the Mother House of the Missionaries of Charity and began many new works, teaching, providing care to the sick, treating lepers and starting a hospice for the dying. By the end of the '50s the order had grown to around 100 sisters.

At the same time, her diary records an inner destitution seemingly at odds with her joyful demeanor and the growing power and impact of her Message. In 1956 she wrote, "I am longing with a painful longing to be all for God—to be holy in such a way that Jesus can live His life to the full in me. The more I want Him, the less I am wanted. I want to love Him as He has not been loved—and yet there is that separation, that terrible emptiness, that feeling of absence of God. For more than four years I find no help…"

This inner sense of emptiness and distance from God would continue almost unabated for the rest of her life. For many years she struggled and almost

*Her Valley of Wholeness continued (and seems to overlap the beginning of her **Releasing Stage**) with a difficult time of working alone.*

*The Releasing stage was a time of **Apprenticeship** for Teresa. She functioned within her calling role but in a smaller sphere of influence as she learned the ropes.*

This season was one of upward growth and expansion in her life mission.

God continued forming her Life Message of quenching the thirst of Christ.

*Her **Valley of Identity** is kicked off by a change in her relationship with God.*

*Teresa began to **Take on the Full Mantle of her Calling Identity** as she accepted her interior desolation (the lack of the felt presence of God) as part of her call.*

*A releasing of great favor and opportunity in a new, global sphere of influence marked Teresa's entry into the **Fulfillment Stage**.*

Her mission moved outside Calcutta to the rest of India.

*During the early years of this stage her job was further refined into a **Convergent Role** that fit her organizational and leadership gifts.*

despaired at this "agony of desolation [that] is so great."

In 1958, the consolation of God's felt presence returned, but a month later it was gone again. But that event, along with the appearance of a new spiritual director, seemed to catalyze a change in her. Although the pain didn't go away, she began to see her darkness as an identification with those she was called to serve, a drawing into the pain they experienced in order to be part of their redemption. Her spiritual director relates that instead of a curse, she began to see her unquenched thirst for God as a "special share she had in Jesus' passion… a mysterious link that united her to Jesus." She had prayed repeatedly to be part of quenching the thirst Christ spoke of on the cross, and now she accepted the experience of that thirst as a core part of her calling.

She wrote to her sisters in 1961, "My dear children, without our suffering, our work would just be social work, good and helpful, but it would not be the work of Jesus Christ, not part of the redemption. Jesus wanted to help us by sharing our life, our loneliness and our agony… Only by being one with us has He redeemed us. We are allowed to do the same: all the desolation of the poor people, not only their material poverty but their spiritual destitution must be redeemed, and we must have our share in it." Acceptance of her calling identity as one who thirsts to see Christ's thirst satisfied launched her into her Fulfillment stage.

Fulfillment

In 1960, at the age of 50, Mother Teresa took her first extended trip abroad, speaking and meeting people throughout the United States and Europe. It brought much funding and favor to her mission. On her way home she stopped in Rome to deliver the petition to make her order pontifical. This process normally took 30 to 50 years, but with her usual determination she decided to ask after only ten. The probationary period for her new society came to an end as well, and for the first time the Missionaries of Charity were able to expand beyond Calcutta.

As her notoriety increased, so did her travel. She delegated more tasks to make room for the time she was on the road. Being treated as a celebrity did not affect her—her total abandonment to God gave her a freedom from being influenced by honor or criticism. She simply accepted whatever was given and used it to further her mission. In one humorous incident, the Pope visited India, where he drove around in a white Cadillac donated to him by Americans living in India. Upon his return to Rome, he in turn donated it to Mother Teresa. Instead of driving it, she wasted no time raffling it off to have more to give to the poor.

In 1965, the Pope gave the Missionaries of Charity authority to operate throughout the world. Two years later, in 1967, Mother Teresa opened her first home outside of India in Venezuela. Requests for homes began to pour in from different countries. Within a few years, Mother Teresa was able to open a new home within seven days of receiving a request. No money was spent to start a new work–everything was donated and provided for by the people and community that each home would serve. Nuns were trained in India and then sent around the world to new homes to continue the same routine and work they had learned.

Her work expanded into many other countries.

In 1975, at age 65, Mother Teresa celebrated the Silver Jubilee (25-year anniversary) of the society with 1100 sisters and 80 homes around the world. By then the work was enormous. For instance, in 1979 the sisters provided medical services to four million patients, treated 258,000 lepers and ran 107 slum schools. During the Diamond Jubilee (1990), Teresa was able to open a work in her home country of Albania for the first time. Drana had already passed away, having never seen her Agnes since she left Skopje in 1928.

Great blessing and success came in her Fulfillment years: a ten-fold expansion of workers.

At the age of 75, her frail health and demanding lifestyle (for instance, she slept two to four hours each night), required her to begin delegating more and more work. At age 79, she was diagnosed with heart disease and fitted with a pacemaker. She continued in her role as leader of the movement until Sister Nirmala was elected as her first successor in 1997. Mother Teresa died later that year at 87, knowing that the organization she had built from the ground up would continue to quench the thirst of her dear Savior.

Thinking beyond her life span, Teresa took steps to put into place a successor to preserve her legacy.

Where Do We Go from Here?

So far, we've taken a brief tour through the timeline, explored the definition of call and looked at the life stories of two leaders. The next step is to actually do a personal timeline—that's the focus of the following chapter. Instead of only learning these patterns from other people's lives, we want to rough out your timeline now, so that as you read the rest of the book, you can correlate their stories to your own experiences.

4: MAPPING YOUR JOURNEY

Now that you have a basic understanding of the model, let's create your timeline! We'll sketch out a rough version here to help you make the most of the rest of the book. As you read through this section, compare the stories of what others have experienced at each stage with your own.

You have two options for creating a timeline. You can use the timeline worksheets provided in this chapter to do one on paper, or you can go to www.TheCallingJourney.com and walk through the same process using our free, interactive Timeline Builder tool. The Timeline Builder lets you type in the labels you want on your timeline, save it and come back later, or print it out in color.

The process is fairly straightforward. We identity the key Valleys in your timeline, and the Stages simply fall into place in between.

The first step is to do a rough sketch of the ups and downs of your calling journey to date. Next, you'll pick out the key events, map them onto the standard timeline and identify the three major Valleys. Fill in the dates when each season starts and ends and you'll have a personal timeline. You should be able to complete the process in under an hour.

Depending on your age, you may not have gone through all the stages yet. If at any point in the process you bring your timeline up to the present, just skip the remaining stages and go straight to *Step 5: Verifying Your Timeline* on page 49. The timeline is most useful for those in their late twenties onward. If you have only experienced one or two stages, the temptation is to try to cram all the ups and downs of the entire timeline into a few years. But if you are in your twenties, it is virtually certain that you have not progressed beyond Preparation, Natural Promotion or the Valley of Dependence. The diagram showing the average stage lengths on page 49 will help you keep your story in proper perspective.

If you get stuck or aren't sure how something from your life fits the model, that's OK. There is a lot more to learn in the ensuing chapters that will help you make sense of your journey! Cross references are included for each point on the timeline so you can find answers to a specific question. There is also a glossary in Appendix A that will help you with the labels and terms.

The point of doing a timeline is to get perspective on the journey. So don't stop once you've roughed out your diagram! The remainder of the book explains each phase of the journey in detail, using stories of how other leaders experienced that season, an explanation of what God is doing in it, and tips for how you can make the most of the stage. Fully grasping what the journey is all about will engender a deep awe and respect in you for how God's sovereign hand permeates every event of your life.

What the Map Measures

Let's take a moment to clarify what the timeline displays. The map uses upward, downward, and flat lines to represent your internal sense **at that time** *of whether you were going forward, backward or nowhere in your call. If you went through a season where at the time your call seemed to be receding into the mist, graph that period with a downward line, even if 20 years later it seems like it was an invaluable growth experience. Since the purpose of this map is to offer perspective on the challenges you face right now, it's designed to describe what the road is like as you travel it.*

Also, the timeline measures progress toward your call, *not how you feel about life. If things are going pretty well and you are enjoying yourself, but you are coasting when it comes to your call, that's a flat line. And a period where you are sweating a tough task but making great progress toward your destiny is mapped trending upward.*

Here's a more in-depth look at what the different types of lines represent:

- **Upward Lines** *represent times when you feel you are functioning within your area of call and or are moving toward it. For example, Mother Teresa's graph trends upward throughout Preparation, because she spent the stage within her area of calling (as a missionary in India) moving toward her life work (serving the poor).*

- **Flat Lines** *are periods when you are functioning outside of your area of call or don't feel you are making much progress toward it. The time Joseph spent in prison during his Preparation stage is basically flat. Joseph was functioning outside his area of call, and much of the time it didn't seem like his life was going anywhere.*

- **Downward Lines** *represent difficult periods when it feels like your call is getting farther away. Maybe you are losing influence, position or opportunity in your area of call. Or you may be in a season of processing where you are trying to save a marriage, deal with a thorny habit or keep a business unit from going under. The fact that you are facing challenges doesn't necessarily mean you are in a valley: valleys are only those times where your call seems to be getting farther away.*

Step 1: Identify Transitions

First, we're going to list the major seasons and transitions in your life and (if you are a visual person) do a preliminary timeline sketch. The idea is to map the ups and downs of *how you felt at the time* about your progress toward your call. For instance, if in your early twenties you had a couple of rocky years where you felt trapped in a nowhere job and God was distant, list or graph the trend as downward for that period. Even if later in life you came to see it as a rich season of inner growth, you would still graph it as a downward stage because that's how you felt at the time.

The timeline is meant to track major seasons in life. To keep the focus on these larger themes, *draw your map with a minimum increment of six months to a year.* For instance, if things went really badly for a month and then you bounced back to normal, don't put that in your list. If you include too much detail, the bigger patterns get lost in the weeds.

Examples of Upward Seasons
- *Doors open and new opportunities come*
- *You learn valuable things and grow*
- *You do productive work related to your call*
- *You experience promotion or advancement*

Examples of Downward Seasons
- *An extended time of adversity*
- *Your call feels farther away than a year ago*
- *You are demoted or ejected from a role*
- *A time of inner crisis or reevaluation*

Examples of Flat Seasons
- *Life is fine but you aren't going anywhere*
- *You feel directionless or are coasting*
- *You're functioning outside your area of call*
- *You wish God would move you on*

In the major transitions you are looking at, you take a fundamentally different kind of role or become a different person, and your graph usually changes direction. In the example below, major transitions are this person's year without work at 22 and getting his first real job. He counts going to college as a minor transition because his graph continued moving in the same direction.

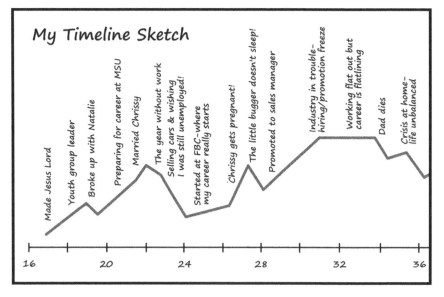

On the next page, sketch out your timeline based on *how you felt at the time* about your progress toward your call. You can either start drawing right away or choose to first list your major seasons and transitions in the table and then transfer them to the graph.

Key Events and Major Transitions	Age	Length	Trend
Example: My Wild and Radical period at ASU	19	2 years	upward
My Lordship Commitment			

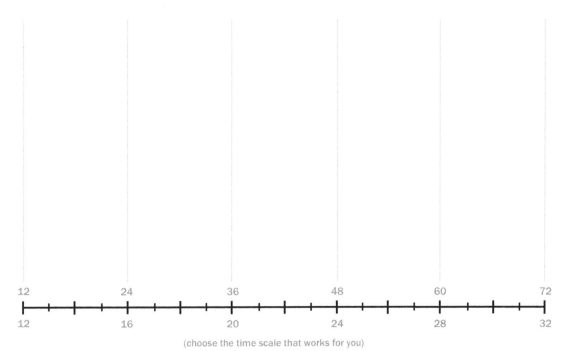

| 12 | 24 | 36 | 48 | 60 | 72 |
| 12 | 16 | 20 | 24 | 28 | 32 |

(choose the time scale that works for you)

Step 2a: Natural Promotion and the Valley of Dependence

Now we'll transfer key events from your sketch over to the standard timeline. You can work with the stages in order or start in the middle (to do so, just choose the place in your story that most clearly fits a certain point on the timeline, and work outward from there). Remember, not everything has to fit! The point is not to force your life to fit the timeline, but to see what the timeline can teach you about your life.

Your journey begins when you make Jesus Lord of your decisions as well as savior of your soul. Mark the Lordship decision on the diagram below.

The first stage, Natural Promotion (see chapter 5), averages one to five years of rapid advancement, with God's grace working through your natural, unrefined abilities. Doors open, you grow by leaps and bounds, God takes you on miraculous faith adventures, and entering your call seems just around the corner. This season corresponds to Joseph's teen years as the gifted dreamer and favored son.

> **Valley of Dependence**
> - *Averages 2.5 years in length*
> - *A tough time of failure or adversity*
> - *A negative event or character flaw (i.e. arrogance or self-sufficiency) leads you into the Valley*
> - *Life fails to match expectations; causing doubt, fear of missing it or anger at God*
> - *"Kicking against the pricks"—you fight against entering the valley*
> - *Wrong beliefs about God are challenged*
> - *You live a new dependence on God*

The Valley of Dependence which follows (see box) is seen at the time as a period of failure or adversity. Expectations are dashed and the call seems to grow distant. (Note: one valley may include a cluster of several major transitions in your list.) This season is when Joseph lost his favored position and was enslaved.

Enter your Natural Promotion stage and Valley of Dependence below. If you don't seem to have a valley right after Natural Promotion, try the alternate graph on the next page.

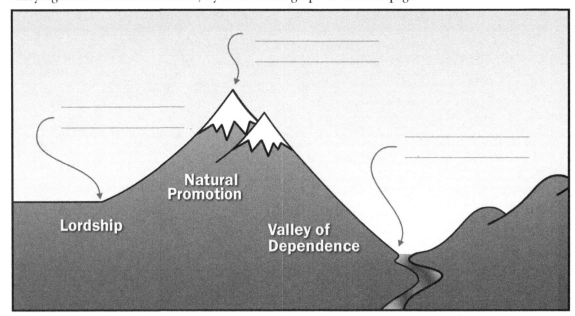

Step 2b: Descent before Lordship Option

For some people, the Valley of Dependence comes first, then Natural Promotion. This reversal of the stage order, called *Descent before Lordship,* is most common for individuals who grew up in a Christian environment and then ran from God for a season as a teen or adult. In this pattern, the low point of the valley (see diagram below) is where you take Jesus as Lord of your life, and the upward Natural Promotion stage afterward continues right into Preparation. The boundary between the two is often where you take on a Preparation Role. Mother Teresa's life demonstrates this pattern: her Valley of Dependence starts with her father's death, and Lordship and Natural Promotion came later.

If this variation sounds like a better fit for your story than the standard timeline, use this version of the graph. The Descent before Lordship pattern is described in detail on pages 57.

> **"I'm an Optimist; I Don't Have Valleys!"**
> *If you have a naturally optimistic personality, you may have difficulty at first identifying any valleys or downward-trending seasons. Here are a couple of helpful tips:*
>
> *1. Ask your spouse. Often what you see with rose-colored glasses is viewed more objectively by your mate.*
> *2. Think back to what you felt at the time. In hindsight, your personality will tend to see the good in whatever happened. Remembering how you felt at the time can offer a more accurate picture of whether this was truly a valley.*
> *3. Be aware of your defenses. Optimistic people sometimes deal with stress or conflict through denying or ignoring it, or trying to put a happy face on it. Awareness of how your natural defense mechanisms function can help show you where the valleys are.*

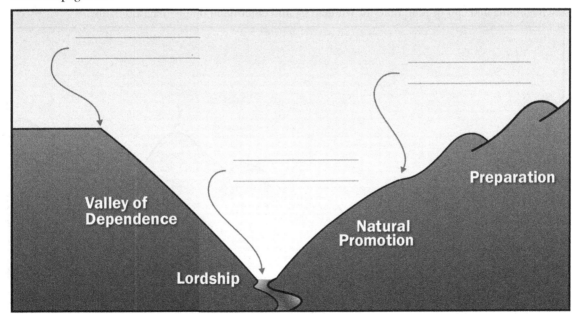

Valley of Dependence

Lordship

Natural Promotion

Preparation

Step 3a: Preparation and the Valley of Wholeness

After the Valley of Dependence the Preparation Stage begins (see chapter 7). It usually lasts five to 15 years, and focuses on developing the general skills and experience you need to fulfill your call. Often the stage kicks off when you enter a Preparation Role God uses to systematically develop you. For some, this stage is a time of increasing influence and effectiveness within their area of call, while others go through it outside their area of call and may experience it as a flat season with little outward progress toward their destiny.

> ### Valley of Wholeness Characteristics
> - *Averages one to three years long*
> - *Often triggered by family or relational issues, life balance, unrefined gifts or hidden sins*
> - *The valley most likely to be entered voluntarily (you request help instead of being forced to get it)*
> - *Less prominent or sometimes skipped by those in the Inside Preparation pattern*
> - *A Day of Release where those leaders in Outside Preparation are suddenly promoted into their calling arena*

The stage ends with a Valley of Wholeness, a second time of adversity when God surfaces internal issues that could trip you up in your Fulfillment years. Leaders often report dealing with life balance issues, relational problems, family/marital issues or secret sins here.

For leaders who are prepared outside their calling vocation, the key issue in the Valley of Wholeness is often grappling with the lack of outward progress toward their destiny and how that affects their relationship with God. Joseph's last two years in prison are a good example of this pattern.

On the graph below, mark the start of your Preparation stage (usually the same as the end of your Valley of Dependence/Natural Promotion stage). Then find the events on your timeline sketch that signify the beginning and end of your Valley of Wholeness, and enter them on the diagram below.

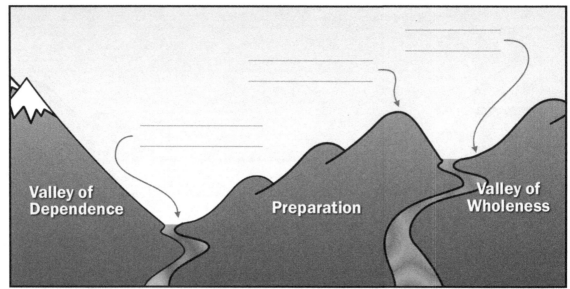

Step 3b: Inside or Outside Preparation

Some leaders go through Preparation within their area of call, and others outside it. If your call is to business leadership and you spent this stage running a company, your story fits the *Inside Preparation* pattern. You would map this stage as an ascending line (as on the previous page), representing an upward time of growth and productivity. Mother Teresa's story fits this pattern.

However, God chooses to prepare some leaders in a vocation that seems unconnected to their destiny. If your call is to business leadership but your primary Preparation role is as a stay-at-home mom, your story fits the *Outside Preparation* pattern (see below). Here, Preparation is more of a flat line, and the final portion of the stage may be experienced as a stagnant time where you wonder if you'll ever reach your call. Joseph's story fits this pattern.

Outside Preparation is usually connected with an exciting Day of Release (see page 104) after the Valley of Wholeness, when God suddenly moves you into a primary role in your area of call. This day (marked by the third arrow below) often includes a career change, geographical move or recruitment by a senior leader into a new, larger sphere of influence. Use the graph on the previous page for Inside Preparation, or the one below for Outside Preparation.

> **Help! This isn't working!**
> *If you are having trouble mapping out your timeline:*
>
> - *Be sure to graph your experiences based on how you felt at the time, instead of in hindsight.*
> - *Instead of beginning at Lordship, start at a point where your story obviously fits the timeline, and work forward and backward from there.*
> - *Get a Calling Coach. These coaches, vailable through www.TheCallingJourney.com, are specially trained to walk you through the process of developing and understanding your timeline.*
> - *Get perspective from a spouse or friend on what your major transitions are and how they fit.*

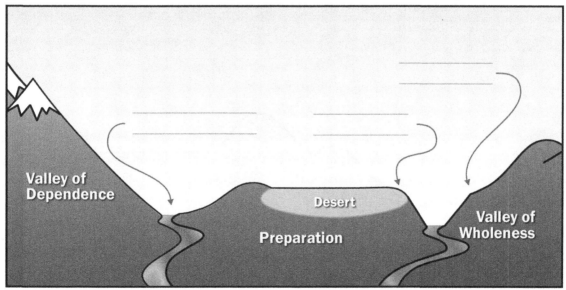

Step 4: Releasing and the Valley of Identity

After the Valley of Wholeness, leaders move into the Releasing stage (see page 128), an upward season of increasing responsibility and impact within their area of calling. This positive season averages about a decade in length. Often leaders look back on this time as an apprenticeship to the call, where they learn the ropes in a limited role or under the tutelage of another leader.

This stage culminates with a third valley, which usually takes place 15 to 30 years from the start of your calling journey and lasts several years. This Valley of Identity (see page 141) is often triggered by a significant loss of favor and influence, and/or ejection from a long-time role.

> **Valley of Identity Characteristics**
> - *Averages four years in length*
> - *Stripping of identity in work*
> - *Often triggered by ejection from long-time role or a great loss*
> - *Loss of influence and favor, financial reverses*
> - *Focus moves from doing to being*
> - *From focus on my own accomplishments to finding success in the success of others*
> - *Taking on the mantle of your calling identity*
> - *Learning to present yourself as who you are*

For those in Inside Preparation, it commonly includes a flat, wilderness season. Leaders in Outside Preparation tend to have a shorter valley followed by a brief Interlude before they move into Fulfillment.

In this valley, God works to free you from grounding your identity in work, moves your focus from doing to being and develops in you a healthy detachment from your calling (you move from *needing* to do your call to being free to do it as a gift to him). This retooling time challenges you to believe that you **are now** who you are called to be, and to present yourself to others as that person. You are commissioned to take a big risk for the sake of your call and to craft a Convergent Role that allows you to function in your best abilities. These steps move you into the Fulfillment stage (see page 159).

Identify your Valley of Identity and the Releasing stage before it and label them.

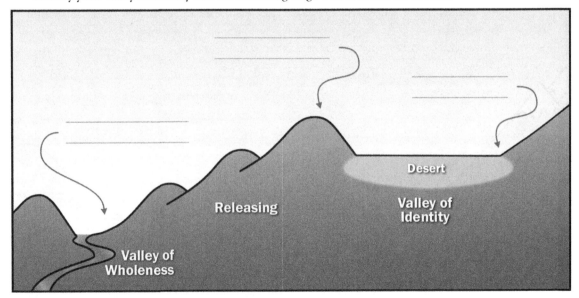

Step 5: Verify Your Timeline

While there is no "right" length for a stage or valley, a good way to verify that you're on track is to compare the length of the stages of your diagram with the averages. The graphic below represents the average of many leaders' timelines. The "length" is the average time those leaders spent in that stage, while the "Range" in the diagram is the window within which about 85% of those people fell. For example, the average person's timeline would have a Preparation stage about ten years long. 85% of leaders would spend at least six years but not more than 15 years in that stage.

So if your Preparation stage lasts between six and 15 years, you are right in the ballpark. If it is longer or shorter than that, it doesn't necessarily mean your timeline is incorrect, especially if you have one of the mitigating factors in the box at left. However, since the length of the stage is outside the norm you might want to go back and double check.

> **Why Stage Lengths Differ**
>
> - *If you made Jesus your Lord in childhood, your Natural Promotion stage may be longer.*
> - *If you got off course or backslid for a period of time, that stage may be longer.*
> - *If you made Jesus Lord in your thirties or later, all your stages will tend to be shorter.*
> - *It is common for younger leaders to overestimate their progress.*
> - *God may just choose to take you on a longer or shorter path. It's his call.*

Two large, blank diagrams are provided on pages 50 and 51 for you to combine what you've done so far into a final version of your timeline. Feel free to add learnings, key events or anything else that would make your timeline more meaningful to you. If you'd like a nice color version that you can hang on the wall, or want to use the Descent Before Lordship Pattern, just go to the on-line Timeline Builder application at www.TheCallingJourney.com, fill in the labels you came up with and print it out.

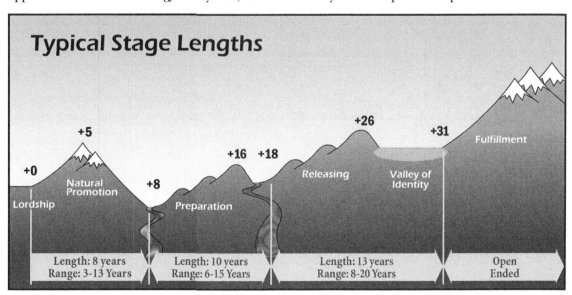

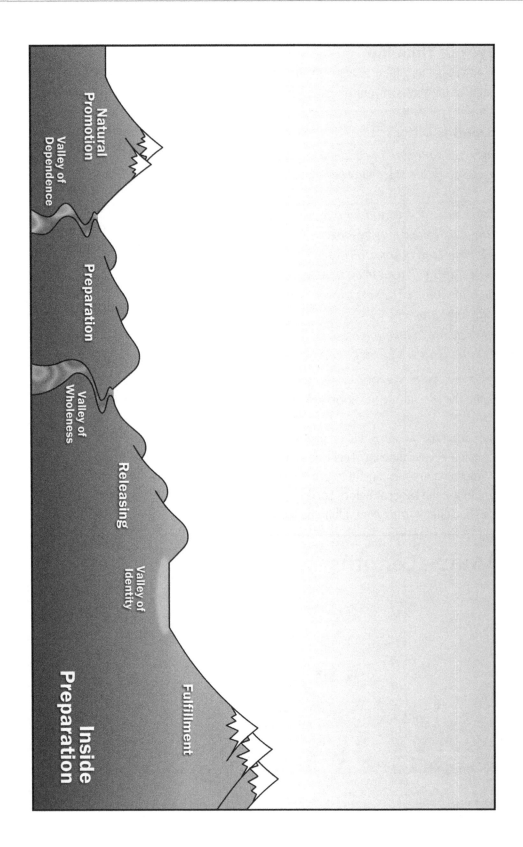

My Timeline (Inside Preparation)

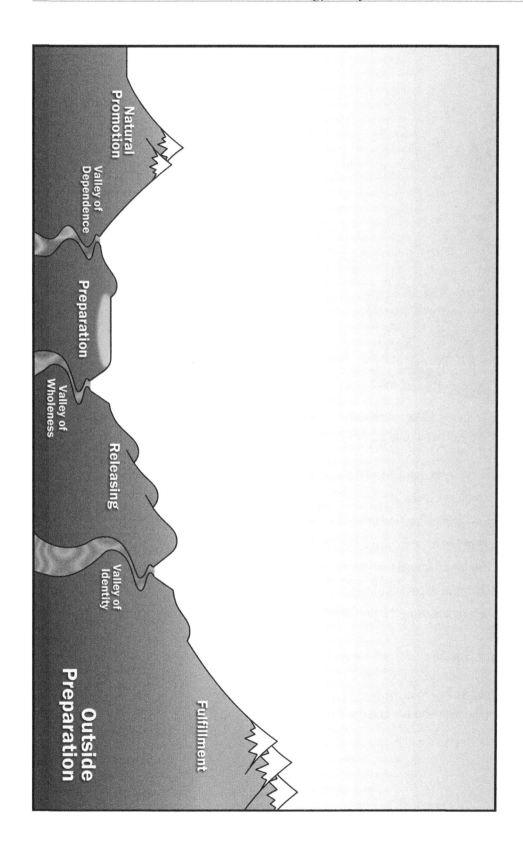

SECTION II

Now that you've completed a personal calling timeline, let's delve a little deeper into what that timeline can show you about God's activity in your life. In this section you will discover:

- More about the sovereign God who redeems everything you experience for good;
- How other leaders experience the stage you are in, and what they learned from it;
- Specific steps for meeting God in and making the most of your current stage;
- The process of Life Message formation, and how to identify the Messages God is planting in you;
- What you can look forward to in the next few years of your calling journey;
- How to identify the stages your loved ones are in and understand their life stories;
- How to coach others using the perspective of the Calling Journey model.

The best way to learn the model is through the stories of others. In the next few chapters, you'll hear from dozens of leaders like you, from all ages and walks of life, as they describe their experiences on the calling journey. The perspective in those stories can save you from a lot of preventable pain and speed you on down the path God has laid out for you.

5: NATURAL PROMOTION STAGE

O ne well known traveler is William Wilberforce, an English evangelical who spearheaded the effort to have slavery outlawed in the British Empire. His life was recently popularized in the movie, *Amazing Grace.* This account (co-written with Dr. Myra Dingman) chronicles the first stages of his calling journey.

William Wilberforce[9] was born in 1759 as the only child of a wealthy Yorkshire merchant. His mother Elizabeth envisioned a great destiny for her son and encouraged his development and nurture from a young age. William later described his upbringing and parents as "religious to the Old School," meaning a nominal commitment to the Church of England with "no true conception of the spiritual nature and aim of Christianity."

William's father and sister died when he was nine, and after his mother became seriously ill she sent her son to live with his aunt and uncle. Their fervent evangelicalism was much more profound than he had experienced at home, and William loved them as if they had been his own parents. During those years he developed the beginnings of faith in Christ and was introduced to leading Christian figures of the day such as the revivalist George Whitfield. He also met John Newton, the slave-trader-turned-Calvinist-pastor who penned the hymn, "Amazing Grace," and who would later mentor William during

Wilberforce benefitted from a Christian upbringing.

---

9   All quotes from William Wilberforce are taken from Kevin Belmonte, *William Wilberforce: A Hero for Humanity* (Grand Rapids, Zondervan, 2002) or John Stoughton, *William Wilberforce* (Charleston, Forgotten Books).

some of the difficult periods of his calling journey.

This tranquil period in his life ended when his mother, fearing that he had become "completely Methodist," brought him back home. "I was so much attached to them, I was almost brokenhearted," William recalled later. Back home, he gradually turned away from faith and adapted to his mother's world of society, card-playing, and partying.

*In this **Descent before Lordship** variation of the timeline, the descent into Valley of Dependence comes before Lordship and Natural Promotion.*

At 17, William enrolled in St. John's College in Cambridge, where he was shocked to discover "as licentious a set of men as can well be conceived." He soon fit in and became quite popular, excelling in social activities like drinking, and hosting dinners, but not in his studies. His natural abilities—a charismatic personality, adroitness at conversation and his exceptional singing voice—made friends and opened doors for him.

During his college years Wilberforce became friends with William Pitt, a classmate who later became the Prime Minister of England. Together, they decided to run for election from their respective counties. Financially

Wilberforce's natural abilities produced great outward successes.

independent after inheriting his uncle's fortune, William was elected to Parliament at the very young age of 21. He soon enrolled

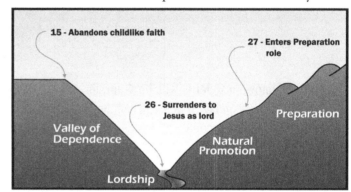

in several men's clubs where he continued his life of gambling and drinking while enjoying his new-found public stature. All of his God-given eloquence, demeanor and abilities were employed in a "life of ruin and dereliction." He later admitted, "The first years in Parliament I did nothing—nothing to any purpose. My own distinction was my darling object."

These successes were undermined by his self-focused life and character flaws.

At 25, William was set to travel to Europe with his childhood tutor, John Milner. When those plans went awry, Milner's brother, Isaac, took his place. Unaware that this brilliant Cambridge scientist was also an evangelical, Wilberforce was surprised to find someone he could respect intellectually who also held a genuine Christian worldview. Together, they read Doddridge's *Rise and Progress of Religion*, and the following year the Greek New Testament. William began to reflect deeply on his life, which led to a period of intense sorrow and depression. "I am sure that no human creature could suffer more than I did for some months," he later wrote of the last throes of his Valley of Dependence. Finally his personal struggle with faith came to a close as he made

*The **Valley of Dependence** is often a painful time of learning our need for God.*

Jesus his Lord in late 1784.

In the year of accelerated growth that made up his Natural Promotion stage, Wilberforce reevaluated his life and his priorities. He began to rise early to pray and read the Bible, cancelled all of his gentlemen's club memberships and worked to make better use of his time. Greatly regretting the years he had wasted in school, he dedicated himself to an ambitious reading program of eight hours a day in the classics to make up for lost time. William wrote letters to his closest friends, including Prime Minister Pitt, about his transformation and the "great change" that had taken place in him.

He also began to question whether he should leave his position in Parliament to become a minister. At the time, evangelicalism was viewed as nonconformist and those evangelicals in public life were ridiculed and scorned. After agonizing over the implications if it should become public, Wilberforce finally arranged to meet secretly with John Newton, a prominent evangelical. Newton encouraged him to see his current position as a divine calling on his life. William wrote later that year, "My walk… is a public one; my business is in the world; and I must mix in assemblies of men, or quit the post which Providence seems to have assigned me."

In a conversation under an oak tree at 27, Pitt (now Prime Minister) offered the challenge that further clarified William's calling and catapulted him into his Preparation role: "Wilberforce, why don't you give notice of a motion on the subject of slave trade?"

It was no small objective. The slave trade was a huge part of the British economy. Some commentators have likened it to removing the housing market or the defense industry from the current U.S. economy, solely on humanitarian grounds. After six months of prayer and questioning, Wilberforce wrote in his diary that, "God Almighty has set before me two great objects: the suppression of the slave trade and the reformation of manners [morals]." This decision moved him into his Preparation role as a legislator working on the slavery issue, and launched him into the Preparation stage.

> *Wilberforce wrestled through whether this adventure was truly a call from God.*

Lordship happens at the bottom of the valley.

*The **Natural Promotion** period is characterized by accelerated growth and living radically for God.*

Wilberforce first saw politics as a calling through the influence of a leader he had met earlier in life.

*A **Calling Event** later during this stage focused him on the slavery issue.*

The sense that God can do anything is common during this stage.

Wilberforce's life is an excellent example of how the first stages in the calling journey play out in the life of a political leader. Let's look at some of the key characteristics of Natural Promotion.

Lordship: the First Step

The key event of the Natural Promotion stage is making Jesus Lord of your life. Lordship is the trigger that initiates our first upward season of Natural Promotion, when we feel we are aligned with God's call on our life and moving toward it. Most of the time, making the Lordship commitment is also the starting point of the calling journey. The exception is the Descent before Lordship pattern, where leaders like Wilberforce experience the valley before their Lordship commitment.

The significance of Lordship for a calling timeline is that we are embracing God's mission for our life. Salvation makes me part of the family; but like Joseph, we still have to decide[10] to embrace the family calling. In effect, Lordship is joining the family business. When you say, "God, I surrender—I want you to be in charge of the course of my life," it's as if a son of the owner has chosen to join the family enterprise. You are still family, but now dad is also your boss. You have always had a shared

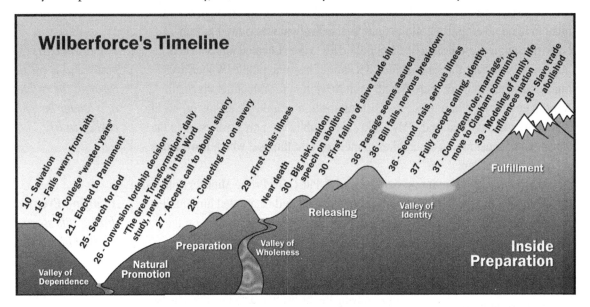

relationship; now you also have shared goals, dreams and labors.

Once you take a job in the company, all the resources of that business can be brought to bear to develop you as an employee and maximize your contribution to the corporate mission. If you never join the business, you'll still inherit it someday, but you won't get access to the employee benefits in the meantime! The choice to let your maker make the decisions and be your boss is the foundation on which your unique calling in this life is built.

Wilberforce knew about Jesus as a child, and experienced salvation at around 12 years of age. But for a 10-year period he wasn't living for God or recognizing the claims of God's mission on his life. It wasn't until he made Jesus Lord that he began to ponder what God wanted him to do with his life.

At times the Lordship commitment comes gradually. Drew, a professional jazz musician, sees his Lordship decision as something that formed over the course of a particular year in the Navy. "There was a man on the boat, an older sailor, whom I was living with while they were overhauling the ship. He rented me a room. He was a serious Christian who took me under his wing and was just relentless about

---

10   I think the biblical norm is for salvation and Lordship to happen together, but in current North American culture these are often separate events.

The Descent before Lordship Case Study

Normally, leaders experience a period of upward promotion before the first descent. But sometimes this pattern is reversed.

Allen grew up as the son of a prominent ministry leader and accepted Jesus as his savior as a child. Although he led Bible studies, brought friends to the Lord and did all the things good Christian kids do, he struggled to accept a faith shared by a workaholic father who didn't seem interested in his life. At 20, Allen dropped out of church, dropped out of college and dropped out of his parents' lives.

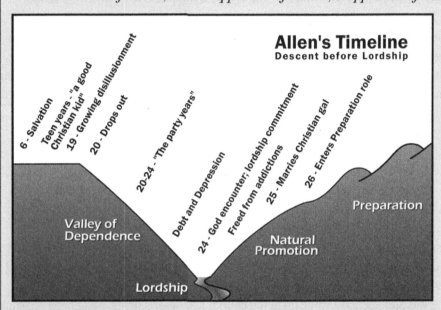

"I had no sense of purpose in life. But I did have dreams," he remarks mischievously. *"My dreams at that time were to get drunk, have sex with a beautiful woman, fly first class, speak to very large audiences, drive a Ferrari on the autobahn, and scuba dive the Great Barrier Reef."*

But four years of partying, drinking and debt led him only into depression. "One night I heard a very clear voice from God: 'There are two paths you can go down. You can die in two weeks in a car accident, drunk and stoned, and you will go to heaven. You have really messed up your life, and it won't last much longer. Or, you can choose option two and live for me. I can't tell you what it will look like, because it will scare you. I know your dreams—they are weenie dreams—but my dreams for you are much bigger."

"'Weenie dreams' is exactly the word he used," Allen laughs. After deciding to make Jesus his Lord that night, Allen got serious about living for him, and at that point his timeline (see above) shoots back upward. He stopped partying, experienced a miraculous deliverance from his addictions, and married a great Christian gal within a year of that God encounter.

In Allen's story, the progression is descent>Lordship>promotion. This variation seems to occur most often in leaders who grew up in a Christian environment but experienced a trauma that caused them to run from their upbringing. If you have a major season of difficulty leading up to your Lordship commitment, and none within a few years afterward, this version of the map may fit you best.

telling me about Jesus. He invited me to church every time he saw me. [It was during that time that] I knew that God would be authoring my life and I would follow." Drew points to that entire year as his time of making Jesus Lord instead of to a particular moment.

For others, the Lordship decision is more dramatic. Dave ran as far away from his dysfunctional home as possible when he went to college. "I smoked as much pot as I could get my hands on and was totally miserable," he recalls. "In my sophomore year I was working as a waiter. One night they overscheduled, so I decided to go home. I looked at myself in the mirror in the locker room—I was skin-and-bones, and weighed 118 pounds—and thought, 'This cannot possibly be what God has for me.'"

"So I called my mom and came clean about everything I was doing… I knew I needed to be either radically for God or against him. So I decided to be radically for him. It wasn't long before I was going to four or five Bible studies a week, out witnessing on the boardwalk at the beach… and then preaching and delivering food and Bibles in Mexico every weekend." On that night in the locker room Dave joined the business of the Kingdom, and the journey to his calling began.

Gordon's life story provides another example of the impact of the Lordship decision on one's relationship with God. "Up until I was 24 I was on the fire insurance plan," he laughs. "From 18 until 24 I partied a lot. I was dating an older woman from work, and one Saturday night we were out getting drunk and high. By God's grace I had never gotten into being sexually active to that point. When I dropped her off at her home, she stood in her doorway—I remember very clearly—and said, 'If you don't come in and sleep with me I will never speak to you again.'"

"That was a very spiritual experience. A scripture came to me at that moment: 'Resist the devil and he will flee from you; draw near to God and he will draw near to you.' I had memorized it as a kid, and my mom had put it on the fridge. I turned and just literally ran."

"The next morning was Sunday, and I woke up to the church next door singing. I had been resisting God for so long, and I decided, 'I am not going to do this anymore.' So I flushed my pot down the toilet, went to church, and never looked back."

Some individuals connect their Lordship commitment to a calling event where God spells out their life mission. For Jane, that moment came at 19, during a summer doing Bible schools out in the fields for the children of migrant workers. "I went to 25 different farms over the summer, and we did Bible school right beside the potato fields where the parents were working. Some parents would let us work with their kids and some wouldn't. That bothered me… and I wondered why, if we were safe and wanting to help and right in plain view the whole time, why they wouldn't want us to help their kids."

"What I discovered was that it had to do with how their employers treated them. The employer had a big role in the migrant workers' eternities. If they were getting substandard housing, being underpaid, or not getting paid for overtime… they were not open to the Gospel. The real gatekeeper for these lives wasn't the Bible school teacher, but the employer! And the opposite was also true. At the farms that treated them with dignity—like human beings, and as peers who were just being hired to do a job—at those places, not only did the migrants want their children to be with us, but they would come over themselves and hang out with us and hear the Gospel when their workday was over."

Her supervisor had strongly encouraged her to consider a career in missions, and at the end of the summer he asked what she had decided. "I told him I was called to be a missionary to the corporate world. I thought he would be proud of me, but he said, 'You can't do that. There is no seminary around that will teach you to do that—that job doesn't exist!'"

Jane recalls with a smile, "I put my hands on my hips and said, 'You are not God. You aren't the one who called me, and you can't tell me I can't be what God called me to be.'" She went on to carry out that mission by leading a 200 million dollar initiative at a Fortune 50 company.

You may wonder why the timeline map doesn't always start at the moment when a person receives a specific, personal calling instead of when they surrender to the general call to make Jesus Lord. From talking to hundreds of leaders about their calling, I've found that many stellar individuals who are living for Christ cannot point to a specific, identifiable moment (a "calling event") that set the course for their lives. For about half of all leaders, the call seems to be progressively revealed through many experiences over a course of years or decades. In fact, many faithful leaders do not come to full clarity on their calling until late in the Releasing stage, when they are in their forties or fifties.[11] So if you don't have one dramatic moment early in life where God speaks to you about your call, that's pretty normal. No matter when in life you come to understand your specific, personal call, your timeline starts when you accept your general calling to make Jesus Lord.

> ### Natural Promotion Characteristics
>
> - *Begins immediately after Lordship*
> - *Usually one to nine years long (longest if Lordship commitment made at an early age)*
> - *Confirmation of call or Calling Events*
> - *Rapid promotion based on natural ability*
> - *Faith Adventures*
> - *Being wild and radical for God*
> - *A sense that God can do anything*
> - *God gives a taste of functioning in your call*
> - *Self-sufficiency, hubris or ignoring counsel may lead you into the Valley of Dependence*

One of the most eye-opening patterns I saw while researching this book was the power this Lordship commitment unleashes in the lives of those who are called. When you make that one-time decision to follow with all your heart, God takes you seriously. There may still be times your faith wavers, or even when you try to escape from your call. Even Jesus grappled with those questions at Gethsemane. But God will see you through the struggle. If you haven't yet said, 'Jesus, I want you to own my life, be in charge, steer my course'—do it now!

Wild and Radical for God

After you've taken the step of making a Lordship commitment, the exciting ride of the first upward season of Natural Promotion immediately follows. This upward season averages about five years in length, although it can occasionally last a decade, particularly if the person makes a serious commitment to Christ at a young age. It's a time we get radical for God. For instance, Wilberforce began praying daily, studying eight hours a day, dropped out of his gambling clubs and began telling friends about what

---

11   For a more complete treatment of this topic, see the *Christian Life Coaching Handbook* by Tony Stoltzfus.

Jesus had done in his life. He also met with a great opportunity to oppose the slave trade, experienced confirmation of his calling and saw rapid advancement in his leadership.

Lisa's story is another that captures the flavor of this season. "I was very excited at the beginning. I took my pastor out to Pizza Hut and shared the Gospel with him. I was asking, 'How come you never told me that Jesus died on the cross for me?' I thought the first night [after I got saved] that I wanted God to take me wherever he wanted me to go. I started reading about missionaries and loved all the stories. I didn't so much feel called, but I wanted to be used of God, and reading about radical people who gave their lives helped me."

"I took the youth group on a boat trip and shared the Gospel with all of them. [This kind of thing] continued throughout high school. I was very active in school. At home, I took the approach of denial—helping everyone else with their problems and escaping [a father's alcoholism at home] by being involved in everything at school. I was a very happy person and a growing Christian."

In this stage, a big helping of God's grace working through our human capacity gives us a wonderful taste of what living in our calling will be like. For Lisa, that was evangelism and discipling people one on one, a role that was later an integral part of her call. We respond to God out of what we have, and at this point in life what we have is raw natural abilities, lots of energy and relatively unrefined character. This stage will display both the great potential locked within and the critical limitations of our natural selves.

Calling Events and Confirmation

About half of the leaders I've worked with over the years can pinpoint a clear Calling Event early in life[12], and often it comes during this stage. Wilberforce had several: his conversation with Newton who encouraged him to stay in Parliament, the conversation where Pitt challenged him to take on the slave trade, and the revelation he recorded in his journal of the two great objects God had set before him.

Margaret's story is another good example. The summer after her second year of college, the career path she'd set out upon was suddenly blocked. She had been taking business classes, planning go back to a previous job, but the company was sold and that door closed.

> **Calling Event**
> *A specific experience where God reveals a major piece of your life call.*

"I went out in the pasture and sat under a tree, trying to decide what to do with my life. There weren't too many options [for women] in those days. I had always said that I didn't want to be a teacher, but as I thought about it, I was drawn to teaching. I felt that God said, 'This is the best option for you at this point. This career uses the skills that you have.' I told him that if he would arrange my schedule to graduate in two years I would become a teacher. I wrote to the man in charge of the Teacher Education department asking about changing majors, and got a letter back with a schedule that would graduate me in two years. So that is what I did."

Confirmations of call from personal successes, evidence of our gifts in action or significant people in our lives are even more common. A few years earlier, Margaret caught the attention of Orpha, a literature and speech teacher in her high school. Recognizing Margaret's natural communication

---

12   For the other half, calling seems to be revealed progressively over time. Often it is not until the Releasing stage or Valley of Identity that leaders become really clear on what God is calling them to do.

abilities, Orpha took her under her wing and became a key mentor and sponsor. She entered Margaret in county- and state-level speaking competitions, wrote letters of commendation on her behalf, and sponsored her into teaching positions in a summer Bible school. Margaret looks back fondly on her relationship with Orpha as "a big influence in my life" and an important affirmation of her speaking and writing abilities. Later, in her Fulfillment stage, Margaret used the same abilities Orpha fostered in her as a prominent community leader and top officer of a large, international women's organization.

Faith Adventures

Faith building seems to be one of God's important objectives in this stage. Over and over, leaders relate stories of the Faith Adventures God took them on: journeys of obedience where they were compelled to depend on God alone, and saw him divinely supply their needs just in time. One older pastor I interviewed recounted how he hitchhiked from California to Massachusetts 50 years ago to pioneer a campus ministry, and led the first person who gave him a ride to the Lord. Another young entrepreneur felt called to take a bus to Mexico City with no money or place to stay, and God supplied lodging and transportation through someone he met on the bus. A third leader felt called to go to college debt free, and while he worked hard during those years, he also had several instances where God sovereignly provided just in time with just enough to meet the need.

> ### Exercise: Building an Altar
>
> *At the end of his Natural Promotion stage, Abraham reached the Promised Land. One of the first things he did was to build an altar. The altar was a physical representation of the fact that God had called him, and a place to worship him for his faithfulness in fulfilling it.*
>
> *You can build your own altar by recording what God has revealed to you about your call. A Revelation Journal is a place where you write down words, confirmations or affirmations, inner knowings about your call and more. As you go through life, a record of what God has spoken and fulfilled becomes a place of worship around God's love and faithfulness.*
>
> *A detailed set of steps for creating a Revelation Journal can be found in the book,* A Leader's Life Purpose Workbook.

Abraham's first call offers a great biblical picture of a faith adventure: God said, "Go to the land *that I will show you.*" Imagine—loading your entire family and your family business into the truck for a major move without knowing where you are going or how to get there!

The Natural Promotion stage is the time of life to do that kind of crazy stuff. We are challenged to step out and depend on God without a plan, in order to see him meet us on the way. That's a Faith Adventure. Doors of opportunity open; we walk through them and live on the radical edge for God.

Rapid Promotion and a Taste of the Call

Another characteristic of this period is rapid promotion: unusual favor from God, significant early leadership positions and great results. Cynthia began this stage working in a mental health center with sex offenders. Feeling constrained by rules against talking about Jesus in her role, she considered moving on. One day God directed her to a particular neighborhood, to a certain address she had never been. On entering the building, she discovered it housed an inner city justice ministry—just the kind of thing she was looking for. Cynthia was soon hired, and among other things did Bible studies in a juvenile prison and roamed dangerous housing projects mentoring young women coming out of the juvenile justice system. "I received lots of affirmation from youth and parents, and the programs were well known and respected," she remembers. Her ministry career advanced rapidly and new doors seemed to open whenever she needed one.

The upward-trending portion of the Natural Promotion stage is a preview of what it will be like to live in our call. Only when we are several stages down the road do we see it for what it is: a God-given taste of the thrilling destiny we have coming if we will follow him through the wilderness to reach it. But at the time, it feels like we have already landed on our feet in our destiny role.

Drew, the jazz musician, was touring with a successful band during this period of life. He loved being on stage and thought he'd found a long-term gig. 'This is it!" he remembers thinking. "This is the life I want to live!" But the band was short-lived, and it was years down the road until his dream of being a professional musician came to pass.

Perils for Parents

Parents tend to struggle when their young adults go through this stage. We *so* want our kids to settle down, get an education, find a career, get a real job—to be successful, at least by our cultural standards. But they seem to be going in the opposite direction. They blow off college to go to an unaccredited ministry school, or change majors in the middle of their senior year, or turn down a great job opportunity with Microsoft to work for peanuts at a start-up company. They dive in, naïvely believe that everything will work out for them financially, when you see no visible means of support. They are shockingly uninformed about the cold, unyielding realities of life. Will they *ever* settle down and become responsible adults?

Things get even more agonizing as God takes them into the Valley of Dependence. Your worst fears come to pass as the things you vainly tried to warn them about come back to bite them. The start-up folds and your first born is stuck living on a friend's couch with no money. The fiancé you were always wary of dumps your son and breaks his heart, or your darling daughter goes to the mission field and returns depressed and demoralized a year later because she couldn't raise the support she needed to stay. It's painful to see your kids fail. You begin to wonder if you have somehow failed them as a parent.

This is a great example of the difference understanding the timeline can make. If you don't understand God's ways, and see success in terms of outward accomplishment, it looks like something is wrong. But in reality, God is in the crazy things your kids are doing. We learn dependence on him best by banging into our own limitations.

An analogy of what's happening in this stage might help. The common joke is that if it wasn't for physical attraction, men would never get around to getting married, let alone procreation. Building a marriage is hard work, especially in the first few years. But God has a plan. He uses hormones to motivate us to find a life partner, and as the hormones fade, a deeper love flowers in their place. But if it wasn't for the hormones, building a deeply loving relationship is so much work that we'd never make the leap.

Calling is similar. Living God's mission for your life is challenging, hard work. Worse, the times of greatest struggle seem to arrive toward the beginning of the journey, while the best of the rewards come near the end. The Natural Promotion stage is like a shot of calling hormones. God lets us taste and see the wild adventure of living for him without a safety net, and that experience ruins us for ordinary life. Having once tasted divine provision, we hunger for more of the call. Without the life-long yearning this season plants in us, most of us would never get started on the calling journey, let alone finish it.

It is vitally important to be crazy for God when you are young. If you can't sell out for him when you have no family, no payments to make and no responsibilities to tie you to the world, how will you ever do it when you have them? While our cultural conditioning says that these are the years to embrace the world system and do what will make us successful in it, God is moving in the opposite direction to inoculate us against investing the best years of our lives into things that will ultimately never satisfy. I think that's pretty cool of him to do that for our kids.

So parents, relax. Your kids need to be radical when they are young. The years to be focused and serious will come. And failing big when they are young isn't so bad, either. The bigger the calling, the greater a young leader needs what only failure can teach: the limitations of one's natural abilities and need for utter dependence on God.

In fact, God can do even greater things with failure. It is likely that the centerpiece of your sons' and daughters' callings, the Life Messages that will give the greatest satisfaction and impact of anything in their lives, will be birthed out of the failure or adversity experienced early in life. God will reveal himself as Redeemer to them—and through them—by how he meets them in those times. You can trust God to look out for them: he means all this for good.

Characteristics Case Study

All these characteristics of the Natural Promotion stage come into play in Kara's story. She grew up in a large church where her father was minister of music. After making a Lordship commitment at a camp at age 14, she immediately moved into the upward-trending portion of the stage. She sought out places to serve in her youth group, got involved in her church's music ministry, served on a pastoral search committee, and even organized a prayer gathering at her school that was publicized in a national magazine. These activities highlighted her leadership gifts and (in retrospect) confirmed her calling to speak value and acceptance into the lives of others.

At another camp several years after the first Kara discovered that God could speak

Natural Promotion Characteristics

- *Begins immediately after Lordship*
- *Usually one to nine years long (longest if Lordship commitment made at an early age)*
- *Confirmation of call or Calling Events*
- *Rapid promotion based on natural ability*
- *Faith Adventures*
- *Being wild and radical for God*
- *A sense that God can do anything*
- *God gives a taste of functioning in your call*
- *Self-sufficiency, hubris or ignoring counsel may lead you into the Valley of Dependence*

directly to her on a daily basis, and that revelation threw gasoline on the fire. "I started taking literally that God could do anything," she recounts. "I was witnessing to anyone, and getting together with friends to worship and listen to God's voice. It wasn't my folks' thing, but they loved it and encouraged it."

Kara is a good example of the wild and radical bent of this life stage. Our exuberance about life in Jesus spills out in every direction, often evidenced in things like witnessing to others, going to every church service in sight, taking joy in acts of service, spending hours in prayer or Bible study, or ignoring other responsibilities to invest in our life with God.

After four years at a Christian college—"I was still in a big bubble"—Kara took some classes in public relations in Washington D.C. While she was there she experienced an important Calling Event. "I remember sitting in a café with a bunch of gals talking about the Gospel, and I felt the Lord say, "This is what you are going to be doing while you are in D.C." Her congressman found out she was in the area, and invited her to do a six-week internship there. The next week she got a call from a friend of a friend, who asked if Kara wanted to live with her on Capitol Hill. She took a leap of faith and signed a year lease, with no idea what she would do when the internship was over. One thing led to another, and she got a job with a Christian statesmanship center doing discipleship. In this Faith Adventure, she experienced going out on a limb based on God's leading, and seeing him open doors and provide at just the right time.

Kara was getting a taste of what living her call would look like. "I had a very profound experience there [in D.C.]," she recounts. "I noticed for the first time that there were a lot of hurting people behind the façade. Everyone is ambitious, but many are clueless about their personal lives. I got to sing in front of senators and disciple older women. I thought I'd found my dream job!"

However, operating at this level of our call this early in life only happens with a heaping helping of God's grace. The longer Kara stayed in her new role, the more her sense of lacking something fundamental began to percolate to the surface. "I began to flounder," she remarks. "I started to question if who I was was enough for what I was doing. I didn't know anything about policy. I was ignorant about the issues that these people were dealing with. I began to realize how big the world is and how small I was, and how little influence I actually have. I wasn't in a controlled environment where everyone accepted me anymore. Walking into the Senate, I realized that I didn't have anything to offer."

Kara was legitimately afraid of becoming like the driven, stressed-out people she was serving. "I didn't want the lifestyle I saw everyone living," she recalls. "I didn't want the 80-hour work week. But if I am not this, if this is not where I belong—then who am I? I began to wonder if I should just move back home to Colorado. Everyone here was so serious. My spirit was being squelched, but I didn't know how to name it or what to do about it."

Kara had the opportunity, she had God's favor, and she had the natural talent and ability to succeed in a role that fit her destiny. But with an unusual wisdom for her age, she intuitively knew something was missing. *She was not the person she needed to be to do what she was born to do.* And so, at the moment of our greatest success to this point, God prepares to take us down an unexpected, shadowed path—the Valley of Dependence.

Making the Most of Natural Promotion

So what does it look like to lean into God's purposes for you in this stage of life? The task of the Natural Promotion stage is to make Jesus Lord of your life and firmly fix your course toward your calling. Being ruined for the ordinary is part of the learning agenda, so you will be challenged to leave your comfort zone and do the extraordinary. Most people go through this stage in their teens and twenties, and there is no time to be wild and radical and do crazy things for God like when you are young and he is Lord! Step out in faith, take risks and hold things lightly as God rearranges your life.

Since this season is more about your formation than your accomplishments, don't waste a lot of effort trying to make sure you are in the perfect job or role. "Whatever your hand finds to do, do it with all your might," is the rule for this season. If God seems to be in it, do it. The goal is not to set yourself up for success in the world system of power and wealth, but to fix your heart toward following Jesus wherever he goes. The rich young ruler story is a great example of God's call to someone at this point in life to leave behind the prospect of worldly success and just follow him.

> ### The One Step You Must Take
> *The single most important thing you can do for your calling journey is find a mentor who is farther along on the journey. Do it now!*

I encourage people in their late teens and early twenties not to worry too much about getting on the career track right away. The US Department of Labor says that the average US worker today will change careers three to five times during their lifetime. That's a different vocational world than what their parents experienced. While the conventional wisdom of the past was to go straight to college and then into your career, in today's world accumulating a wide variety of experiences instead of focusing in on one area may better help young people develop into who they need to be to succeed in life.

For example, one young couple in our small group took a trip all the way around the globe in their mid-twenties. They lived with missionaries in the jungles, immersed themselves in other cultures, took wonderful pictures and got some great insight on their life's direction. Now that they've come back, they are starting a family and settling down for the long haul. But that trip is a powerful memory and guide to their discernment of what God made them for. It may be 15, 20 or even 25 years before it will be possible for them to take an adventure like that again. What a great decision to do the wild, risky thing when you are young!

My daughter is 17, and her dream is to enroll in an unaccredited ministry school once she gets out of high school. We're actually moving from one coast to the other and planning for her to graduate a year early to help her achieve that dream. Yes, I do want her to go to college someday. But even more, I want her to grow in hearing and following God's voice.

After I completed my own college degree, instead of going to grad school I worked part time for five years so I could gallivant around the country with a band, run a men's discipleship house, lead small groups, and devote myself to full-time volunteer ministry. Those were great years, and I could not do what I am doing today without them. I left a lot of money on the table by not becoming an engineer, but looking back, that was a great decision. I believe as my daughter follows her dreams that God will make her career path turn out well for her, too.

Temptations

Just as each stage of the journey has unique growth tasks, it also has unique temptations. The most obvious one in the Natural Promotion is to think more highly of yourself than you ought to think. When we first commit to Christ (especially if we are young adults) the world is our oyster, and by golly, we are going to go out and change it tomorrow. Those stuck-in-the-mud senior leaders with their life experience just don't get it. And when God abundantly blesses our early efforts, it is easy to think that nothing will be impossible for us, and we're going onward and upward from there on out.

> ### Summary of Key Learnings
> - *Our promotion begins immediately after our Lordship commitment.*
> - *While most of us make Jesus Lord, go upward through Natural Promotion and then descend into the valley, for some the progression is valley>Lordship>ascent (the Descent before Lordship pattern).*
> - *In the upward portion of this stage we get a taste of functioning in our calling.*
> - *Getting perspective on our stage from older leaders or mentors is vital to traveling well.*
> - *Key Task: "Whatever your hand finds to do, do it with all your might." Accumulate a wide variety of experiences. Be radical for God.*

Sometimes when you are young, no one can tell you anything. I think God smiles at that. The gift of being young is that sometimes you are too naïve to know that something is impossible, so you just go out and make it happen. The down side of walking in that uninformed faith is that you lumber into potholes that are glaringly obvious to anyone who has been down that road before.

It can be difficult to separate the wisdom of age from the cynicism of those who have stopped believing and want you to stop hoping, too. The solution is not to surrender your idealism, nor is it to just stop listening to your elders altogether. Instead, *listen to the people who are actually out changing the world, and are doing it for the good of others.* The cynics and critics and gadflies will sit on the sidelines and tell you everything you lack and what can't be done. Don't listen. The manipulators and the self-serving will try to recruit you to make their own dreams of grandeur come true. Don't join. The controllers will want to take charge of your life, or sabotage your efforts if you refuse because you aren't with them. Walk away.

The people to listen to, the ones with real wisdom, will gladly welcome you into the arena, find out what you are called to, and do what they can to help God's dream for you happen in your life. Great leaders follow God's dream, not their own. And because it is God they follow, they can tell when God's dream is in others, and they'll invest in it for his sake.

Natural Promotion Reflection Questions

1. When in your life did you make Jesus Lord of your decisions and your future as well as savior of your soul?

2. In the years immediately after your Lordship commitment, which of the stage characteristics (box on page 68) did you experience?

3. What was/is God doing in your heart during these years?

4. When did the upward season of promotion and favor come to an end, and what triggered that change?

Bible Study Guide: Natural Promotion

Look for the stage characteristics in the box at right in the lives of these biblical characters. What might have been going on inside these leaders as they walked through these experiences?

> ### Natural Promotion Characteristics
>
> - *Begins immediately after Lordship*
> - *Usually one to nine years long (longest if Lordship commitment made at and early age)*
> - *Confirmation of call or Calling Events*
> - *Rapid promotion based on natural ability*
> - *Faith Adventures*
> - *Being wild and radical for God*
> - *A sense that God can do anything*
> - *God gives a taste of functioning in your call*
> - *Self-sufficiency, hubris or ignoring counsel may lead you into the Valley of Dependence*

1. **Paul**, from his salvation/Lordship experience to the descent where he was shipped off to Tarsus (Acts 9:1-31).

3. **David,** From his anointing by Samuel until the conflict with Saul that led him into the Valley of Dependence (I Sam. 16-18).

4. **Joseph**, from his growing-up years of favor to being sold into Egypt (Gen. 37:1-36).

5. **Moses,** from his first sense of call (when he "went out and saw his people" and attempted in his natural abilities to save them) until his exile in Midian (Ex. 2:11-21).

6. **Abraham**, from when he obeyed the call to go to the Promised Land until the famine forced him to leave it for Egypt (Gen. 12:1-10).

7. **Jesus**, when his early functioning in his gifts was truncated by his parents (Luke 2:40-52).

6: THE VALLEY OF DEPENDENCE

A missionary friend of mine likes to recount a story about Loren Cunningham, the founder of Youth with a Mission and the University of the Nations in Hawaii. Responding to criticism about how he was handling the challenges of setting up a ground-breaking international institution from scratch, Cunningham replied, "Hey—it's my first University! Maybe when I've got three or four under my belt I'll make fewer mistakes."

> **The Valley of Dependence**
>
> *The first major season of adversity on the calling journey, which God uses to shape your Life Messages and build reliance on him instead of your raw gifts and natural abilities.*

The Valley of Dependence is that kind of first: the first big dip in our map, the first time God uses an extended season of difficulty to shape us for our destiny. The fact that we are walking an unfamiliar road makes this a challenging season—it is rare to see someone go through it with the equanimity Cunningham showed later in life. Once we have several transitions under our belts, we navigate them much more easily.

To this point, our road on the calling journey has taken us steadily upward[13]. We've gotten the great job, been promoted, seen God act, or taken a leap of faith and landed on our feet. When living in the place of favor and promotion is all we've known, we naturally expect things to go on like that forever. We take it as a given that when you make Jesus Lord, life is onward-and-upward forever. When life suddenly and dramatically fails to meet our lofty expectations, a crash is inevitable.

Let's pick up Cynthia's story. She came to Christ at 23 and had lived an all-out Christian life ever since. While praying at 24 about her work as a therapist, she saw a picture of herself crossing the ocean

---

13   Assuming that our story fits the standard timeline and not the Descent before Lordship variant.

and being free to talk about Jesus in her counseling sessions, something she couldn't do in her current job. That calling event led her to become a missionary.

So she and her new husband left for a missions training program in Amsterdam. "We went on outreaches and saw miracles and healings—that was wild and new. I thought, 'This is really the Kingdom of God that we thought existed...' I learned about unreached people groups and felt strongly called to go to places with no church."

So at 30, Cynthia and Brad left for central Asia. "I went so full of faith that we would quickly see a huge move of God and many miracles take place," she declares. "I was sure that we would see lots of people come to the Lord and many churches planted quickly. Instead, I got pregnant—twice, in 15 months! I wasn't prepared for this at all. I didn't know anything about being a mother. There was no one there to teach me anything, and I felt completely isolated because I didn't know the language. I couldn't talk to people, so I had to take everything to God."

"What made it worse was that I was in a setting where women were nothing. Before, Brad and I had always ministered together. But now Brad got all the opportunities, and I often felt overlooked and unseen. I felt like an idiot: I couldn't do anything."

"I spent two or three years in the wilderness working on identity issues. Sometimes I felt like I was going to die in this place that was so far from my home and what had given me affirmation before. I finally reached the point where I surrendered depending on myself and my own ability. It wasn't until then that God allowed any fruit at all to come from what I did. Before that, I was always comparing myself with others around me, and it felt like there was pressure on us to show results in ministry. People would compare me to others in ministry and ask me why they were seeing much fruit and I wasn't. That time brought me to a place of dependence, of knowing I'm his daughter whether I produce any fruit or not. It was about putting my identity in him, not in my ministry or how 'successful' I am."

The Jolt

Cynthia's story is a good example of many of the key characteristics of the Valley of Dependence.

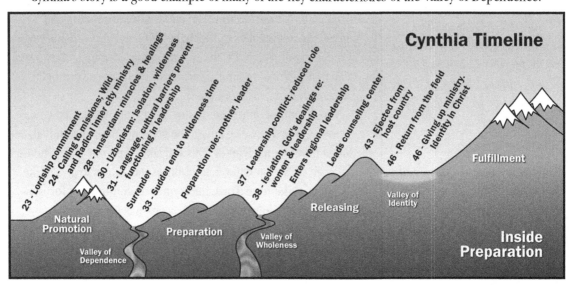

This season lasts an average of two-and-a-half years, and is usually triggered by a negative event (or series of events) that disrupts our happy existence and moves the focus from outward productivity to inner renovation. For Cynthia, that trigger was a geographic move that created language, cultural and gender barriers to her functioning in leadership. Transitioning from ministry into motherhood, feeling rejected by the authority figures over her and leaving family and friends behind brought Cynthia to a crisis. As she cried out to God in her pain, he redeemed it. Instead of crippling her, that crisis became a mirror that allowed Cynthia to see the limitations of her natural abilities, and drew her to deeper intimacy and dependence on God.

Valley of Dependence Characteristics

- *Focus: Dependence*
- *Averages 2.5 years in length*
- *A negative trigger event leads us into the valley*
- *Our character flaw (i.e. arrogance or self-sufficiency) often contributes to the crash*
- *Difficult time of failure or adversity*
- *Formation of key Life Messages*
- *Life not meeting expectations causes doubt, fear of missing it, feeling lost, anger at God, cynicism*
- *"Kicking against the pricks"—we fight against entering the valley*
- *We ask God to get us out of our circumstances and he explicitly refuses*
- *Isolation or rejection by friend or authority figure*

Cynthia's being call is "to be a person of courage—having the inner strength from him to do whatever he asks, knowing he will lead me to victory." Can you see the connection between that Message and her Valley of Dependence? God redeemed her situation by using it to make her into the person she was born to be. The inner strength of Jesus—the courage to do whatever the Father asks—has been incarnated in Cynthia through this difficult experience. What at first seemed meant for evil, God turned into good. This valley is about meeting the Great Redeemer in the midst of our limitations and learning to depend on him.

There is a river at the bottom of the Valley of Dependence—a stream in the desert. You will find water in your valleys, because God is there. The sign that you are in the center of his will in a valley season isn't that everything outwardly is going well, or that God feels close. It is thirst. Thirst is what leads you to dig a deep well, down to the heart of your being, and when you do you'll hit water.

The three valleys in our timeline each reshape our identity in different ways. Because they touch our deepest selves, the events that trigger them tend to be ones that challenge who we think we are. When our identity is bound up in a role, like Cynthia's was, losing the role means losing our identity. That leads to anxiety, uncertainty, self-doubt and questioning our standing with God.

Cynthia's overconfidence and heightened expectations about the big ministry God would bestow on her also contributed to the pain of her crash. She took for granted that she was on an uninterrupted path that would lead her smoothly onward and upward to her call. It was a natural assumption, given what she'd experienced to that point in life. However, Cynthia didn't anticipate motherhood, language difficulties or gender issues blocking that path.

The failure of life to meet our expectations causes much of the angst of the Valley of Dependence.

Our entire experience to this point of walking with Jesus as Lord is an exciting upward season of favor and growth. We've had a taste of our call, and believe that full release is just around the corner. Our experience feels like real, New Testament Christianity, so we naturally expect it to continue this way for the rest of our lives. We may have even looked down on other believers we know who aren't living the way we are. So when God unexpectedly takes us into the desert, the place we thought we'd never go, the house of beliefs we live in is stripped down to the bare studs. These are the times when God does his best work of interior renovation.

Interior Renovation

Making extraordinary changes to our identity usually requires extraordinary circumstances. Amy's story is another example of how God redeems our greatest pain and uses it to accomplish his purposes. Growing up in a home without a father, "I became depressed and insecure, introverted… and emotionally needy," Amy recounts. "I grew up in the lie of needing to have a man to fulfill me and complete me."

She felt called to ministry, so she married a youth pastor, thinking that was the path that would take her there. It wasn't long before things went sour. When he began to have emotional affairs, "I tried to confront it but he was in denial," Amy recalls. "I got pregnant, thinking 'surely if we have a child this will fix everything.' But it didn't. One day he called me up from a hotel to say that he was with another woman… It was evident [his affairs] were turning physical. I was so upset I had a miscarriage. Then he resigned from the church because he decided Christianity was not for him! In one week I lost my baby, my ministry and my marriage."

Because her husband never acknowledged to their church that he had done anything wrong—"he lied to cover up everything"—only a few friends close to Amy knew what had really happened. Isolated from her church home, frightened by her husband's growing violence and rejected by the authority figures in her life, Amy came to a crossroads in her faith.

"How do you respond to that kind of loss?" she asks. "I said, 'God, if this is what you have for me, I don't want it.' So I went back to the old coping mechanisms modeled in my family and started drinking. I remember one night having a wine cooler in one hand and a Bible in the other, saying, 'What am I going to do? Which one will I choose?'"

"I remembered what the bottle had done to my step fathers, and I didn't want to go down that road. So I threw away the bottle and threw myself into the Word, staying up nights and crying out to God… I had to find a new church, a new home, new friends and new everything. But I grew by leaps and bounds, just me and God there in my little apartment with my worship CDs and my Bible."

A beautiful smile crosses Amy's face when she talks about the fruit of that season. "What that time produced in me was a complete surrender, a desperation for God. It thrust me into a deeper faith and trust in God and who I am in him. I know that I know that I know now that I can trust in him and his Word. I wouldn't trade that for anything."

Hubris

A major negative event is what usually leads us into the Valley of Dependence. Sometimes, that event grows out of our own arrogance, character flaws or determination to move forward regardless of the warning signs. Ethan's story is a good example. Growing up, he seemed singled out for a great future. As a teen, he became part of the altar ministry team at his church and prayed for a number of people who were supernaturally healed. He taught in the youth group and at times in adult Sunday schools, sang solos, and was president of the youth group. His picture of the future was "I would go to seminary, be a youth pastor and then a senior pastor."

However, Ethan recalls, "I was arrogant. I didn't know how to interpret the power I seemingly had. I thought I was more favored than others and had more insight."

While interviewing for a job one summer, on the spur of the moment he decided to check out a summer camp he passed on the way home. "I went on a day all the female counselors were out sunbathing. The camp looked pretty after the rain, but at the job interview that morning it had been all dreary and gray. So I decided to work at the camp for the girls and the atmosphere."

His first year at college was difficult. People in his new circles were highly suspicious of Ethan's supernatural experiences, and Ethan felt more and more isolated in his faith. Then the crisis hit. "At 19, the girl I thought I was going to marry suddenly broke it off. I had been seeing her for two-and-a-half years. The same week, my parents had a violent fight and my mom left. And soon after the pastor that had mentored me was asked to step down after people discovered he'd had multiple affairs with women in the church. His son was my best friend."

Ethan was stunned. "I had never experienced any trauma in my life. I was completely knocked off balance. I stuffed the emotion because I had no one to talk to, stuffed it inside." He ended up letting himself be seduced ("it wasn't hard"), and lost his virginity. Upset, angry at himself and unsure how to handle his own blunders, Ethan avoided the girl for months. Later he learned that she was pregnant and had gotten an abortion.

"I was in a conservative, pro-life group and had violated both. I carried a lot of shame for years for that… The temptation was to isolate myself and avoid connections—to not open up so I wouldn't be hurt again." Not understanding how to meet God in his valley, and isolated from the perspective he desperately needed to do so, Ethan's relationship with God was put out of joint instead of being healed (Heb. 12:13). He became cynical about his past God-encounters.

Finally, after almost a decade of functioning out of shame, God used a marital crisis and the near death of a child in Ethan's Valley of Wholeness to break open those wounds and bring healing.

> *The enemy's agenda for our first valley is to try to get us to believe it came from God, that God is powerless to stop it, or that God is not there.*

The Enemy's Agenda

Ethan's experience reveals that the enemy also has an agenda for us in the Valley of Dependence. God wants to teach us how to meet him in times of adversity as the Great Redeemer. His purpose is that we come out of the Valley knowing and trusting his goodness to us more deeply, no matter what circumstances bring.

The adversary's plan is to co-opt this time to make an assault on God's character. Instead of intimately identifying with Jesus' cry ("My God, my God, why have you forsaken me?") and looking forward to the end of the story (Jesus' triumphant resurrection), Satan wants us to get all wrapped up in the pain and lose hope. If he can get us to believe we have been abandoned in the valley, that God cannot be trusted, or that God is not there, he wins. When instead of being healed we allow the enemy to put our brokenness out of joint, the result is doubt, cynicism, bitterness and continuing pain.

The contrast between these two agendas cuts to the very purpose and meaning of suffering. We suffer because we live in a broken, fallen world. That world is redeemed by God entering into it in the form of a man, taking on the brokenness of the world and making what was meant for evil turn out for good. By entering the brokenness, it is transformed by Jesus' life and brought into his Kingdom. This is God's plan for bringing his Kingdom to creation and the human race.

God does not cause our suffering, nor does he take over the world by force to stop it. *He redeems it,* working first through his Son, and then through his Son living in us. To experience the pain of living in the world and allow Jesus to redeem it is participating in Jesus' mission. It is filling up the sufferings of Christ (Col. 1:24).

More than even redemption, this is about intimately knowing the Redeemer. At the core of Jesus' identity, the thing that most defines who he is, is the fact that he came down out of love and suffered for us, in order to redeem us. He is the Suffering Servant, now glorified as the Great Redeemer. When we participate in suffering and redemption, we begin to grasp the essence of who he is through our shared experience. Meeting him in the pain of that suffering and the passion of that redemption allows us to know him in a way we never could otherwise.

That's what Paul refers to as "the fellowship of his sufferings" (Phil. 3:10). When I suffer and then am redeemed, I experience both the fellowship of his sufferings as I grasp the essence of who he is and the power of his resurrection as I participate in his redemption of the world.

I Will Not Let You Go

It should come as no surprise, then, that leaders often report specifically asking God to let them out of the Valley of Dependence, and God just as specifically answering, "No." That's what Brian experienced. At 23, he went through "the most miserable time of my life in terms of inner struggle… that was stirred up by some things in my wife's past. I couldn't get over some of what she had done. I tried all the different things the books said to get better. I prayed, fasted, cried, read, consulted mentors and counselors, but nothing worked. It took a year of being in a real black hole before it went away."

"In the end, it was all about my self-righteousness. I had so much pride—I judged everybody. God was digging down in me to get all the garbage out. The year before [during Brian's Natural Promotion] was all about God loving me, healing me and being my dad. This was more of a challenge to be a man. God was saying, 'I am going to let you lay in this hole until you give up this self-righteousness thing.'"

"I kept wanting him to do it overnight, and he wouldn't. I begged, I pleaded, I cried out for months to get out of this, and he said, 'No.'"

"This was where I developed my hatred for formulas [that I used to live by], because nothing worked. I was disappointed with God, mad with God, begged him to let me die. I wanted God to go away. I tried it both ways, trying to get him to do what I wanted him to do—then I began to realize that God wasn't going to do what I wanted him to do. I realized I couldn't command or manipulate God."

"When it was over, I was a different person. It was the first time I got the idea that there was a speck in my own eye. People had told me it was there, but before then I really didn't believe it."

While Brian wanted out of his painful circumstances, God—knowing that the pain actually came from within Brian instead of from without—entered into them in order to heal him. An important lesson of the Valley of Dependence is that *adversity exposes and breaks up the compacted soil of the heart* so that the seed of God's life can penetrate and take root. Therefore, painful times contain the greatest potential for heart transformation.

> ### Identifying Your Life Messages
> *A great exercise during or after a Valley season is to identify the Life Messages God is forming in you and encapsulate them in memorable form. For instance, I've created phrases for some of my Messages, like "Being comfortable in the place of brokenness" or "Meeting God in suffering." For others, I use a snippet of scripture, like "All things work together for good," or even a single word that's meaningful to me, like "Authenticity."*
>
> *However you do it, identify the heart of what God has formed in you in this season and remember it! An exercise for identifying and naming Life Messages is included on pg. 126.*

Where the heart is transformed, Life Messages form. Often the Message birthed in our Valley of Dependence becomes the heart of our call. For Brian, coming out of his self-righteous, I've-got-it-under-control pose became an important Life Message. "The things that are most painful leave us with a limp, but that limp is where God's power is," he passionately asserts. "That limp helped to remind me… that I couldn't just fix anything, and that some things were out of my control. It helped me be more humble. I couldn't fix what was inside no matter how much I read, how much I prayed, how many people I talked to. Only he could fix it and he was going to do it in his time."

"I would have been a really horrible husband if I hadn't gone through that!"

God's Agenda for this Valley

There are several key things on God's agenda for us during this valley. Forming our Life Messages is one. Surprisingly, mature leaders often point back to the Valley of Dependence as the source of the Message that is at the heart of their being call. That's profound: the work God does during the painful times, not when everything is going great, is what turns out to produce our greatest legacy.

Life Messages form when we are deeply processed by God and Jesus is embodied in a certain part of our character. For instance, Brian's hard-won Life Message that "the limp is where God's power is" became rooted deeply in his identity during his time of inner struggle. It's a place where he particularly looks like Jesus.

In the valleys, outward progress is put on the shelf for the sake of the inner renovation that forms Jesus within. Since the legacy we leave is the impact of this Jesus-in-us on the people we serve, our greatest contribution is born in secret in our most difficult hours.

I often say, "You win your ministry in your transitions." In other words, what God does in your heart during the isolated, unproductive, questioning valleys is what he will draw out of you in your next productive stage. In the valleys he prunes, for greater growth in the stage that follows. In fact, you can predict where the growth will come based on where he's been pruning you! Life Message formation is important enough that I've included an entire chapter (on page 116) on that topic.

The second key objective of this valley is moving from independence to dependence. While Natural Promotion is about learning I can do anything *with* God, in the Valley of Dependence we learn that we can do nothing *without* him. Over and over, leaders describe this passage as moving them from self-sufficiency and confidence in their own abilities to utter reliance upon God. While the manifestations of God's grace and power in the upward part of the stage build our faith and hope in God, it's the withdrawing of his hand in the descent that reveals where our natural selves leave off and his life begins.

The all-consuming affection God has for each of his children is shown in his willingness to repeatedly take us to the desolate places with him (see Hosea 2:14-15). At first that seems pretty counter-intuitive. If God really loves us, why wouldn't he make everything we do successful and productive? If God wants us to live daily in his power and presence, why does he withdraw it from us? And if God really made us for something, why doesn't he allow us to do it *now*?

> **Valley of Dependence Objectives**
>
> - *Life Message formation*
> - *Move from independence to dependence*
> - *Experience unconditional love*

This gets us to the third objective: that we would know his love. In the first stages of our calling development (and often much later!), most of us live the Christian life as if it depended on us. We pray and witness and work partly out of the joy of our salvation, but also out of fear, trying to prove our worth to our Father. Although he already adopted us when we were naked and lying half-dead in the gutter, our fallen hearts can't really accept that we are loved unconditionally. We can only understand love to the degree that we've been loved, and most of the love we've experienced in life is pretty selfish and transactional. In our belief system, love and approval are things we earn. As long as we are doing great things for God, we are able to maintain the belief that we can earn his acceptance.

Living this way is what God is trying to save us from in the Valley of Dependence! One of the great, life-long works God does in human hearts is convincing us that he simply loves us, without restraint, without condition, without measure. When we believe his love is something to be earned, the only effective way for us to discover unconditional love is to come to the point where we have nothing at all to offer. In our valleys and wilderness times, when we are stripped of our productive work and our pitiful faith is laid bare, God reaches in and gloriously redeems our pain by showing us a love we could never have grasped when things were going well. In the very moment when our failure to do what we think will please him is overwhelming, God delights to say, "I LOVE YOU!"

After prophesying about a difficult time to come for the nation of Israel, Hosea speaks poetically about this process:

> *"Therefore, I am now going to allure her;*
> *I will lead her into the desert and speak tenderly to her*
> *There I will give her back her vineyards,*

And make the Valley of Trouble a door of hope" (Hosea 2:14-15; NIV).

In other words, God is going to take his bride out to the desert to show his love for her. Afterward, he will restore her fruitfulness (the vineyards he had taken away), and make what seemed like a valley of trouble[14] into the doorway to a great future.

Saving Me from Myself

My own Valley of Dependence is a good illustration of this work of love, dependence and Life Message formation. It began with what I call a dangerous prayer. I'd gotten hold of a book on leadership where the author claimed that for the first five to ten years after Jesus' Ascension, no one but the twelve apostles filled any leadership roles in the church because, "you've got to get sanctified before you can lead." Whatever you think of that theology, it gripped me at the time. So at 22 I began to pray consistently, "Lord, take the next five years of my life and just sanctify me!"

If you've been around the block a few times, you can already see the steep learning curve just ahead! I was young, full of the Holy Ghost, full of faith and full of myself (although I never would have seen that at the time). I thought those five years would be crammed full with leadership experiences that would take me onward and upward to greatness. By 28, I'd be preaching to thousands nationwide and be fully functioning in my calling. I actually thought that asking for five years of processing was requesting a *longer* Preparation season than normal, so that I would function in greater power when I was finally released into my life's work! (Actually, my call turned out to be around leadership character development, so the prayer itself was perfectly in line with what God wanted to do in me—I was just two decades or so off in how long I thought preparing for my call would take!)

The first thing that happened was that all my leadership roles came to an end. I had been the lead guitarist and a vocalist in a band that traveled around the country doing worship renewal. Another guy joined the band who was a much better singer and guitarist than me, so I got relegated to running sound from the back. Then we cut an album, the sound engineer got saved, and he joined the band. He was much better on the sound board than me, so I was relegated to gopher. I felt terribly left out and let down. At the same time, the small group I led spontaneously decided to disband one night, because they felt they "were not having a good small group experience." That was a blow.

Then the band disbanded altogether. Suddenly, I was producing next to nothing for God. I began to doubt myself. This wasn't how the radical Christian life was supposed to look, was it? What had I done wrong?

The proverbial nail in the coffin was when God pulled the plug on my devotional life. Up until then, I had been Mr. Discipline himself. I had my hour of power every morning, my Bible study plan, my yearly goals, my monthly goals, my budget where I recorded every penny I spent or earned. I fasted twice a week, I got together for prayer three times a week with a buddy, and I was there every time the church doors were open. As far as I was concerned, if you weren't living that kind of disciplined life, you were a spiritual wimp.

All at once, my disciplined life began to crumble. I couldn't meet my own expectations, and the guilt

---

14   The story behind the Valley of Trouble is in Joshua chapter seven.

and shame that flooded me stole any spiritual energy I had left. It got to where I couldn't *stand* to be with God. I would sit down for devotions, get through one or two verses and then put my Bible down in anguished frustration. I

didn't read any Christian books for a year. Isolated in my church of 20-somethings, there was no one to turn to that had experience with extended wilderness seasons who could give me some perspective.

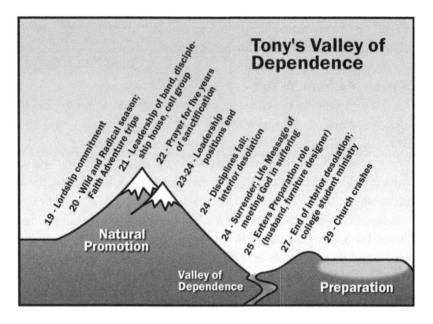

Toward the end (it took me about two years to reach the bottom) I pictured myself sliding down a greased rope in a deep, pitch-black well. I reached the knot at the end of the rope and clung to it for dear life. I had no idea how far I would fall if I let go. Years later, I realized that the knot represented my own efforts to earn God's approval. What would happen to me if I stopped trying to live the disciplined Christian life? Would God reject me? That was a terrifying thought.

Finally, I couldn't hold out any longer. "God," I said to the stony heavens, "I give up. My life is over. I can't live the Christian life. I guess I'll be like one of those guys Paul talks about who get to heaven with all the clothes burnt off their back, because nothing I am doing is worth jack squat. If you can make anything out of my life, you do it; but I'm finished."

I had failed at the most important thing in my life, the only thing that really mattered.

Then something happened that I never anticipated. God started speaking to me again, telling me how much he loved me. Now I was completely undone. That couldn't be God! I rejected and refuted that voice for weeks, until finally it began to dawn on me that God loved me whether I did anything for him or not. I gradually began to understand grace and love in a way I never had before, because I found I was loved when I had nothing to give.

That insight changed my life forever. Jesus loved me for me! As the truth sank in, my drivenness and judgmental nature began to wither. I stopped being so obsessive about spiritual disciplines. Where I had been a graceless person before, I now gave grace to others and me when we failed. I let go of measuring myself so much against the accomplishments of others—of trying to be the next John Wesley. I allowed myself to have limitations, and to be comfortable in the place of brokenness.

Although I hadn't known what God was doing or why, and I fought him tooth and nail much of the way, Jesus saved me from a life of addiction to outward religious tripe. I'll be eternally grateful!

The core of my Life Message/being call was birthed during that time. One of my great takeaways from this incident was realizing that God would leverage my outward circumstances to work on my inward character. I became aware of how adversity creates a great climate for incarnation, and began a lifetime habit of growing by leaning into difficulty instead of avoiding it, and learning how to meet God in even the smallest of failures and reverses. The theme of meeting God in adversity and being transformed at the heart level is the key Message of my life—the heart of my call. I would never have come to embody that part of Jesus without going through a painful Valley of Dependence. The best part of me would be missing. My life's legacy will be built on how I embody and communicate what God first taught me in that valley.

Making the Most of the Valley of Dependence

What can you do to make the most of this valley? The first question most people ask in that regard is, "How can I get it over with as quickly as possible and get back to a productive life? What's the secret to doing this faster?"

> *You can't make the seasons go faster: God's best is to move through them at the pace he determines.*

The answer is, you can't make this valley go faster than what God has planned. And why would you want to, when your legacy depends on how profoundly you engage God during this time? Going through the stages faster than others does not make you a better or more faithful Christian (it does betray a need to compare yourself to others and find worth in being better than them). Striving to get to the next stage only distracts you from the real agenda: deeply meeting God where you are at. Nothing will make your journey seem longer than wishing you were someplace you are not.

The single most important thing you can do in the valleys is to change perspective. Stop looking at your circumstances from a human vantage point ("It hurts!") and see it from God's point of view ("This is making me like Jesus."). Dwelling on the pain, injustice or adversity you are suffering leads nowhere. Even focusing on practical steps of action misses the point. This is about how the Great Redeemer can sift your identity and implant himself in your innermost self.

The key is to engage your situation with your heart. While you'll learn practical lessons about how to handle difficulty, that's not going deep enough. The valleys are for learning about who you are: what drives you, the wrong beliefs that hold you back, the hidden wounds and holes in your heart that bleed when life touches them. This time is about inward change and intimate fellowship with just you and God.

So here are some simple to-dos for this season:

- **Let Go Gracefully**
  In most valleys, your productivity drops or even stops. God is OK with that—in fact; he is helping you detach your identity from these external things on purpose, and making room in your life for you to go deep. Stop kicking against the goads and fighting your descent, and accept that he is at work in this.

- **Cozy up to God**
  Hang out with him. Like King David, share your anger, your doubts, your questions and your frustrations. If your situation has you isolated, learn to depend on him even more. God is going

to be doing most of the work on this one—you just need to give him room to do it.

- **Tune into God's Agenda**
  Get your focus off what is going wrong, and onto what God wants to do in you. Instead of begging him to protect or deliver you from your situation, as if he is not doing his job, start asking him what's on his agenda.

- **Engage with Your Heart**
  Your circumstances are a mirror that reveals what's in your heart. Now is the time to go deep and see what God wants to reveal (the questions on page 123 and 124 can help). He's not doing it because you are bad, but so he can heal you.

- **Find a Mentor**
  Having an older, go-to person who understands the seasons of life and has been there can make all the difference. When you doubt yourself or wonder what to do, it sure helps to have a respected friend say, "Yeah, I've been there, too."

> ### Summary of Key Learnings
> - *The Valley of Dependence is the first major time where God uses adversity to shape us.*
> - *Valleys are about internal growth, not outward productivity.*
> - *When we meet God in suffering and he redeems it, we come to know the essence of who Jesus is.*
> - *Perspective and engaging with the heart are the keys to making the most of this valley.*
> - *Key tasks are forming Life Messages, moving from self-sufficiency to dependence and experiencing unconditional love.*

Valleys impact our emotions in predictable ways. If you are experiencing self-doubt, anger at God, fear of missing it, lack of direction, or wondering why God won't deliver you from your circumstances—that's normal for this stage. Confusion about what to think and believe is a natural by-product of the shaking of your core belief system. This shaking is a good thing when you allow God to use it to mold your heart. We all hold beliefs that are built on hurt, misconceptions about God or reaction to injustice. Just as intense heat causes the impurities in metal to float to the surface, exposure to adversity reveals the beliefs we live out of and smelts out the dross. Without exposure to heat, these underlying drives can become strongholds that hinder us for a lifetime.

Perspective from older leaders can be a real difference-maker in sorting all this out. For instance, Hunter didn't seem that distressed by an up-and-down Valley of Dependence that included a frustrating internship, he and his fiancé both losing their jobs a week after getting engaged, and working for a billionaire who cursed him out every day for six solid months. While he has a high-challenge, positive personality, Hunter's rootedness in the midst of that storm was still very unusual.

When I asked what made his experience relatively benign, he immediately replied, "I've always had great mentors. I can't even imagine what it would be like to live without them." During his descent he met regularly with a mentor figure who challenged him, helped him navigate the heart issues that rose to the surface and offered encouragement and perspective along the way. If there is only one thing you do to facilitate your calling journey, make it this: cultivate relationships with older leaders who can give you perspective when you need it.

The Valley of Dependence can be a lonely, confusing time. However, if you go to the deep places with God in it, years later you will look back on that time as so important that without it you would be unable to fulfill your destiny. God is at work in the valleys, making you into the person you need to be to do what you were born to do.

David said, "Even if the way goes through Death Valley, I'm not afraid when you walk at my side" (Ps. 23:4; MSG). The Great Redeemer is at your side and on your side, and you can look forward to meeting him in ways you've never known before. The desert truly is a beautiful place.

Valley of Dependence Reflection Questions

- Take a look at the stage characteristics on page 82. Which years in your life best fit this description?

- Does the first part of your calling journey follow the usual Lordship>promotion>valley pattern, or does your big, early crash come before your Lordship commitment and Natural Promotion stage? (See the two different maps on page 44.)

- How did God meet you in these years? What did this season teach you about who you are, and who he is?

Bible Study Guide: The Valley of Dependence

Use the questions below and the stage characteristics (see box) to study the Valley of Dependence in these biblical leaders' lives.

1. **David,** (I Sam. 18-22:5). Note the growing conflict with Saul, and the multiple negative events around the beginning of David's descent. What was different in the outcome of David's plots to save himself (escaping to Gath; or using his wife to cover for him) versus when he inquired of the Lord about his direction? How was David learning dependence on God?

> ### Valley of Dependence Characteristics
> - *Focus: Dependence*
> - *Averages 2.5 years in length*
> - *A negative trigger event leads us into the valley*
> - *Our character flaw (i.e. arrogance or self-sufficiency) often contributes to the crash*
> - *Difficult time of failure or adversity*
> - *Formation of key Life Messages*
> - *Life not meeting expectations causes doubt, fear of missing it, feeling lost, anger at God, cynicism*
> - *"Kicking against the pricks"—we fight against entering the valley*
> - *We ask God to get us out of our circumstances and he explicitly refuses*
> - *Isolation or rejection by friend or authority figure*

3. **Abraham**, from the famine that forced him to leave the Promised Land to the renewal of the promise (Gen. 12:10-13:17). Note the contrast between his plot to save himself in Egypt by calling his wife his sister, to his trusting the call to God by offering Lot the first choice of the land. In what circumstances did God renew or expand Abraham's call?

4. **Moses**, when his first attempts to save his people collapsed and he fled the country (Ex. 2:11-22). What was he attempting to do when he killed the Egyptian? (Hint: what made Pharaoh decide to drive a member of the royal family out of the country for killing a lowly foreman?)

7: PREPARATION

The Preparation stage begins where the Valley of Dependence ends. We have entered a new level of dependence on God and have a more sober view of what it is really going to take to reach our destiny. Knowing that all our dreams aren't going to happen right now, we turn our attention to the hard work of Preparation in the roles and responsibilities in front of us. An apt depiction of this phase is seen in Jesus' journey in the years of obscurity where he "kept increasing in wisdom and in stature, and in favor with God and man" before he was released into public ministry at age 30.

The Preparation stage is a long season, six years at a minimum and more often ten or 15. During this time we gain practical skills, life experience and fruits of the spirit needed in our Fulfillment years. We're learning the general competencies of the Christian life: healthy relationships, how to hear God's voice, conflict skills, overcoming obstacles, faithfulness, integrity and the like. While we are having an impact, God's agenda is more about our personal growth than our fruitfulness.

Many years ago, I heard a denominational leader voice a truth about Preparation that has always stayed with me. "Up until you are 40 it's all about you," he asserted. "Any actual ministry you get done before that is gravy." What he was saying is that until midlife, God is focused more on preparing you than on your productivity. That's a profound statement of how God functions as an investor. I like to voice it this way: "A year of your impact when you are 50 is worth ten years when you are 25."

God takes a long time to prepare us because creating people who can *do* great works out of their natural abilities is not enough. He is after leaders who can reveal the Christ incarnated in their character *through* those works. He is making ambassadors.

An ambassador does much more than travel to foreign countries—that's a tourist. An ambassador goes as a fully empowered, official representative of the home country, steeped in its values and trained to represent its interests. You are not an ambassador unless you carry the authority of your home country within your person. Your Preparation as an ambassador is long because God is making you into an official representative who carries the image of his son in your identity.

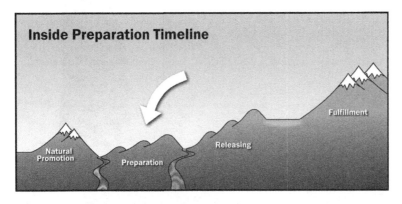

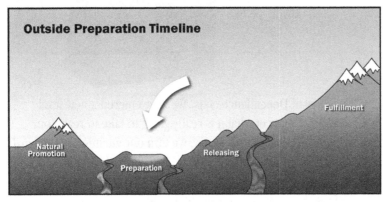

Inside vs. Outside Preparation

In the Preparation stage, there are two different paths that both lead to the same destination: *Inside Preparation* and *Outside Preparation*. Here are the two timelines, shown together for comparison, Inside Preparation above and Outside Preparation below. The area where they differ is highlighted.

Those who are prepared inside their area of call experience the journey differently than those whose refining takes place outside their calling arena. Neither course is intrinsically better or faster than the other—the best version of the timeline for you is the one God chooses for you. The stages and valleys are the same in both, but what happens during those periods is slightly different.

Below is a table showing the most common differences leaders experience between the two:

	Inside Preparation	Outside Preparation
Vocational role:	Within area of call in both Preparation and Releasing	Outside area of call until the Releasing stage
Preparation stage experienced as:	Upward to bigger and better things; increase	Fruitful but disconnected from call; later part a stagnant period
Developmental focus:	Specific and General skills learned together	General skills in Preparation; specific skills in Releasing
Most significant transition:	Valley of Identity	Day of Release
Wilderness time during:	Valley of Identity	Preparation stage
Day of Release:	No	Yes

The lives of Joseph and William Wilberforce (see pages 10 and 53) are good illustrations of these two paths. Joseph's life exemplifies the Outside Preparation pattern, while Wilberforce's story demonstrates most of the key characteristics of Inside Preparation:

	Wilberforce (Inside)	**Joseph (Outside)**
Vocational role:	Wilberforce spent his entire career *inside* politics. His primary role was in Parliament in both his Preparation and Releasing stages.	During his Preparation years in Egypt (until the beginning of his Releasing stage when he got out of prison) he worked as a slave, *outside* his area of calling.
Preparation stage experienced as:	Wilberforce experienced the Preparation stage as one of *increasing* influence and ability in his area of call.	Joseph likely experienced the Preparation stage as *fruitful but disconnected* from his call and maybe as a wilderness time (especially his prison years).
Developmental focus:	He built both *Specific and General skills* in politics, public speaking and advocacy at the same time in his Preparation phase.	Joseph mainly cultivated *General skills* like Egyptian language and customs in Preparation, and learned the *Specific skills* needed for his political role on the job in Releasing.
Most significant transition:	Wilberforce's Valley of Identity, when he considered abandoning his cause, was longer and more significant than his Valley of Wholeness.	The role shift at Joseph's Day of Release (from prison to Pharaoh's right-hand) was a more significant transition than reconciling with his brothers in the Valley of Identity, where he stayed in the same role and sphere of influence.
Wilderness (flat line) experienced during:	Wilberforce's major wilderness time occurred during his Valley of Identity.	Joseph's major wilderness time occurred in prison during his later Preparation years.
Day of Release:	Wilberforce's story does not include a Day of Release.	Leaving prison and taking over the Egyptian economy was Joseph's Day of Release.

Celebrate the Difference

Let's look at some contemporary examples of the difference. Drew, the jazz musician, is an example of Outside Preparation. He spent his Preparation years driving a forklift and then working for a company that manufactured guitars. Playing in a band was something he did on the side. At his Day of Release, he transitioned from making instruments to playing them. Taking a part-time teaching job allowed him to invest half of his work time in building a music career—a major turning point in his calling journey. It was only after his Valley of Identity that he left outside work behind and struck out on his own as a full-time jazz musician. Moving into that convergent role launched him into his Fulfillment years.

Jeff is a counselor and marriage coach who spent his Preparation stage in the counseling arena, working with troubled youth. A child of divorce, Jeff's call is about bringing healing to relationships, especially marriages. While that first job was a tough row to hoe and not a great fit, Jeff was functioning within his

> ### Inside or Outside Preparation?
> *Answer these four questions to determine which fits you best:*
>
> - **Where is your primary role?**
>   *If you are working vocationally in your area of call during Preparation, you are probably in the Inside Preparation pattern. If your primary role (paid or unpaid) is outside your calling area, that's Outside Preparation.*
>
> - **Is there a Day of Release after your Valley of Wholeness?**
>   *Outside Preparation includes a significant career transition into one's area of call here, while those in Inside Preparation tend to continue along the same basic career track.*
>
> - **Does your story fit the Day of Release characteristics?**
>   *Those in Outside Preparation display a specific set of symptoms around the Day of Release (see pg. 115) that are not normally present in the Inside Preparation graph.*
>
> - **Which transition is most significant?**
>   *In Inside Preparation, the Valley of Identity tends to be the major one, often lasting three to eight years and involving a wilderness season when favor and opportunity are removed. In Outside Preparation, the Day of Release to be the more significant transition.*

area of calling during that time, so his story fits the Inside Preparation pattern best.

If you are in the middle of Preparation and aren't sure which path you are on, that's OK. The objective here is not to find the "right" thing you are supposed to be doing, but to meet God and learn all you can wherever you are. The Inside/Outside Preparation distinction is clearest in hindsight. Whether or not you have a Day of Release at the end of the stage (see chapter 9) is the most reliable indicator of which path God has you on.

General and Specific Skills

Our calling and our job are not the same thing—in fact, the earlier in the calling journey we are, the less likely they are to overlap. A good picture for thinking about the relationship between our primary role and our call is a funnel. Early in our calling journey, we are at the top of the funnel, and the playing field is pretty large. There are many responsibilities, roles or jobs we can take on that will ready us for our calling. As we move farther along the journey, the funnel of options narrows, and there are fewer roles available that fit what we need to develop us. Finally, when we reach the neck of the funnel,

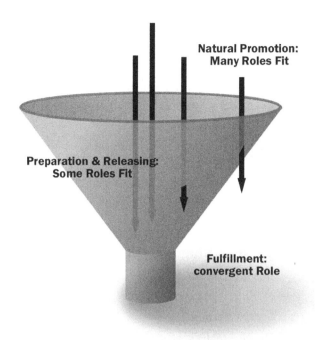

Natural Promotion:
Many Roles Fit

Preparation & Releasing:
Some Roles Fit

Fulfillment:
convergent Role

we need to move into a narrowly-defined convergent role that fits us well to fulfill our destiny.

Early in the calling journey, the role is less important than the skills we are learning. God will use whatever we are doing to prepare us. But the closer we get to Fulfillment, the more important is the role.

The key to understanding where to focus your energy if you are in Outside Preparation is thinking in terms of Specific and General Skills. General skills (like emotional intelligence) apply to virtually any role, while specific skills are particular to a certain job or career. For instance, if you are a stay-at-home mom, changing a diaper is a job-specific skill. There aren't too many corporate careers that require it! However, changing diapers also trains you in the general skill of taking care of the need at hand even when the situation stinks. That quality is in great demand in any number of careers!

If you are working outside your area of calling in this stage, God is developing your general skills. Later in life, you'll find that the broad competencies you learned in this stage (things like responsibility, time management, keeping commitments, managing money, or relational skills) translate readily over to your destiny role. In my furniture design job, I learned sales, copy writing, customer service, and project management, as well as people skills like relating to strong personalities, handling conflict and working on a team. Those are all abilities I rely on heavily today. Specific skills are like icing on the cake of general skills that adapt them to a particular job.

Here's an example of how to use this concept. Say you are contemplating a mid-life career change from business owner to ministry leader. If you have engaged God well in your Preparation stage, you already have most of the general skills and character competencies (i.e. communication, visioning, generosity, or humility) you need to succeed. The task that remains is to adapt those general skills to the specific requirements of your new

Specific Skills	General Skills
Fixing a copier	Troubleshooting
Making a shopping list	Planning
Sticking to a family budget	Delayed gratification
Doing chores at home	Being a self-starter
Doing status reports	Accountability
Paying your taxes	Honesty when no one sees
Disciplining your kids	Conflict skills

career. For instance, you'll need to understand the particular lingo of the ministry world, the values ministry leaders function out of, how networking is done among ministry leaders, and the difference between working with paid employees versus a volunteer organization.

You are switching careers, but you are not starting from scratch! Instead, you are building on the general character and competencies God has developed in you during your Preparation years

Preparation Characteristics

Kevin is a businessman whose journey provides a great example of the overall flavor of the Preparation stage. After spending several years earning next to nothing while digging his family business out of a deep hole (his Valley of Dependence), at 26 Kevin began to build a life. He bought his first house ("I literally had nothing when I moved in—just two garbage bags of clothes"), got married the next year, and began to apply himself to growing spiritually. "We started to get involved [in church] and grow together—doing studies together, getting in the Word, building friendships around Christ."

Especially in the early stage of the Calling Journey, God does as much or more work in us through marriage, family, church, and community as he does through our vocation. We are learning to manage not only a job, but our personal lives, family relationships, spiritual lives and much more. For instance, Kevin's commitment to financial giving flourished in this season, as he and his wife learned to follow God's leading together in their gifts to a church, a Christian school and families in need.

> ### Preparation Stage Characteristics
> - *Normally six to 15 years long*
> - *Usually starts three to eight years after Lordship commitment*
> - *Onset may be marked by Season of Healing or entry into a new Preparation Role*
> - *Leader gains experience and skills needed for his/her destiny role*
> - *A focus on growing in ability to take responsibility and lead*
> - *Sense of being prepared for God's future*
> - *Living in tension—I have a call but am not yet released to it*
> - *May be prepared inside or outside area of calling area (see pg. 84)*

On the career front in this season, "there was opportunity after opportunity," Kevin remembers. "We just kept growing the business." This kind of upward movement toward bigger-and-better is common for those prepared inside their area of call. With each new step, Kevin learned business and management skills that are vital to his ability to fulfill his calling. One major task was reshaping the company's culture and values. "When I first came in our company had an awful reputation. But we turned it around and ran it according to the golden rule."

In his Preparation stage, Kevin worked on basic competencies of the Christian life. As his sphere of influence and productive service expanded, God also took him through experiences like remaking his company's culture that developed his ability to bring biblical principles to bear in the workplace.

Entering a Preparation Role

The end of the Valley of Dependence and the beginning of Preparation is often marked by our entry into a Preparation Role that's our primary vocation during the stage. Steve's story is a good example. When he came to Christ and made Jesus Lord in his thirties, he sold his company, told all his business buddies he was going into the ministry and started preparing for seminary. They all thought he was crazy, but doing something wild and radical like that seemed like a natural response to the way God had touched his life.

"I sold my business, put a couple hundred K in the bank, and signed up to go to seminary," Steve recalls. "Two months before I was supposed to start, my wife challenged me, 'You think you've got it all figured out, Steve. You've got enough time to go to seminary, enough money in the bank, enough time to have sex with me, but do you have enough time to be father to your daughters?' That really hit me between the eyes. As I thought about it, I realized I was trying to prove myself to God. I wasn't going to seminary for the right reasons. So I withdrew and decided to go back to business."

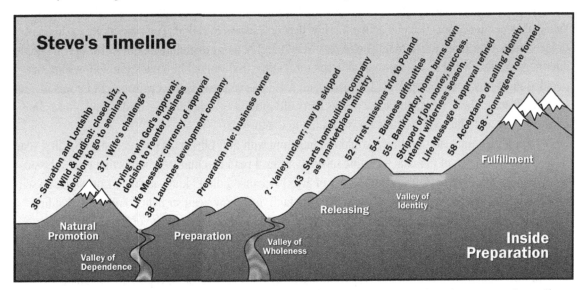

Retracing his steps after so confidently leaving the business world behind took Steve into his Valley of Dependence. "It was humbling to have to explain to my family, friends and business associates that I had changed course again and was back," Steve says, "But I now had a clear sense of direction. The marketplace was where I was supposed to be."

Steve entered into the Preparation phase when he launched a new business and stepped into his Preparation Role as a business owner. He had made Jesus Lord of his life, experienced a radical Natural Promotion season of selling out and planning to go to the ministry, then a sobering Valley of Dependence where his motives were challenged and he was humbled before his friends. By starting over, Steve was able to build biblical values and objectives into the heart of his company. Even though he came to Christ well into his thirties, his story tracks through the normal stages of the calling journey (although the later in life you make your Lordship commitment, the more they tend to be shortened).

The Season of Healing

Sometimes, the Preparation years begin with what I call "A Season of Healing." After a difficult time of heart surgery in the Valley of Dependence, God, with the tenderness of a good father, grants us an interlude of joy and refreshment before we dive into the next task. For instance, during her Valley of Dependence, Kara went from working with U.S. senators on Capitol Hill to doing paperwork "in a back office at the end of a dark hall in a smelly building, with no influence at all." She hated it. After two hard years of dying to self in that job, then six weeks with no work at all (and a husband in grad school she was supposed to be supporting), her Valley of Dependence came to an end when she took a new job in her church. This people-oriented role fit her extroverted personality and allowed her to accomplish something meaningful, and she flourished there. "I am in a new job and am moving in my gifts," she says enthusiastically, "and the fear of lack of influence and being small is much less prevalent. I don't question life as much when I am operating in my gifts."

For some, the Season of Healing is a time when everything just goes well for a while, and we recover our equilibrium. For others, it is a period of deep fellowship with God in a place of isolation. Greg's Valley of Dependence was what he called a "slow descent" away from God. The risk-taking excitement of his new stock trading job, a first taste of real wealth and hanging around with guys who weren't going anywhere spiritually led to several years of stagnation. After God yanked him back into fellowship, Greg decided the best way to start moving forward again was to leave the negative environment he was in and get a fresh start. There were only a few places he could move as a commodities trader, and after ruling out New York and Chicago he ended up relocating to California.

"I made a promise to God that I would not hang out with non-Christians on weekends that first year, because… I didn't want to make the same mistake again. I read two hundred books that year [classics from authors like Andrew Murray and Teresa of Avila] because I didn't know anyone. I drowned myself in those books in an attempt to get grounded in the faith, to get my head straight." For Greg, that first year was a Season of Healing, marked by intense fellowship with God in a place of isolation.

Living in Tension

An uncomfortable quality of the Preparation season is living in tension, especially for those in Outside Preparation. How do you relate to God when he has given you a mission but you aren't yet doing it? Your peers are getting onto the career track and entering into their area of calling, and you are stuck in a dead end job or trapped in a small world that doesn't offer the opportunities you need to move forward. Every time you come before God, the uncompleted mission of your life is lurking in the background. You no longer believe you can just go out and kill an Egyptian like Moses did and make it happen in your own strength. You can't scheme and manipulate it into being as Jacob tried to do. A fact of life you live with every day is that you are not doing what you are called to do. If you begin to feel you have missed your call or that God has passed you by, it's hard to have an open relationship with God.

In the desert times, we learn to be at peace and trust him enough to walk together in the dark. It's there we are taught to be content in any and all circumstances, because there we discover "the secret of being filled and going hungry, both of having abundance and suffering need: I can do all things through him who strengthens me" (Phil. 4:12-13). Even when it looks like our call is going nowhere, God is in control. His agenda for us in desert times is to let go gracefully, put what we can't do in his hands and practice trusting our future to him.

Our agenda, however, is usually to fix what blocks our desired future, eliminate the tension we feel, and get moving again at a pace that makes us feel useful and important. However, "kicking against the pricks" and trying to get out of Outside Preparation is the surest way to stay there longer. *If I cannot be content until my call is moving forward at my pace, it is not really in God's hands.*

I didn't handle this tension particularly well in my own life. I worked outside my area of call for a decade and a half, and just about every year I asked God to release me from my job and move me on. Year after year, I heard nothing about leaving. It was only in the last few years that I began to realize that a big part of the curriculum was contentment, and I couldn't graduate until I learned to be at peace where God had placed me.

In the Preparation stage, you are still in school. It doesn't feel like you are doing "it" because you aren't supposed to be. That's really OK with God—he designed life to work that way. So relax, be where you are at, and focus on wringing all the juice out of the situation you are in, instead of wishing you were somewhere else. Like many leaders, when you reach the Fulfillment stage you'll look back and say, "I didn't realize it at the time, but I couldn't be living my call without what I learned in those years."

Making the Most of Preparation

Preparation is about building your core abilities as a leader. So how can you best engage God's purposes in this stage? The key is to cultivate trusting God for your future and focus on applying yourself to the task at hand. Fretting about your progress and trying to make your call happen is a distraction. So make your peace with the fact that you aren't there yet.

While entering the fullness of your call may be years in the future, this is no time to sit on your hands. Develop the foundational skills and character that will support your calling in the future. Become a great husband and father or wife and mother. Complete your schooling. Build a consistent devotional life. Cultivate lasting friendships with people who challenge you to grow. Hone your strengths and practical skills by functioning in leadership.

Focus less on climbing the ladder at work than on finding roles that will develop you as a person and a leader. This is a time when you'll have significant energy to invest in yourself through your career, family and church roles. Later in life, executing your responsibilities will take much more of your time and attention. So be intentional about using this season of life for personal growth!

This stage builds disciplined foundations for your Releasing and Fulfillment years. If the

---

Summary of Key Learnings

- *The Preparation stage often begins with a Season of Healing or moving into a Preparation Role.*

- *Some leaders go through Preparation within their area of call, while others travel it outside of their vocation.*

- *The leader's task is to find the general skills needed for his/her calling role and work at developing them.*

- *Known character issues that aren't addressed here can blow up your calling later in life.*

foundations aren't solid, everything built on them is in jeopardy. When prominent leaders crash and burn later in life, very often the problem can be traced back to personal issues they were aware of during this period but failed to address. If there is conflict in your marriage, even if you can cope with things as they are, *take responsibility and deal with it, now!* The fallout from a divorce at 45 or 50 can easily cut the impact of your life in half. If you are an aggressive leader who tends to get tripped up by your blind spots, surround yourself with people who have the confidence and depth of relationship with you to call you on it. Nothing is sadder to me than to coach a leader of great influence and find that their children are estranged, they are just going through the motions in their marriage, or their relationship with God has grown cold in what should be their best years. God has much more for you than that.

Failure to learn to manage your money and get out of debt in these years can hamstring your ability to step out in your call in later stages when it counts the most. If you never deal with your anger toward your dad, or uncover the vow you made to yourself to never be poor again, or address your controlling or people-pleasing tendencies, those issues will grow deeper and more intractable—and more costly to deal with—as the years go by.

Worse, in some measure those flaws will be passed on to whoever you impact. Remember, if calling is about being, *operating in your call is transmitting what is in your being to others.* The people you lead will become like you, not so much in what you do as in who you are. Your character flaws are transmitted along with the Jesus in you, and the weeds grow up in your followers along with the wheat.

God is determined to let his children sow with him in spite of our contaminated seed. Instead of pulling us off the job and uprooting the good with the bad, he simply lets it all grow up and then sorts it out at the end of the age. The fact that God is using us greatly is no proof that we are in great shape—we may be sowing more weeds than we are wheat! Progress on the calling journey is measured by how deeply we meet God and allow him to shape us along the way, not by outward accomplishments.

God's emphasis on refining early in life is actually a wonderful gift. When God deals with a leader's flaws, it affects everyone in that leader's sphere of influence. For instance, if you are an organizational leader prone to hubris and overconfidence, how do you imagine God might deal with that weakness? I would say you are most likely to deal with that flaw when you overreach and your organization experiences a big failure. If that happens, some of your innocent employees might lose their jobs or have to work a lot harder to clean up the mess. Everyone you lead gets to eat the fruit of God's dealings in your life.

So make your biggest mistakes when you are young. Let God bring the worst of your flesh to the surface and deal with it now, when your followers are relatively few and not too many will be disappointed or wounded by your failings. It is always hard work to undergo heart surgery with God, but it is much tougher when the fallout affects a thousand people instead of only impacting ten. The Preparation years are God's gift to your followers. Use them well!

Making a Plan to Grow

I use an exercise called Five Fingers (see page 94) to help leaders be strategic about developing themselves in the Preparation stage. You identify five competencies and five character qualities—like the five fingers on each hand—that you need to succeed in your call. For instance, if your calling is to run a retreat center, your list might look like this:

Top Five General Skills	Ranking	Notes
1. Basic small business skills	2	My weakest—needs attention
2. Marketing	6	My job gives me lots of practice
3. Spiritual direction	4	Need to take it to the next level
4. Understanding transformation	5	Find ways to formally study this
5. Familiarity w/ spiritual masters	7	I've done a lot of reading already
Top Five Character Qualities	Ranking	Notes
1. Practiced intimacy with God	7	Has always been a strength
2. Ability to let go	4	There is a lot more to learn
3. Authenticity/openness	10	Here's a place I have truly mastered
4. Life balance	5	Ouch! Major changes needed
5. Servant heart	3	I need some refocusing

Once you've identified five competencies and five character qualities, you can create a growth plan to develop yourself in these areas. For instance, if you want to work at familiarity with the spiritual masters, design a reading program for yourself. If effortlessly living a balanced life will be vital to accomplishing your retreat center vision, find disciplined ways to build rest, Sabbath and relationship into your life now. Even if you aren't totally sure what role you'll be filling in ten years, these General skills will still apply.

To do the exercise, flip to the following page.

Preparation Reflection Questions

1. When did your first valley season end?

2. After your Valley of Dependence, when did you first assume a major Preparation role?

3. How well does the season you tentatively identified seem to fit with the characteristics list on page 95?

4. Was your primary role in the Preparation stage inside or outside of your area of call?

5. How long did this season last until your next major transition or season of major dealings of God with your heart? (This season normally lasts six to 15 years.)

Five Fingers Exercise

Use this exercise in the Preparation and Releasing stages to plan how to develop yourself for your call.

Step 1: State the Mission

Jot down your calling or life mission as best you understand it. Don't agonize—just get something down.

Step 2: Identify the Five Fingers

Take a few minutes to envision yourself operating in what you believe will be your calling role. What will you be doing? What responsibilities will you have? It might help to imagine what you'd do on an average day in that role. You don't have to get this exactly right—just take your best shot based on what you know about your call. Once you have a picture of that future role in mind, jot down the top five general skills you will need to succeed at this role. Make a second list of the inner character qualities that will be most important. The two lists below provide some examples of qualities and competencies.

Competencies	Character Qualities
Networking	Merciful to the undeserving
A graduate degree	Humility
Relational skills	Joyful
A certain type of job or life experience	Peace in the midst of conflict and change
Language skills	Ability to wait on God's timing
Cross-cultural communication	Control of tongue
Management skills	Self-disciplined
Proven ability to start a business	Willing to see others get the glory
Public speaking	Courageous
Design or artistic skills	Graceful under pressure
Ability to make tough decisions	Focused
Organizing skills	Principled
Self-management	Doing the right thing
Mentoring/coaching	Secure
Fundraising	Open to feedback
Recruiting	Positive outlook

Step 3: Evaluate Your Development

On a scale of 1 to 10, rank where you feel you are in your development of these qualities. If "10" is the level of competence needed for your ultimate role, and "1" is starting from scratch, where are you at now?

Step 4: Make a Plan

Take one or more of your top five and make a plan to start moving your competence toward a "10." Your plan could include anything that works for you: reading, finding a mentor, even a career change.

Bible Study Guide: The Preparation Stage

Use these questions to explore how the Preparation stage looks in the lives of three prominent biblical leaders.

1. **David:** I Samuel 22:2 describes David's Preparation role. Think about what skills and character qualities leading this group would develop, and jot down a few. Then read chapters 22-26 to learn about David's Preparation journey. How did God develop those skills and qualities in David? What qualities was he developing that you didn't anticipate?

2. **Moses**: Little is said about his 40 years of Preparation in the role of a shepherd. What general skills do you imagine he learned in his role as a shepherd that would be vital to keeping alive a group of Egyptian slaves from the Nile Delta for 40 years in the desert (see Exodus 2:21-3:1)?

3. **Abraham:** Genesis chapters 13-14 describe Abraham's Preparation stage. Abraham's key Life Message is about faith: that believing God is the basis of relationship with him. How does Abraham's story in the Preparation stage work to build that Message within him?

> **Preparation Stage Characteristics**
> - *Normally six to 15 years long*
> - *Usually starts three to eight years after Lordship commitment*
> - *Onset may be marked by Season of Healing or entry into a new Preparation Role*
> - *Leader gains experience and skills needed for his/her destiny role*
> - *Focus on growing in ability to take responsibility and lead*
> - *Sense of being prepared for God's future*
> - *Living in tension—I have a call but am not yet released to it*
> - *May be prepared inside or outside area of calling (see pg. 84)*

8: THE VALLEY OF WHOLENESS

A second period of upheaval in our calling journey is the Valley of Wholeness. In this time of inner renovation, God moves us forward by addressing major character issues we might not see as connected with our ultimate destiny: marriage, family, relationships, life balance, secret sins or unrefined gifts and strengths. Working on them now saves us from being derailed by these issues in our Fulfillment years.

The Valley of Wholeness averages about two years in length and usually takes place from nine to 20 years after our Lordship commitment. This valley is usually the shortest of the three.

Jim's story is typical. "The promotion period for me lasted for a long time," Jim reminisces. "From the time I gave my life to Christ it was sort of an upward, saw-toothed line.[15] Going to college, seeing my girl come to Christ, going to Christ for the Nations Institute, having a revival in my first pastorate… basically, every time I turned around I was being promoted. Then I went to grad school, did some teaching at seminary, and was on the denomination's general board. I got a full scholarship at Notre Dame—[the promotion had lasted] 16 years at that point."

But then Jim came to an unexpected fork in the road. "I was home on Valentine's weekend, and it just hit me that my sons were growing up without their dad around, and that they needed me there. [I saw that] I could not finish this degree and be a dad at the same time, because I was living in Indiana during the week and was only at home [in Illinois] on weekends. They were going to finish high school but I would not be there for them. So I withdrew from the doctoral program and let go of the scholarship for the welfare of my family and the welfare of our sons. I got off the upward trajectory."

---

15   Since Jim followed the Descent Before Lordship path, his Natural Promotion and Preparation stages combine in one long climb as shown on the graph above.

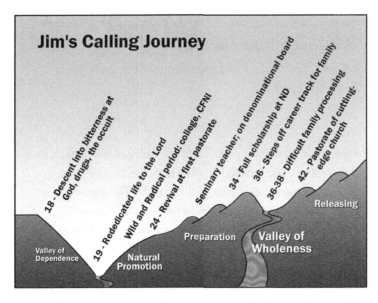

Jim's Calling Journey

18 - Descent into bitterness at God, drugs, the occult

19 - Rededicated life to the Lord

Wild and Radical period: college, CFNI

24 - Revival at first pastorate

Seminary teacher; on denominational board

34 - Full scholarship at ND

36 - Steps off career track for family

36-38 - Difficult family processing

42 - Pastorate of cutting-edge church

Releasing

Valley of Dependence

Natural Promotion

Preparation

Valley of Wholeness

Letting go of what he felt called to and his ability to bring it about was painful. Jim sighs, "Everything I had worked so hard for for almost a decade—I had so much vision, so much tied up with that and with strategies for bringing revival in the denomination. I was walking away from all that, and knowing that I would never come back to it again. But I felt very, very strongly that I should do it. So I took a pastorate to be home more."

Even so, Jim's sons went through a period of rebellion, and the family went into counseling. "One night before Christmas," Jim recalls, "I was so depressed that I lay in bed and cried and slept, and woke up and cried, and slept some more. I was so heartbroken I said to my wife, 'I just can't go to Christmas.' My sons were so mad at me. That's a picture of how low it felt."

Now in his fifties, Jim is an exemplar following the Lord wherever he goes and being content with wherever he has been placed. It is easy to see the connection between his decision to step off the fast track and the obedient contentment that is at the core of his Life Message. The intensity of his Valley of Wholeness was an important part of embedding that Message deep within him.

Jim experienced this valley as a voluntary choice to let go of his calling for the sake of his family. Releasing ownership of our call (the right to have it happen on our terms) is one of the most important lessons the valleys have to offer. We come to the place where we can let go of our need for what a calling gives us without letting go of our hope or getting cynical. I've heard different leaders express it like this:

- *"I reached the point where I could say, God, if this never happens, you are enough for me."*

Valley of Wholeness Characteristics

- *Focuses on Wholeness*
- *One to three years long*
- *Often triggered by family or relational issues, life balance, unrefined gifts or hidden sins*
- *Valley most likely to be entered voluntarily (by asking for help instead of being forced to get it)*
- *Deepening of Life Messages first formed in Valley of Dependence*
- *Less prominent or sometimes skipped by those in the Inside Preparation pattern*
- *Usually connected with a Day of Release for those in Outside Preparation*

- *"I realized that I could be sweeping floors and still fulfill my primary call to my family."*

- *"I was ready to be a janitor if that's what he wanted me to do."*

- *"I had put my identity in my job, and that time of isolation brought me to the place of letting go and getting centered in God again."*

Life Message Refining

Refining and adding to our Life Messages is an important purpose of the Valley of Wholeness. Lis's life is a good example. During her Preparation stage, she traveled all over her country as a mission's leader, starting teams that were going out to cities and villages around the world. "The ministry was growing like crazy," she recounts. "We went from 200 to 500 workers in three or four years."

"Then I got pregnant. I was sick and hospitalized for months—the doctors told me I had to have complete rest and couldn't do anything. I hardly had any visitors, was not allowed to read or watch TV—and I had an identity crisis."

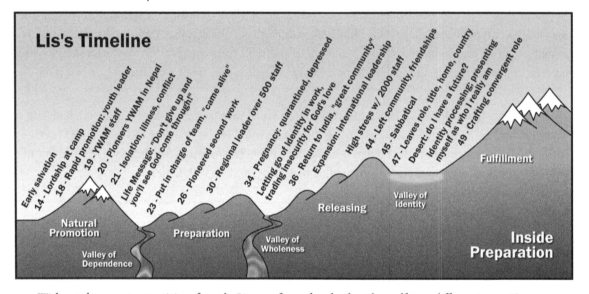

Without the constant activity of work, Lis was forced to look at herself in a different way. "I went into depression after the baby was born," Lis remembers. "The doctor said I might die and the baby might die too—she was only three pounds when she was born. I saw holes in my life, that I needed to go deeper with God. I began to see that I was running on activity but the foundation wasn't solid. I started asking myself, 'Who am I outside of what I am doing?' I needed a new level of revelation of God's deep love for me no matter what I did or who I was. I felt insecure in just being Lis without any ministry identity."

One of Lis's key Life Messages had been birthed years earlier in her Valley of Dependence, when she was sick, alone and imprisoned for the Gospel. That Message was, "Don't give up! If you just keep moving forward and don't give up you'll see God come through." Another Message at the heart of her call is, "Trusting a Great Big God." The Valley of Wholeness drove God's work of faith in Lis's heart to a new depth. In prison, she had learned about facing external circumstances with faith. In the Valley of Wholeness, God removed her fear of going inward.

"It taught me I could face things," Lis asserts. "I could go deeper and be OK, feel safe. In the place I am in today, it would be a total crisis if I had not dealt with the identity thing back then. Now I realize that when I start feeling insecure, I need to go deeper with God."

Secret Sins and Unrefined Strengths

For Evan, things seemed to be looking up at this point in his life. He got the kind of job he'd been seeking for several years, with a small company that gave him "a spot at the table" to influence key decisions. But his new job also let him telecommute from home, and without the structure of working in an office he began turning increasingly to on-line porn.

"I stopped reporting in to accountability partners, and started lying to everyone," Evan recollects. "Finally, I realized I couldn't lead this double life. The most traumatic explosion of my life was bringing my sin to light. I went to my pastor, my wife and my employer, as well as my small group and confessed it. Five guys circled around me, providing ongoing counsel and accountability as I began the process of repentance and restoration."

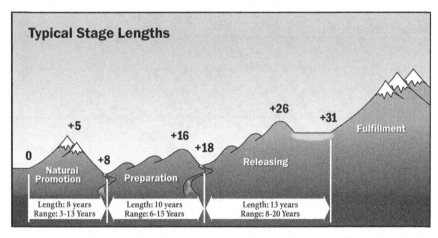

Evan voluntarily chose to bring a secret sin to light and deal with it, preserving his marriage and career. When asked about his Life Messages, Evan confidently replies, "Brokenness in relation to discovering sin in my heart. Grace is another: that there is nothing in and of myself that gains approval from God.

When creating your timeline, it is helpful to know how long the stages usually last. The graph above gives the averages based on our research with present-day leaders. The range is the span of years that fits 85% of the population—your timeline is likely to fall within these windows.

Also, coming to an honest self-assessment before God, and to the freedom to walk openly before him." The connection between Evan's Life Messages and what he experienced in the Valley of Wholeness is obvious.

Sometimes this passage revolves around coming to terms with the flip side of our strengths. Dave is an optimistic, can-do person who always has a million ideas of what can be done to make the world a better place. Since he was a kid, he's been starting businesses and figuring out ways to make money. The flip side of this strength is his tendency to want to do everything now. Dave's personality type and entrepreneurial style often led him to bend the rules to get things done, figuring he could deal with the consequences later.

For instance, he tells about a time during his Preparation stage when he was doing commission sales in a furniture store. He had met with a customer and done all the ground work to get an order, but then on an evening when he was gone a co-worker stole the sale. Instead of going through the channels and taking the issue to his boss, Dave simply tore up the sales receipt and rewrote it using his own name instead of the co-worker's. He ended up losing his job over that incident. It was a tough situation having no job and a family to support, but he still didn't catch on to all of what God was trying to teach him about who he was and how he functioned.

Several years later, Dave began using his business acumen to establish orphanages in Ethiopia. He was making a real difference, but his involvement took time away from his family and put them under financial stress. Things came to a head before another trip, when his wife put her foot down about devoting time to her and the kids. She made him promise not to launch anything new while he was away.

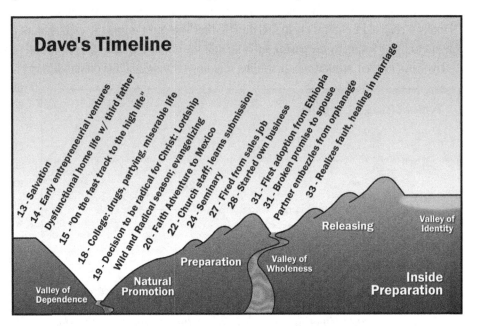

While in Ethiopia, Dave recalls, "I justified it to myself and started a new thing without the approval of my wife. Doing that destroyed a lot of the trust in my marriage. It took a year before she truly forgave me and I realized how much I had hurt her and that I needed to ask forgiveness." Dave was unaware of the impact his free-wheeling ways had on those around him. "The way I thought was, 'If it isn't hurting anyone, I can justify it.' I would do whatever it takes to get something done. You can do that for a while, but then it catches up to you."

In the middle of this difficult time in his marriage, the Dave's initiative in Ethiopia fell apart when his partner absconded with all the funds for the orphanage. "I was working the system instead of waiting for God's timing. For me, learning total reliance on God... has come out of awful experiences."

It took some painful circumstances to get Dave's attention about this area of his character. But his new awareness and responsibility for how he impacts others will be crucial to fulfilling his destiny.

In the midst of a valley's turmoil, we don't realize the contribution it will make to our future. Maybe God waits to show us that connection on purpose, so we engage our character flaws for the sake of relationship with him and others, instead of just to get us where we want to go.

At the time, the Valley of Wholeness is usually perceived as a period of waiting or a step backward. To embrace it as part of God's growth plan requires the perspective of repeatedly experiencing failure, meeting God in the midst of it, and seeing how he redeems it to move us toward our call. At first, our approach to suffering is one of endurance. But endurance produces character in us, and after experiencing that process repeatedly, we begin to approach adversity with hope—the hope that it will transform us. And that hope is never disappointed, because through it we come face to face with the Great Redeemer, who has been at work all along, turning our worst into his best. With that kind of attitude, "…we can't round up enough containers to hold everything God generously pours into our lives through the Holy Spirit" (Rom. 5:3-5; MSG).

Making the Most of the Valleys

The valleys offer an upper-level course in letting go of blame-shifting or a victim posture and learning to willingly lie down on God's operating table. Walking through a valley according to God's purposes means letting it be about you, not about what people or circumstances have done to you. Here's what one leader who lost a role and the ministry he built in a valley season has to say about navigating these times:

> **Summary of Key Learnings**
> - *The second valley deals with issues that seem unrelated to one's call but could undermine it later.*
> - *The Valley of Wholeness helps us let go of our need for our calling and be content with God alone.*
> - *This valley is an important part of forming the Life Messages that make up our being call.*
> - *The key to navigating the valleys is dealing with God instead of blaming people or circumstances.*

> *"The theme of pointing the finger at myself was what got me through the time of processing. God was saying, 'You can't do anything about them, so let me deal with you.' That's what carried me out of that. It hurt like hell, but the Lord was there. Early on, when I was still bleeding internally a year or two later, I started to tell people, 'I didn't know the Lord like I do now.' I had never been broken before to the degree that he was able to come in at this level of intimacy. In the last few years, I've been able to submit to him and bring my heart to him in a deeper way… I've said, 'Lord if you never make a way for me to rise again or do a big thing, if I am just where I am at now and have your presence, I'm content with that.'"*

If you are in the Valley of Wholeness, here are three key things to focus on:

- **Choose to Enter**
  If a hidden problem or secret sin is nagging at you, voluntarily choose to deal with it rather than having it forced on you by circumstances.

- **Take Time**
  Instead of fighting against the season, lean in by setting aside significant time for reflection and inner renovation, even when it seems to take away from what you want to accomplish. In the valleys, God brings outward endeavors to an end to create time for inward retooling.

- **Point the Finger at Yourself**
  Make your conversation with God about who you are instead of what you do; and about the things in you that need to change instead of what needs to change in others

If you are in Outside Preparation, this valley has special significance. The next chapter covers the special challenges and joys of this period for those prepared outside their area of call.

Valley of Wholeness Reflection Questions

1. What event(s) seemed to bring your Preparation stage to a close? Locate your Preparation stage using chapter seven, and see if there is a clear ending point.

2. Do you have a Day of Release, and if so where is it located? Find a significant career transition where you move into your area of call that fits the Day of Release characteristics (see page 115)?

3. Do you have a season of transition or upheaval ten to 20 years after your Lordship commitment? Compare your journey to the average stage lengths chart on page 99 for some hints as to when your Valley of Wholeness might have occurred.

4. Does this transition fit the characteristics of the Valley of Wholeness? Compare the season you tentatively identified to the characteristics list on page 103.

Bible Study Guide: The Valley of Wholeness

Look for the stage characteristics in each of these examples. Note that all three leaders went through Outside Preparation. How are these leaders experiencing this valley season?

1. **David**. As he neared the end of a long desert season on the run, what was happening inside David? (See I Samuel 27.) Why did David go to Philistia? What were the implications for his call if he stayed, or if he went to war against his own people? What was God dealing with in his heart during that time? In II Samuel 1, David was released into his call but lost his best friend. What was going on inside him there? (I Sam. 27, 29-31, II Sam. 1)

> ### Valley of Wholeness Characteristics
>
> - *Focuses on Wholeness*
> - *One to three years long*
> - *Often triggered by family or relational issues, life balance, unrefined gifts or hidden sins*
> - *Valley most likely to be entered voluntarily (by asking for help instead of being forced to get it)*
> - *Deepening of Life Messages first formed in Valley of Dependence*
> - *Less prominent or sometimes skipped by those in the Inside Preparation pattern*
> - *Usually connected with a Day of Release for those in Outside Preparation*

3. **Moses.** His Valley of Wholeness ended around the time of the burning bush (see Exodus 3-4). In his Natural Promotion stage, Moses got way out in front of God when he killed the Egyptian overseer. How did 40 years in the desert change the way he pursued his call? The story also highlights Moses' failure to circumcise his son, an apparent conflict with his wife over the issue and God's dealings with him on it. How would having uncircumcised children (and a lack of clarity in his own house about religious allegiance) have affected the pursuit of his calling?

4. **Jesus'** Valley of Wholeness ended with his forty day fast in the wilderness (see Luke 4:1-14). Think about the three temptations in terms of his calling. How was Jesus being tempted to misuse his gifts and calling, or to enter his call in an inappropriate way? How do/did you experience those temptations in your own journey?

9: THE DAY OF RELEASE

The Valley of Wholeness has special significance for leaders who are being prepared outside their area of call, because it is closely tied to the Day of Release. The Day of Release is a sudden transition when a leader in Outside Preparation is promoted into his or her area of calling. This joyful, exciting moment at the onset of the Releasing stage is filled with a sense of God's favor and action on that leader's behalf. After years lying dormant, the dream is coming to pass!

This transition, unique to those in Outside Preparation, is often marked by a change of vocation, a geographic move or the conclusion of an intentional period of study and training. While the day[16] itself is a time of celebration, the years immediately preceding it are often when leaders in Outside Preparation feel most abandoned by God on the journey.

> **The Day of Release**
>
> *A sudden transition when a leader in Outside Preparation is promoted into his or her area of calling at the beginning of the Releasing stage.*

David's life story offers an excellent example of the key characteristics of the Day of Release. While still a teen, David is anointed as the future king, then experiences a stratosphere ascent during his Natural Promotion stage. From the youngest of eight sons of a backcountry sheep-herder, David rises from obscurity to become a royal musician in the throne room, then a national hero and savior of the king's reputation for killing Goliath (as head and shoulders taller than anyone else in the army, Saul was the obvious choice to go and face the giant). Best friend of the heir to the throne, sung about in the streets of the capital, married to the king's daughter,

---

16   The transition doesn't necessarily take place in one 24-hour day. We call it a day because it happens far too quickly to call it a season or a stage.

David is "prospering in all his ways, because the Lord was with him" (I Sam. 18:14).

While David isn't recorded as doing anything overtly rebellious, Saul has good reason to fear his designs on the throne. So just when the sky seems to be the limit for David, Saul turns on him, and he is thrown out of golden-boy status into his Valley of Dependence. On the run, David tells Ahimelech the priest he is on an official errand for the king, a lie which brings terrible consequences to the priests of Nob. He loses his wife (who is eventually given to another man), goes into exile, feigns insanity to preserve his life from the Philistine king, and ships his parents off to the safety of a foreign country.

At this point, the prophet Gad shows up with a word from God how to handle his valley. David returns to Israel, and retreats to a cave in the desert. While this shot of perspective seems to calm the worst of the chaos, the once-great hero is now a fugitive on the run from the leader who controls his arena of call.

I love the leadership assignment God gives David as his Preparation role: "Everyone who was in distress, and everyone who was in debt, and everyone who was discontented gathered to him; and he

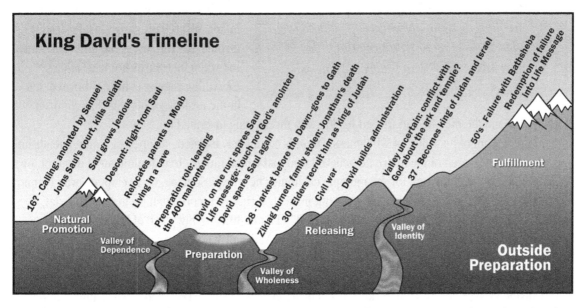

became captain over them" (I Sam. 22:2). David gets to lead the 400 malcontents—the undisciplined, the troublemakers and the law breakers—and mold them into an army. I'm sure he felt his Preparation role was a huge come-down from the heady days in the palace. But if he could lead that group, he could lead anyone. Many of these same misfits became warriors in his band of mighty men, who were strong supporters of his kingship and a loyal core that stuck with him even during the Absalom affair.

David spends five to ten years roaming the wilderness before the arrival of his Day of Release. He is betrayed several times, suffers the death of his key mentor Samuel and spares Saul's life twice with nothing to show for it but empty, face-saving words of false repentance. A decade after being anointed by Samuel, the kingship seems farther away than ever. David begins to lose hope.

"Then David said to himself, 'Now I will perish one day by the hand of Saul. There is nothing better for me than to escape into the land of the Philistines. Saul then will despair of searching for me anymore in all the territory of Israel, and I will escape from his hand.' So David arose and crossed over, he and the six hundred men who were with him, to Achish the son of Maoch, king of Gath" (I Sam. 27:1-2).

A year or so later, the Philistine kings go to war with Israel, and Achish asks David to fight with him. In despair that his call will ever happen, David readily agrees. At least he is back in a palace, bodyguard to a king, leader of a band of troops, part of an army—almost like the old days with Saul. David seems to be flirting with the false opportunity of becoming a leader among the Philistines.

> ### Characteristics of the Day of Release
>
> - *Darkest before the Dawn*
> - *False Opportunities to compromise your call*
> - *Being recruited into your calling sphere*
> - *Major transition from a vocation outside your area of call to one inside it*
> - *Abrupt promotion to a much larger sphere*
> - *Often includes a geographical move*
> - *Functioning as an apprentice to your calling, often under a more senior mentor or leader*
> - *Must take a big risk to believe in your call*

David is about to go to war against the nation he is called to lead. That traitorous act would have precluded him ever becoming the Israelite king. God steps in and sovereignly saves David's destiny through the distrust of the Philistine kings, but when he returns home to Ziklag everything is gone—his city burned, his home destroyed, his wife and children kidnapped, and the men he had trusted his life with threatening to stone him.

At the bottom of his Valley of Wholeness, David is completely isolated, stripped of family, friends and possessions, and bereft of the future he believed God had called him to. In that moment of desperation, he could choose to curse God for the multiple calamities he is experiencing, or give up, or even blame himself for blowing it and sink into despair. But instead, scripture records that on that terrible day, David "…strengthened himself in the Lord his God" (I Sam. 30:6). A big piece of David's Life Message of being a man after God's own heart was formed in his Valley of Wholeness.

The Darkness before the Dawn

Outside Preparation is often darkest just before the dawn. David's Day of Release is almost upon him, but God has intentionally withheld the timetable for David's promotion and kept the map of his journey hidden away. As far as David can see, the wilderness season he is in is endless, and he is farther away from his life call than ever.

For those in Outside Preparation, the greatest feelings of abandonment and hopelessness about the call come toward the end of the Preparation season. As it drags on with no end in sight, the big questions of the heart percolate to the surface. Will my calling ever happen? Am I trapped in this job, doomed to a life that is less than my hopes and dreams? And where is God in all this? I was so sure that he called me, but now—did I make all that up? Were those early days when he met me at every turn just a dream? Have I fallen out of his favor, overlooked and forgotten as he moves on to work with people he cares about more than me? Or worse, is he even real at all?

The Scriptures tell us that endurance is a virtue—something that produces character, which produces hope, which will not disappoint us. The end of the Preparation stage is a place for that kind of simple endurance. The answers we seek will not come until God's time. Sometimes, the only thing that gets us through is not hope or faith but the determination just to hang on and not give up. That was enough to get David to his destiny.

In later years we can truly say, "My worst times came when my dreams were just around the corner." God seems to use this moment, just before our unexpected release, to accomplish a critical work in our hearts. Our own plans to find a path to our call have failed. Every person or opportunity we depended on to get us there has let us down. Circumstances force us to decide: will I hope against all evidence that God will fulfill this deep desire of my heart, or will I settle for a mediocre life of watered-down dreams? Like David, only when every other crutch has been knocked away do we experience

---

Despising the Past

On Moses' Day of Release, the first thing God asked of him was to "remove your sandals from your feet, for the place on which you are standing is holy ground" (Ex. 3:5).

What was the place where Moses was standing? The desert. He had spent the last 40 years in his Preparation stage there, functioning outside of his area of call. The desert is the place he fled to after abandoning his mission to save his own skin. He worked in this "back side of the wilderness" as an unknown shepherd leading a flock of dirty, smelly, stupid sheep through a dustbowl land. It was a far cry from being a prince of Egypt who was called to lead an entire nation out of captivity. The desert symbolized the most desolate, dry, insignificant, seemingly-off-course years of Moses' life—and yet God called it "holy ground."

A place is holy ground when God is there. By naming the desert holy ground, God was telling Moses that his desert years weren't wasted. God had been at work there all along, preparing Moses for his life's work. In fact, Moses was finally ready to fulfill his God-given mission precisely because he spent those formative years in the desert.

At that moment in his life, it was crucial that Moses grasp this truth. For him to truly reveal God as "I AM," the one who was present at that moment to redeem the Hebrews, Moses first needed to see how the great I AM had been present to redeem every experience on his own calling journey.

Whenever you enter a new stage, the temptation is to disparage the season you've been in instead of recognizing it as holy ground. Ever catch yourself saying, "I'm glad I've grown beyond that," or "That was just a phase I was going through," or "I should have known better?" Those statements reveal that you see past difficulties as embarrassing failures instead of displays of God's redemptive power in the life of someone who really needs help.

In God's economy, every stage you go through is holy ground. You were where you were supposed to be for that time in your life, and you couldn't be where you are now without having gone through it. The proper perspective on past stages is to celebrate how God met you in your weaknesses, not disparage how you used to be. It is a disservice to the travelers that follow you to pretend that the stage they are in is any less than God's best.

standing in God alone.

But then, to put all our hope in him, and have him suddenly unlock our dreams! What an incredible revelation of God's love! The great desire on God's heart is that I would understand—he loves *me!* This blessing of release is for me and no one else, from him alone. It is not a second-hand-smoke blessing that I got because I was around another person that God specially loves, or I am part of some other work he blesses. God specially loves *me,* and blesses the work he has assigned to *me.* It is not an accident of fate that brought this opportunity—God himself went out of his way to bring it for *me!* Sometimes we are isolated because the removal of every other source of help is the only way we can understand our Father alone is the one providing for us.

If you are in a wilderness time, it is because God believes you can handle it. He believes in you more than you believe in yourself. He believes you are at the place of maturity where he can withdraw the feeling of his presence and you will not turn away. He believes your love for him is more than something you offer to get your emotional needs met. He believes in you.

I worked for a furniture company for fifteen years in my Preparation stage. Stuck in a little town in Indiana, outside my area of call and with no prospects for getting into it, I was beginning to despair that it would ever happen. Then a leader recruited me out of the wilderness and into my calling sphere. What a joy! But because he was the one who promoted me, a part of me believed that fulfilling my calling was dependent on his favor. That belief made me terribly vulnerable.

When I found myself in a place where I had to confront that leader, the fear of losing my calling if I lost his favor was paralyzing. I agonized over what to say, waited too long, violated my own values and standards, and finally did a trembling, angry job of saying what needed to be said. Everything I had feared ended up coming to pass—I lost his favor, and with it much of my network, my home, my community, my church and the majority of my income.

God redeemed what had happened to me, and immediately put me into a place of even larger influence. By bringing the ugliness of my fears and responses to the light, I began to be transformed. But I had handled the situation so poorly and so much of what God had for me remained unfinished that he arranged for me to go around that mountain once more a few years later, again with great loss of opportunity and income, to hammer into me a confident foundation that he alone would bring my calling to pass. Meeting God in the midst of those experiences has given me such a great freedom and security that I am able to function in the midst of conflict in a way I never could before.

Placing the hope of your calling even partially in a person or job or opportunity can cause you great distress. If your circumstances are causing you to fear losing your calling, grab hold of the opportunity to place all your eggs in God's basket. You'll be glad you did.

Recruiting

One sign your Preparation season is nearing an end is that people start recruiting you to things that resemble your calling. At the Day of Release, leaders in Outside Preparation normally switch careers to move into their area of call. For you to enter this new field without having to start all over at the bottom, at the level commensurate with God's groundwork in your life, you need a sponsor to recognize your true abilities and recruit you into a role that will make full use of them. In Joseph's case, the butler recommended him to a key leader who recognized his gifts and recruited him out of prison. In the same way, Aaron went to find Moses in the desert at the time of his release, and Barnabas went to Tarsus to find Saul. John the Baptist recognized who Jesus was before anyone else, and sponsored him into his own sphere of ministry, even though it meant that John's ministry would decrease as he pointed people to Jesus.

Jeannette's story followed a similar pattern. After a period of questioning brought on by a serious injury, she made Jesus Lord at 23 and entered a period of rapid promotion. During the next few years she joined a committed church, built significant relationships with other believers and toured the country with a worship band. After a number of years working happily as a chemist, at 29 she took a volunteer role overseeing cell groups in her church. Jeannette began to realize she had a passion for church planting and cell group ministry.

"At one point, people in our church had to write life goals and ten year goals. I remember writing a life goal to be involved in church planting—some very small number like five [churches]," she laughs. "Up to that time I had no designs on being in ministry. I was pretty happy with my life. I had a great-paying job, I'd bought a house, and I thought I was doing well and having fun. I was involved in a small group, but not a whole lot of doing ministry. It felt like a normal Christian life where I was doing what I was supposed to be doing."

Responding to her growing sense of call, at 32 Jeannette became part of a church planting team in

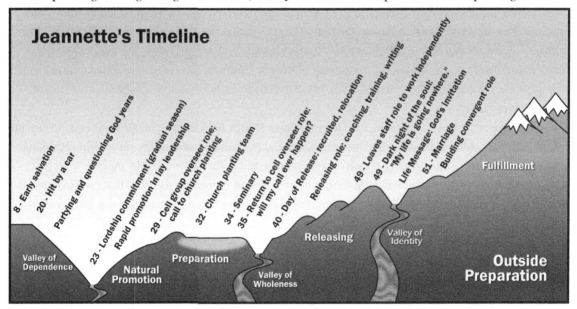

her local church that eventually went out and planted a new work. After two years of high involvement there as a lay leader, she took a year off to go to seminary.

Moving back to her original church at 35 triggered Jeannette's Valley of Wholeness. "I was again doing cell oversight at [my original church]. I knew something bigger and different was coming down the road. But in those years in between I felt stuck, doing the same job of giving oversight to cells for the third time. I wondered, 'Is anything ever going to happen?' As is often the case for those in Outside

Preparation, Jeannette's Valley of Wholeness involved wrestling with her apparent lack of progress toward her call.

Suddenly, after she finished seminary, her life underwent a "huge transition." Jeannette met a well-known church planting consultant, and was recruited to come and work for him. At age 40 she moved across the country to apprentice under this leader, and started training, coaching and writing curriculum in his vastly-larger, international sphere of influence. Saying "yes" to this great opportunity represents Jeanette's Day of Release and the beginning of her Releasing stage. Over the next ten years she worked with dozens of church plants and cell churches as a coach and consultant, far surpassing her early dream of being involved with five church plants in her lifetime.

The leader who recruited Jeannette greatly accelerated her calling journey. Using the favor, influence and name recognition he had accumulated over a lifetime, he opened doors for Jeannette, giving her access to opportunities that would never have come to her on her own. This kind of sponsorship is a crucial function of leaders in the Fulfillment stage. In Fulfillment, God moves us from finding satisfaction in our own successes to getting our greatest joy from the success of others. One of the greatest legacies of mature leaders is their part in the legacies of the many others they have promoted.

False Opportunities

Not all opportunities are God's best. After keeping the dream alive for years on the run in the deserts of Palestine, David's hope for a better future began to run out. That discouragement led to some poor choices. By attaching himself to the king of Gath, David regained the outward appearance that he was moving toward his call. The similarities to his early role with Saul are striking—the king's right-hand man, trusted body guard, leader of a contingent of troops. However, this role represented a fundamental compromise of what God had revealed about his call. David was born to be a leader of Israel, not of Israel's chief enemy.

False Opportunities like this one tend to come to us shortly before the sponsor God sends to recruit us into our Day of Release. As leaders around us sense our readiness and ability, they begin recruiting us to their ventures. The challenge is one of discernment and faith: can you rightly evaluate which opportunities really fit, and do you have the confidence in God to pass up the ones that compromise your values or don't fit your call? After years of closed doors, the false opportunities can be incredibly enticing.

I once worked with a couple who had dreamed for years of running a retreat center for pastors and missionaries who needed a place of rest. After a long time without much movement, and no idea where the money for their dream was ever going to come from, a businessman appeared out of the blue and offered them a million-dollar resort to run as a retreat center. What an opportunity!

However, as they began checking it out, one red flag after another popped up. The businessman had a vision, but his wife was not on board with it at all. He talked so fast they barely got in a word in their 'conversations.' He was running the place on weekends and doing his regular job during the week, and never took a Sabbath (not a good pattern for someone who wants to minister rest to others!) He seemed to have no accountability and little connection to a local church. The more this couple looked, the more issues came to the surface. After years of faithful waiting, it was a bitter pill to swallow to decline that offer. However, accepting it would have compromised their values and yoked them with a leader whose character flaws would have constantly undermined the mission they were called to do.

To navigate this season well, you have to be clear on what God has shown you so far about your calling, and believe that God will bring it to pass without any outside help if that's what it takes. One of the most common pitfalls of this stage is allowing yourself to be co-opted by a leader who promises the moon but is really only interested in using you to fulfill his or her own dream.

The Suddenness of the Day

Once David shakes himself free of the false opportunity in Gath and revives his trust in God, his Release is not long in coming. He begins to aggressively consult God through Abiathar the priest (something it didn't seem he had done in a while), and is directed to pursue the raiders who had burned his city. Everything he lost is recovered, and more. Two days later, David learns of Saul's death. The biggest obstacle to his destiny has suddenly been removed. The same messenger brings Saul's crown right to David's doorstep—what an interesting confirmation of David's call!

However, it's a bittersweet moment. At the same time God elevates David, he is mourning for the loss of his best friend, Jonathan, and the damage done to his country. Once again he inquires of the Lord, and is directed to make a geographic move out of exile to Hebron, the heart of his people's territory. With Ziklag burned, there is no longer any reason to stay in Gath. God manages to simultaneously remove the obstacles to David's return to Israel and force him out of his comfort zone in exile. Once he arrives home, the elders of Judah quickly show up and recruit David to be their king. In the space of a few weeks, David goes from having little hope of ever fulfilling his call to a coronation.

Many contemporary leaders also report that their Day of Release came suddenly. Following a stint in China as an English teacher, Dave returned to go to seminary during his Preparation stage. After four years working on his degree, a contact with a distant friend and some divine intervention combined to give him a dream opportunity to serve in a leading church in the black community. The fact that he was hired a week before he graduated was highly unusual. Shortly after moving across the country, he was traveling as the personal assistant of a leader who appeared on the cover of Time magazine, and was writing articles for him that were published nationally. From a low-level job in admissions at a university, David went in a very short time to a position with national influence. It was an exhilarating, satisfying experience.

David's story illustrates six of the characteristics of the Day of Release (see box page 106). In this case, the first two (false opportunities and the darkness before the dawn) don't play a prominent part in his timeline. Your story will not usually display every one of these symptoms, either.

Temptations

Jesus' Preparation occurs outside of his area of calling, while working as a carpenter. During a forty-day fast in his Valley of Wholeness he faces three temptations. Since he has been tempted in every way we are (yet without sin), these temptations may be common ones for those on the cusp of being released into their calling.

Luke records that Jesus is hungry after 40 days without food. The first temptation is to turn a stone into bread. 'If you really have the power of God at your disposal, use it to meet your own needs!' the devil implores. 'If you don't take care of yourself, no one will—not even God.'

A legitimate call is always about the service of others, not self. One of the great temptations on the calling journey is to use what God has given us to get what we want. Maybe our hearts' desire is to have a television ministry, a mansion on a hill, financial independence, the respect of our peers, or even to accomplish something impressive for God. It is so easy to twist a call into something that meets our own need for meaning or significance in life.

Jesus' reply is, "Man shall not live on bread alone, but on every word that proceeds from the mouth of God" (Mt. 4:4). In effect, he says, "Getting my own physical needs met is not what keeps me going. My sense of worth and significance is not tied up in meeting the physical needs of others, either. This is about spiritual life, not things."

In the second temptation, Jesus is taken up into the realm of vision, and sees a picture of what the

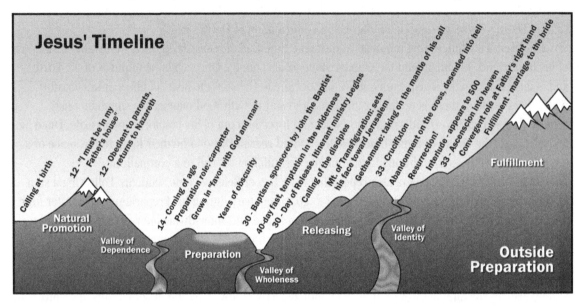

fulfillment of his call could be like. He sees himself ruling in glory over all the nations and peoples of the earth. That's an image of what he was born to be, and something God intends for him. However, in the devil's version of the story, Jesus rules through the power structures of this world as an earthly king, instead of coming as a suffering servant building a kingdom that's not of this world.

For Jesus, the temptation is to take control of his destiny and become a king immediately by using temporal power and earthly power structures to accomplish the mission. Taking this shortcut would bypass the suffering God's plan entails. If Jesus will only compromise the *means*, he can have the *end* without the cross.

Part of the force of this temptation is that it comes at the end of an 18-year season of waiting. The false opportunity to control our destiny and reach it now, on our own terms, is a sore trial after we've waited years for our release and wondered if it would ever come. The temptation to compromise to enter our calling is never stronger than at this point on the timeline.

The Bible is very clear about the results of taking this path. Since Satan has been given the earthly power structures of the world system to give to whomever he wills, taking worldly authority as a ruler in order to fulfill his call would put Jesus in Satan's domain, under Satan's authority. It would make Jesus a servant and worshipper of Satan. In fact, the person to whom Satan eventually *will* give all this worldly authority is the Beast from the Sea, the Anti-Christ (Rev. 13:2). *Attempting to fulfill a God-given calling using the tools of power and control is not God's way.*[17]

This is a terrible temptation for American Christians in this day. We see the ills of our society, are even called by God to address them, and political power to affect those changes seems to be right within our grasp. If we will only make a small compromise in the means, and attempt to enforce His kingdom of love using earthly, governmental power, we can have a Christian society. Instead of taking the long, uncertain road of faith, prayer and suffering to change the culture, political power can let us control the outcome and get quick results right now. Think of the lives we could save! And all we have to do is work the levers of power Jesus abhorred to touch and use the devil's tools to do God's work.

Jesus refuses the offer of worldly power because of the allegiance to the enemy it entails. As you navigate this season, beware of the false opportunities that seem to put your call within your grasp but compromise the heart of it.

The third temptation is about believing in his call and the God behind it. "*IF* you are the son of God…" the devil says, "Prove it! Throw yourself off the 300-foot-high temple wall in broad daylight and prove to everybody (including yourself) that God is with you." So often we want to *know* God's call beyond a shadow of a doubt before we step out in it. This impulse doesn't flow out of our great devotion, but from our need to be in control. We seek confirmation after confirmation along the path because we are afraid to take the big risk that God is real, he has called *us* to do something great and the time is now. And we want *public* confirmation and a *public* word (that's why this test happened in the middle of Jerusalem on the pinnacle of the temple) instead of God's still, small voice in secret, because then we can lean on the faith of others to make up for what we lack in ourselves.

Jesus' response to the tempter is, "You shall not put the Lord your God to the test." After a point, asking for more and more evidence of God's direction is simple unbelief. It's saying to God, "Prove it!" If you find yourself asking God for proof and not hearing anything, it may be time to put away your fleeces and start acting on what he has already told you.

Making the Most of the Day of Release

The key to making the most of this moment in life is simply to go for it. You've been through a long season where the word from God has been, "Not yet." You've yearned to move on, but when the time comes to actually pull up stakes, take a big risk and tackle your calling; you may suddenly realize how comfortable waiting has become!

The end of both the Valley of Wholeness and the Valley of Identity frequently require us to take a big risk for the sake of our calling. We must believe that God has actually called us, and that with him we

---

17   This is not to say Christians should never enter government, but that they should not believe that governmental power is a tool that can build God's kingdom on earth. The very act of using earthly power to enforce what you believe God wants so utterly misrepresents God (as a God of power, enforcement and control) that it actually works against his kingdom.

can do it. Often God requires us to put our money where our mouth is and stake a significant portion of our resources and reputation on that fact. You cannot enter into your calling without risk.

For instance, on his Day of Release at the burning bush, Moses learns he has to go back to Israel and face Pharaoh, the god-king, son of the man he ran for his life from years before. On Joseph's day, he must interpret Pharaoh's dream, risking his future and probably his life that he is genuinely hearing God. David must take over a nation in disarray that was just thrashed in battle, and overcome all the bad blood from Saul's failed kingship. Wilberforce has to try to convince a bunch of cold-blooded politicians to outlaw an entrenched practice that made up a significant percentage of the national economy.

One reason risk is required is that the fuel the kingdom of God runs on is faith. What pleases God is to be believed in and trusted, not following rules or self sacrifice or doing great exploits in his name. "Without faith, it is impossible to please God" (Heb. 11:6). Calling will always be a work of faith. You will never know with absolute certainty what you are supposed to do, whether everything will work out or how God will come through—because if you did, you wouldn't need faith!

The second reason risk is required is that you need the confidence it brings to do what you were created to do. At some point in the

> ## Summary of Key Learnings
>
> - *Those in Outside Preparation have a Day of Release that moves them into their area of call.*
> - *God arranges this day for you to show he specially loves you.*
> - *Sponsoring the Releasing of others is an important task for those in Fulfillment.*
> - *God will not allow you to enter your call without risk.*

pursuit of your call you will need the strength to stand alone with God, with no visible means of support and no one else to lean on, and say, "God called me to this and I am going to see it through no matter what." No one is going to make your call happen for you: if you don't walk this path and pay this price, no one will. And God is so committed to your success that he wants you to enter your call well prepared for those moments. Asking for big risks is one way God prepares you to succeed at your life's work.

Day of Release Reflection Questions

1. Did you go through the Preparation stage with a primary role outside of your area of call? (You must answer "yes" to have a Day of Release in your timeline.)

2. When did you make a major transition to a primary role within your area of call?

3. How well does that moment fit the list of characteristics of the Day of Release (see page 115)?

Bible Study Guide: The Day of Release

Look for how the Day of Release plays out in each of these three characters' lives.

1. **Jesus.** John the Baptist sponsored Jesus at the beginning of his Releasing stage and brought him into a large sphere of influence quickly (see Luke 3:1-22 & 7:18-23, John 1:1-51 & 3:22-36). What specifically did John do that gave Jesus an immediate platform? What resources came Jesus' way from John? What did it cost John to promote Jesus, and how did he handle that?

3. **Moses**. His Day of Release was when he met God at the burning bush. Which of the Day of Release characteristics (see list at right) fit Moses' story? What specifically did he struggle with in accepting the call, and what caused him to keep raising objections? How was Moses' experience of releasing like yours?

> **Characteristics of the Day of Release**
> - *Darkest before the Dawn*
> - *False Opportunities to compromise your call*
> - *Being recruited into your calling sphere*
> - *Major transition from a vocation outside your area of call to one inside it*
> - *Abrupt promotion to a much larger sphere*
> - *Often includes a geographical move*
> - *Functioning as an apprentice to your calling, often under a more senior mentor or leader*
> - *Must take a big risk to believe in your call*

4. **Paul**. He has a conversion story for the ages, a meteoric rise in Christian circles, hob-knobs with Peter the apostle—and then is shipped out of town for his own good when he gets into trouble. Paul returns home to obscurity in Tarsus. The Bible does not record his having disciples or starting a ministry there, and the church as a whole did better after he left town (see Acts 9:1-31). It is years until Barnabas goes to find him and bring him back into ministry at Antioch (Acts 11:25-26). Put yourself in Paul's shoes. What would it have been like to have Barnabas believe in you and sponsor you after all those years? How was Paul's ministry with Barnabas different than it was before he went home to Tarsus? Which of the characteristics in the box fit Paul's Day of Release?

10: FINDING LIFE MESSAGES

L ee, a highly successful business leader in his sixties, can immediately rattle off his life task: "My mission is using my talents to help bring freedom to the captives." How that phrase came to have unique, deep meaning for him offers a window into how Life Messages form.

Lee grew up in a Christian home and made Jesus his Lord early in life. During his Natural Promotion stage in high school, everything seemed to be going up. "I was a star—I had a long-term girlfriend, was the quarterback on the football team and lettered in four sports... I was busy, but I was coasting. I didn't do my homework, wasn't ambitious—I wasn't experiencing a lot of growth as a person."

In college Lee joined the ROTC, found something that caught his interest, and began to excel. As number two in his ROTC class, on graduation he got an Air Force commission and went directly into flight school. "I was in training 14 hours a day... I focus well in a high challenge environment. I was going to use it right away—so between the passion [for flying] and the challenge it was easy."

At 23, both excited and scared, he was sent to Vietnam straight out of flight school. A natural pilot, he was soon flying six or seven missions a week hunting trucks on the Ho Chi Minh Trail. To this point, Lee's life had been mostly about following his dream for flying and having fun—until he was shot down and captured in 1968. That began his Valley of Dependence.

"I stayed in the Hanoi Hilton for five and a half years. When I look back at that experience— especially the first two weeks—God was really taking care of me. I was shot down 250 miles south of Hanoi, so it took two weeks to get there. I was protected in a way that was unreal. The locals tried to kill me several times and the militia protected me. I was bombed and strafed by American fighters several times before I arrived in Hanoi. It also helped that I didn't have any bad injuries from the ejection. We were going pretty fast, and a lot of guys had broken bones or serious injuries from ejecting, but I was in pretty good shape."

"I ended up in a six-and-a-half by seven foot room with three other guys. There were bad times, but we were not high priority targets for torture and mistreatment. We had some mild torture but not like the guys in earlier years. I got close to God and prayed a lot when I was there. One of my roommates was a lapsed Catholic. He would ask us to tell him Bible stories and verses. I remembered stuff from Sunday school, but the well pretty quickly ran dry. I vowed that when I came home I would read the Bible every day."

"I had a lot of shame in me during that time about not doing my homework, slacking off in my studying, not being the leader I ought to be. I guess my sub-conscious was trying to justify being punished, and the only thing it came up with was my being lazy [as the reason I was shot down]."

"We had no books, papers, or magazines, so I had to do a lot of mental work and discipline my mind. All the things that I had resisted and been lazy about as a student I learned to do. I memorized long poems, did math in my head, learned to play chess—it really sharpened me up. I was the lead communicator in my group [keeping in touch with guys in other cells], so I really had to stay focused. I did the tap-code and got good at flashing signals on the wall. I was the most agile, sneakiest, hyperactive guy—I only got caught once, and I managed to talk my way out of it that time. I was maturing spiritually and intellectually, and it gave me confidence that I could deal with almost anything."

The Prison of the Heart

His five years in prison gave Lee an incredible inside perspective on what it was to be a captive. The shame he experienced in captivity became an important theme in how he touched others later in life. Released after the Paris peace talks at 30 years old, Lee returned home to begin his life again. He knew what it was like to be released from an external prison—now God began to teach him about release from the prison of the heart.

Lee married at 31 and became an "instant father"—his new bride already had kids from a previous marriage. "I was a really nice guy," Lee recalls, "but a lot more controlling than I needed to be about the little things. Most things in my life to that point had been life and death, so I tended to treat everything as life and death. The kids didn't benefit from my control, either. I didn't know anything about kids—I hadn't even seen one in six years. The result was that I undermined their confidence."

Lee's Valley of Identity began at 51 when he started to recognize what he was doing to those he loved. "One day I looked around and saw the collateral damage. My wife was depressed. There was some biological background to that, but a lot was from me. I started learning about control. I studied it, I saw it in others, and then I started to see it in myself… Then in 1995 I went to a four-day retreat, ten hours a day. I didn't want to go, but God convinced me. My youngest son was into drugs at the time. I had started to realize that the best way to change him might be changing me."

"The first day, when people went around and talked about who they were and what they were dealing with, I thought they were a bunch of losers. But by the next night I was just weeping. I started to see with empathy, instead of just saying, 'Suck it up and do the right thing.' I started to see my son differently. God showed me that I didn't see myself accurately and I wasn't seeing others the way he saw them. When I saw them like he did, it really touched my heart. I felt more alive after that retreat than I had ever had in my life—I felt like I had gotten some freedom. My wife would say that I am a different person."

"We got marriage counseling at that time, and I committed to continue the growth that had begun.

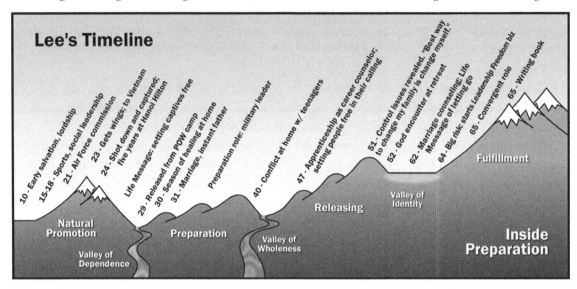

Letting go is a significant part of who I am. Training to be a leadership coach helped me learn to give up control and "telling" and learn how to ask good questions that would be freeing to the other person. The kids call me for advice now—that is a good sign that they are not feeling controlled."

Lee's discoveries about his own heart started to change the way he did business consulting. He began to create situations where the key players could share their pain and shame with the group. "I remember one incident where I got people talking about their struggles. One lady shared some shame, and afterward, another person said, 'I thought that I was the only person that felt that way.'" Another memorable occasion was when an individual in one of his sessions began sharing "about deaths in her family as a kid, and how that had shaped her. Where this woman had been bound by fears, she found a new freedom, and co-workers commented later that she was never the same."

Lee began to have a much deeper impact on people as he worked out of this area of his life. Releasing people from captivity became more and more of a theme in his work. Eventually, he formed a company called Leadership Freedom with a focus on freeing leaders from things that keep them from succeeding. Bringing people out of captivity is now a central part of the consulting work he does with business organizations.

"I have a gift of discernment about bondage," Lee asserts. "I see it in a clear way in others. I've always had an ability to see into other people, but now I have seen so many people get free of lies and pain it is even clearer. I can literally see the spiritual shackles falling off. Because I've been locked up and I know what it means to be free, that is very exciting to me."

The theme of bringing freedom to the captives is Lee's chief Life Message. God met him in situations where he was a captive (both physically in the Hanoi Hilton and in the prison of his wounded heart), the life of Jesus transformed his being, and now that same life flows out of him to others. His Message of freedom is rooted in his life story. Lee is who he is in Christ because of what he and Jesus walked through together. And since that Message is written on his heart—it is part of the very fiber of his being—it pervades everything he does. In his Fulfillment stage, communicating that Message has become Lee's core mission in life. He has crafted a convergent role by creating a consulting business that effectively delivers his Message of freeing the captives to his target audience of business leaders.

What are Life Messages?

I love Lee's story, because it so plainly shows how his Life Message springs from his narrative: the one who was once a captive now sets the captives free. That's how it is for most leaders. Your Message is most likely to grow not out of your greatest successes and accomplishments, but in your place of brokenness and lack.

A Life Message is a place in your heart where you have deeply met Jesus, his life has replaced your natural life, and that incarnation flows out as a Message of Christ to others. Together, these Messages combine to form your being call—the essence of the Christ-in-you that is channeled through your calling role to impact others. Life Messages are individual facets of Christ's character you specially model, while your being call is all those messages rolled together.

> **Definition**
>
> *A Life Message is a place where you have deeply meet Jesus, his life takes the place of your natural life, and that incarnation flows out as a Message of Christ to others.*

Life Messages aren't formed where the best of your natural abilities are *refined*, but where the worst of the natural you is *replaced*. They are not principles you've learned, disciplines you've mastered or even trials you've overcome, but the product of an encounter with God that transforms your innermost self and redefines who you are.

Life Messages are rooted in our core identity. Since changing our identity is extraordinarily hard work, we rarely do it without an extraordinary stimulus. A great touch from God happens most often through an act of extraordinary grace or in the midst of unusually trying circumstances.

In the extraordinary circumstances of a P.O.W. camp, Lee lost control of his destiny and his future. For a get-it-done, hard-charging personality like his, that painful loss of freedom opened his heart to God in a new way. He experienced God's care and presence in the midst of captivity, which deeply touched him, and he experienced what it was like to be free after a long imprisonment.

That experience also gave him the gift of a platform. When you have a story like Lee's, people who need freedom will listen to you because you've been in captivity and met God there. You have real, tested wisdom to offer, and not just platitudes that have never been through the fire. An important by-product of the story behind your Message is that it draws the very people to you who need what you have to give! They sense the power you gained from meeting God in the same difficult place they're in, and you have what they are desperately looking for.

Repeated Processing

The first stamp of Lee's Life Message was imprinted on his heart through encountering Jesus in a

P.O.W. camp. But the work had only begun.

The power of a Life Message is proportional to how much of Jesus is in us in that part of our heart. Therefore, in the most important areas of our call, God is going to process us repeatedly, driving his life deeper and deeper into us each time. This pattern of unusually intense, repeated dealings of God in a particular area of our life is not a sign of sin or weakness, but a sign of call. God has chosen us to go extraordinarily deep with him in this specific place, so that we will have an extra-ordinary revelation of who he is to share with the world.

With Lee, the place God chose to focus in on was control. Lee repeatedly found himself in situations where he lost control, or where exerting control damaged the people he loved. Each incident forced him to practice letting go—in effect, releasing people from the prison of his high expectations. And when he released others and learned to see them with empathy, as God did, he was released to a new level of impact in his life mission as a bondage breaker.

> ### Life Message Characteristics
> *Below are some of the key qualities of a Life Message:*
>
> - **Places of Power**
>   *This is where your story and what you have to offer has the deepest impact on others.*
> - **Drawing**
>   *People who need your Message are instinctively drawn to you, and you are drawn to them.*
> - **Qualification**
>   *You are qualified to speak profoundly to people in similar situations because you've been there and met God in it.*
> - **Soapbox Issues**
>   *Every serious conversation you have seems to get around to your Messages. These are themes you return to over and over, because they represent the most important work God has done in you.*
> - **Tied to Shaping Events**
>   *They tend to be tied to the important shaping events of your life (the crucible they form in).*

All ministry is a function of who you are. You impact people for Christ to the degree that Christ has impacted you. That's what Life Messages are all about—identifying the areas God has most deeply impacted you so that you can build your life mission around them.

More Examples

Paul's ministry offers us a good biblical picture of a Life Message. A key shaping event for him was the extraordinary circumstances of his conversion. He had been persecuting the Christians, thinking that he had all the right answers about what God wanted, and it turned out that he was totally wrong. Paul was the Pharisee of Pharisees, full of religion but empty of love, until God knocked him off his high horse, blinded him, and showed him the depth of his need and the ugliness of his religious arrogance. Is it any wonder that Paul's most important Message is about God's unmerited favor, since he experienced grace in such a profound way? Nobody needed grace like Paul, the foremost of sinners, so nobody grasped it so deeply and nobody can speak about it with as much power as he can. Paul's ministry was built around bringing the Message of grace to those who most needed it—the Gentiles.

Martin Luther is an interesting parallel. Luther was morbidly obsessed with his own sinfulness. He tried literally everything to get rid of his sense of guilt: becoming a priest, confessing every sin he'd ever committed for hours on end, saying "Hail Mary's" while going up and down the steps of St. Peter's on his knees, fasting and engaging in all the "buffeting of the flesh" that was common among monks of that age. No matter what he did, Luther could not feel right with God.

Finally, when he began teaching the book of Romans, he discovered and was deeply impacted by Paul's Life Message of grace. As with Paul, that grace found a perfect vehicle—nobody wanted it or needed it as bad as Luther. Embracing the concept of unmerited favor changed his life, and Luther appropriated Paul's Life Message as his own. *The power of the Protestant Reformation is directly proportional to the depth of Christ's touch of grace in Luther's heart.* The Message that birthed a movement came from the story of Luther's life.

While historical examples give a good picture of the impact of a Message, examining what goes on inside us as they form is easier with contemporary examples. One of my Life Messages, transparency, developed through a difficult shaping event in my late twenties. My home church crashed spectacularly, from 350 all the way down to under a hundred. Though we nursed the body back to health over the next few years, much of the radical, growing edge of our shared life was lost.

At the same time, I was transitioning out of a single lifestyle where I worked half-time, lived in a discipleship house 24x7 and ran around the country doing ministry for free; to having a wife, kids and a full-time job. I no longer had time to spend hours hanging out worshipping and talking about spiritual things with my house mates, and church was no longer spoon-feeding me those kinds of opportunities. So much of my rapid growth in the Natural Promotion stage had been through relationships that I began to wonder, "How do you live the radical Christian life when you have real, adult responsibilities?"

I also bore some major scars from the church breakdown. Deep down, I had believed this church we built was of God, and therefore it wouldn't fail. I expected we'd be together and build the Kingdom together our whole lives. Instead, it fell apart, my best friends left and the best of the dream died.

That event really shook my belief system. I thought God would come through in a certain way, and he didn't. Where was he? If God wasn't going to preserve his own church, what else would he let die? What shook me even further was realizing I was holding back from God, and not giving myself 100% like before. I didn't like that at all, but I didn't know what to do about it, either. So I began pestering God to help me. After several months I got an answer.

"Tony, there's one degree of glory it brings me when you think it will work and so you'll trust me. But there is a whole 'nother degree of glory it brings me when you *know* it won't work and you'll *still* trust me."

As I digested what God was trying to tell me, a major shift began to take place in my belief system. Up until then, the way I built relationships prioritized safety and protection. I would incrementally build trust with people over the course of many months or even years until I felt could share my real self in that relationship without getting hurt. Because I thought in terms of safety, I related to God in that area mainly as a protector. While much of my spiritual growth had been catalyzed through authentic friendships, the problem was that they took years to build, and I no longer had that kind of time.

However, I began to see that there might be a different way. Instead of becoming transparent in tentative, measured steps to protect myself, I could just make the choice to be transparent, whether I knew that the person was safe and trustworthy or not. Living wide open and trusting God even though I knew it wouldn't always work was a way to bring glory to God. I quickly found that when I was willing to take big risks to be authentic, others would do the same—and I could have the deep, authentic relationships I longed for almost any time I took the risk. That shift was life changing.

At the same time, I stopped relating to Jesus only as protector, and began to also share in the fellowship of his sufferings and trust him as my healer. I got to know a whole different side of my best friend. And knowing him as a healer made it possible for me to let go of my need to be protected from everything that might go wrong in life. He was there just as powerfully when he healed my wounds as when he saved me from harm. He shook my belief system, and now I know that even when things are shaken, he can still be trusted.

Over the next few years, I worked out what healthy transparency looked like and disciplined myself to integrate it into my daily life. I also took steps to remember and steward my story (see box below). While the Message itself comes from a God-encounter, you still have to steward what you've been given through discipline and reflection, until it is firmly implanted in your habits and your heart. The more you are conscious of your Messages, know the story behind them and have studied their application, the more powerful they are.

Making Messages

Making Messages is one of the more unilateral things God does. He decides where he is going to

---

Stewarding Your Story

Since your Messages were formed through encountering God in your shaping events, one of your most important ministry tools is the story behind your Message. Remembering the details of how God met you is crucial! Here are some reflection questions that will help you commit the important details of your story to memory:

1. *What circumstances led up to this shaping event?*
2. *When did you first realize God was up to something? What got your attention?*
3. *What defenses in you did God have to get around to get you to engage him instead of blame shifting or playing the victim?*
4. *What were you thinking at the time? What emotions did you experience? What questions were you asking?*
5. *How did you encounter God in the midst of this experience?*
6. *What changed about your identity, core beliefs, values or being?*
7. *Who was the Jesus you met in this? (i.e. redeemer, lover, provider, master, etc.)*
8. *What difference has this God encounter made in how you function now?*

meet us, he creates or leverages the circumstances that get our attention and he motivates us to engage him at the heart level. And when we do, it is Jesus that invades and transforms our hearts, too. Our job consists of two things: recognizing where he is already at work and choosing to go there with him.

God can make living in our brokenness so painful that we are compelled to recognize our need to change. But he would much rather teach us to be attentive to what he is doing. The earlier we recognize God is at work and lean into it, the less painful the surgery is. Here's the key: since it takes extraordinary circumstances to change our identity, *every time we experience extraordinary circumstances is potential Life Message formation time.* Pretty simple, huh? And once you master meeting him in extraordinary circumstances, you can learn to go to the heart level and be transformed in **any** circumstance, large or small.

> **Doing and Being Calls**
> *Every time we experience extraordinary circumstances is potential Life Message formation time.*

What are the clues that God may be knocking on the door of your heart? Here are some common symptoms with questions to help you reflect on what's happening:

- God has brought me into a difficult situation like this several times.
  What are the common elements in the way I respond, and are my responses biblical?

- This affects me much more deeply than the circumstances warrant.
  Why does this touch me so deeply? What in my past does this situation stir up?

- I find myself blaming others or making excuses for myself.
  What am I afraid of? Why do I need someone or something else to blame?

- I experience strong negative emotions here like fear, anger, or grief.
  Where is that coming from? What is the hole in my heart this exposes?

- I am not hearing God speak to me as much as usual.
  Am I not hearing because I'm asking the wrong questions? What does his silence show me?

- Something I am doing isn't working that usually worked before.
  What's changed? Is God asking something new of me?

- I've tried all the obvious practical steps and nothing changes.
  What would it look like if I stopped trying to address the outward behavior and started looking for what drives or motivates me to do it?

- I am challenged in an area or get negative feedback from others several times.
  What are they seeing that I don't see? What part of this is my problem?

- I have failed at something significant, or am in significant adversity.
  How does God want to redeem this by redeeming something in me?

Once we realize we are in an extraordinary moment, it's time for the second key step. *We need to engage God at the level of our hearts,* not our heads, our behavior, or externals. The questions above are designed to do just that. Notice that they are about my motives, my identity, my fundamental drives, and what God's growth agenda is for me. None of them ask what needs to change in the other person.

Here's an example of how to apply this to a real life situation. Let's say that one of your valley times is triggered by a son rebelling, doing drugs or just closing himself off from you. The broken relationship and brokenness in your son's life is painful.

There are many different ways you can engage the situation. Focusing on getting your son in a better school or changing his attitude is externalizing the issue. Bemoaning how he is making your life difficult is taking a victim posture. Maybe you tend to shrink back inside yourself and hope the problem goes away, or spend your devotions every day crying out to God in prayer to save him. None of these responses put the focus on what God wants to do in **you**. One of the most well-worn defensives we use to protect our hearts is asking God to deal with other people's problems instead of our own.

A step in the right direction might be resolving to spend more time being there for him, or practicing the art of listening instead of nagging at him about his grades and his personal habits. These are good, practical steps, but they do not get down to the level of your heart. The focus is on using discipline to control your outward behavior, not discovering *why* you are a poor listener, or why you feel compelled to tell your son what he is doing wrong.

Reading books on anger and control can give us some good tips on self-management, but books alone tend to get us engaging with our heads and not our hearts. With our heads we think of things to *do* different, but what God wants is to come and dwell within us and replace the heart of the old dad with a new one. Dealing with God at the heart level means asking questions like these:

- How is what my son is doing a reflection of who I am as a father?

- What drives me to try so hard to control what he does?

- What do I gain by not paying attention to him or not giving him the time he needs? What does that say about me?

- How are my wounds and needs driving my responses? How do those needs impact him?

- I keep reacting to him—why? Where is this situation touching a hole in my heart?

- He's told me I am a jerk when he is angry—what part of that is true?

- Who does Jesus want to be for me here in my own brokenness?

- Why is it so hard for me to ask these questions?

Wrestling with God at this deep level is what forms Life Messages. Conversely, failure to engage God in our transitions means that instead of experiencing a quantum leap in our effectiveness, our impact on others is about the same as it was before the transition. That's a tragic waste of the adversity we went through! Fortunately, once we've made him Lord, God is pretty good at taking us to where we need to go.

Discovering Life Messages

I often find that leaders have gone through a valley season, met God deeply in it, but still have trouble articulating the Message God planted in them during that time. Sometimes we don't even realize or remember how we met God in challenging circumstances. The exercises on the next two pages (adapted from *A Leader's Life Purpose Workbook*) will help you identify your Life Messages.

Exercise: Identifying Life Messages

Set aside half an hour or so in a quiet place and reflect back on your life story. You're going to identify the major shaping events in your life and tease out the Life Messages formed in them. Since valleys are important shaping times, you'll start there. Remember that Messages are formed in the heart. You aren't looking for skills you developed, principles or practical lessons you learned, but for places where the natural, human you was replaced with the heart of Christ.

Step 1: List Shaping Events

Jot down each valley in your timeline, and the major events in that valley that shaped you. If you want to go deeper, list some other major shaping events in your life as well.

> **Example:** *The birth of my first child.*

Step 2: Identify the Impact

How did each experience on your list shape who you are? How are you a different person at the core of your being because you went through it?

> **Example:** *The wonder and awe of creating life deeply touched me. And how God makes and sustains it in spite of all the things I do wrong. It put together a larger thing God was doing about seeing what is really important in life—people, relationships, living in the now—instead of the worries about performance and fears of the future.*

Step 3: Meeting God

How did you encounter God in this experience? How did your heart and your character take on the likeness of Christ through it? Who is the Jesus you met here, and what is his name?

> **Example:** *I felt I understood my Creator in a new way, and his ability to work through my flaws and still make something flawless. I am much more at rest, more able to live with myself, because I realized that he is OK with me as I am, and he wants me to co-create with him.*

Step 4: The Meeting Becomes a Message

What is the Life Message this encounter built into you for others? What quality of Jesus' character do you powerfully embody because of this? What did God do in your heart that you are highly motivated to bring to others' hearts? The Message is not what you went through, or how it shaped you—it's about how Jesus met you in the valley, and the part of him that is now in you because of it.

> **Example**: *My Message: "He works through the flawed to make the flawless."*

Step 5: Confirmation

Does this theme play an important part in your life now? Does it fit the characteristics of a Life Message (see the box on page 120)?

Exercise: Life Messages in Action

Here's a second way to identify Life Messages that starts with how they work themselves out in your life today.

Step 1: Identify Indicators

Below are four key indicators of the presence of a Life Message, with reflection questions for each. Jot down your responses to the questions on a blank sheet of paper.

- **Themes**: What are your Soapbox Issues? These are the themes you come back to over and over when you are helping or serving others. What are you always talking passionately about? What do you most yearn to impart to people?

- **Impact**: Where are your places of greatest impact? What do you seem to impart to other people there? What Messages do they consistently learn or draw from you?

- **Qualification:** Are there situations you can speak into where others can't, because of what you've been through? Where have you met God in suffering in a way that opens the door to other's hearts? What is the Message you have for people in that situation?

- **Drawing:** What people are you most drawn to help? Who is drawn to you? What are they looking for, and what do you most want them to receive from you?

Step 2: Identify Potential Messages

Step back and look over what you jotted down. What themes did you write about under several of the indicators? Which ones are you most strongly attracted to? These are your Life Message candidates.

Step 3: Name the Message

Create a memorable name or short phrase for each Life Message. A single word, a pithy phrase or a fragment of scripture can be perfect—make it something that sticks with you. And record the story of how that Message developed in your life (there's an exercise on page 126)! The stories behind your Life Messages are some of your most powerful tools for impacting others—so don't let the memory fade.

11: RELEASING

Jon's calling journey has followed an interesting path, from ministry to business back to a combination of the two. He grew up in a Christian home with parents who were involved with Campus Crusade, and accepted Jesus at an early age. Lordship was something he embraced progressively. At 16, Jon "felt God was calling me to full-time ministry—it was clear as a bell." He pursued that path through college, functioning out of a surfeit of youthful idealism and experiencing great success as a leader. "Everybody would have looked at me and said, 'he's going to really be something—pastor a big church, be a traveling speaker.'"

"After I got out of school, I think God was calling me to seminary, but I decided to go to work for Campus Crusade. That was what I wanted to do. There were closed doors, but I just pushed through… I was unwilling to consider that maybe Campus Crusade was not the place I was supposed to be. I was following me, not him."

That decision led him into his Valley of Dependence. "My first year of marriage I couldn't raise support," Jon recalls. "It was horrible. Combined with the financial pressure was the fact that we couldn't even get to our assignment because we had no money. After 15 months it was clear it wasn't going to work. I went through six to nine months of depression where I was totally unmotivated. I had dreamed that dream since I was 16, and drunk the Kool-Aid of trying to change the world. It really was death of a vision for me. I felt that I had really screwed it up—like Moses, I had hit the rock and now there was no way I was ever going to go into the Promised Land."

Finally, after two years in the valley Jon "got a real job" and settled down to serve as a lay person and build a career in his Preparation Role.

Over the next 12 years, Jon worked in sales for an engineering company, climbed the corporate ladder and then helped launch several entrepreneurial ventures. His success was what led him into his Valley of Wholeness. The pressure of doing start-ups had pushed Jon into living an unbalanced life—too much stress, too much work and too much travel. Plus, his kids were reaching an age where he wanted to be home more. So at age 36, Jon had to make a major decision about the direction of his life.

"Up until then, I had thought I would keep doing start-ups, one after another," Jon admits. "But it became clear that God was saying, 'You need to move on, I have something different for you.'"

Since he felt like he had missed God's direction during his first valley, Jon was not about to get out ahead of God again in this transition. "As I was praying about doing something different, I had another key hearing-from-God point in my life. In a moment, I was very quickly able to write down the job criteria he had for me: I would work for someone I knew, that person would be a believer, I would do very little travel, and there would be no Interstate between me and work. The job market at that time was tough… but within a week I had five solid opportunities that met that set of criteria." Jon ended up taking a position as president of a large, well-known company.

While his Valley of Wholeness brought a major change in his career path, there was not a lot of angst for Jon around the decision to let go of being an entrepreneur. "It just seemed logical at the time to make a shift," he remarks. But the opportunities created by his move into the Releasing season caught him by surprise.

Jon's new job "changed things a lot, because I was working for a believer. The line between my professional life and my ministry disappeared… Before, I could do things personally, one-on-one

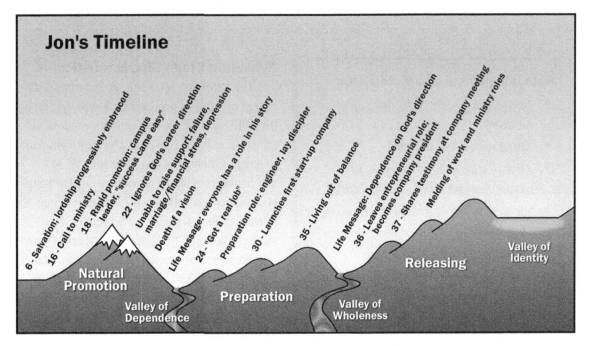

stuff, but I couldn't leverage my position to influence people [to Christ]. Now, I find myself in a place where everyone wants time with me, wants to know what I have to say and what I'm thinking because I'm the president. I said to myself, "Wow! Now I really have a platform of real influence to make a real difference in people's lives."

"It took me about a year to sort out some rules of engagement for how to share my faith. I began to do talks at sales meetings and company meetings that were like what I learned to do at Campus Crusade, where we'd give a talk about how to get better grades or have more fun with a teaser at the end for the Gospel. One early thing I did was about how your identity is tied to your effectiveness in the workplace—that to maximize your effectiveness means sorting out your identity." (Finding your role and your identity in God's big story is Jon's key Life Message.)

"Toward the end of the talk, I began to mention the need to fix your identity in something solid. I said, 'I'm not sure where that solid thing is for you, but here is where it is for me.' Then I basically shared my testimony. I said, 'That may not resonate for you, but find what does. If it does resonate'—I had brought enough copies of *The Purpose Driven Life* for everyone—'I challenged them if they wanted to go that way to read this book and come back to me and talk about it. Guys started coming at me, saying, 'You got to help me figure this out.' It's been like that ever since."

"All this stems from the influence I have as the president of the company. I know God is in this because I didn't try to make any of this happen—I just ended up here. And I have the satisfaction of just doing what I am designed to do. Trying to have an influence for the kingdom and running a successful company aren't two different things for me anymore. Being excellent at my job gives me influence that I can then leverage for the kingdom."

Now 42 years old and seven years into his Releasing stage role, Jon states, "For the first time in my life, I am not hoping to be in the ministry any more. I'm OK where I am. It sounds a little strange for a driver like me to say, but I've become almost ambivalent about it—if it happens, it happens."

Releasing Stage Characteristics

- *Begins an average of 18 years after Lordship*
- *Average length nine years*
- *Time of expansion—increase of accomplishment and responsibility*
- *Includes a Day of Release for those in Outside Preparation*
- *Big risk required to move into it*
- *Sense of apprenticeship to your calling*
- *Building General and Specific skills*
- *Temptation to coast later in stage*

Releasing Stage Characteristics

The Releasing stage is a second extended period of outward productivity where we develop the skills, experience and network we need to fulfill our calling. This stage averages eight years in length (although it can be as long as 20), and begins roughly 18 years after our Lordship commitment. For those who start the calling journey in their teens or early twenties, this stage is filled with the growing-up years of your own teenagers or moving to empty-nester status. For mothers, the parenting role often starts to decrease, leading to major changes in roles and responsibilities during or between the second and third valleys.

The general flavor of this stage is of upward movement on our calling journey. We are building both General competencies and the Specific skills needed for our calling role, and our sphere of influence increases with our growing abilities. We may be climbing up the organizational chart, heading up a larger entity or taking positions of greater responsibility. As our sphere of influence increases, our network and circle of relationships increases with it. We accomplish a lot in this stage, and are more effective than we've ever been to this point.

Jon's transition was both a release into a larger sphere of influence and an increase in his ability to actually function in his calling. The coming together of his professional role with his sense of call is a crucial transition. Jon felt called to ministry, and now ministry is part and parcel of his job. He is functioning much of the time out of his Life Message of helping others find their role in God's larger story—he just isn't doing it in a church.

Sometimes in the Preparation stage we almost feel we are under restraint, constrained to a small sphere and actively limited in what we can do. For Jon, his prior roles contained limitations on when and how he could share his faith. But in the Releasing stage those boundaries have largely been removed.

If you haven't reached the Fulfillment stage yet, it may be hard to tell the difference between Releasing and Fulfillment. Jon is certainly functioning at a high level of satisfaction and effectiveness in his current role. But the promise of the Fulfillment stage is that there is still more ahead for Jon—even more depth in his core Messages, greater freedom to function in his calling, and another quantum leap in effectiveness. His current role is only an apprenticeship for the impact he will have in Fulfillment.

The Big Risk

At the beginning of the Releasing stage, God often requires leaders (especially those in Outside Preparation) to take a big risk for the sake of their calling. Forty years after he'd run away from Pharaoh and abandoned his mission, an obscure, desert shepherd ("every shepherd is an abomination to the Egyptians") named Moses had to go back and face his giant. God called him to confront the most powerful king in that part of the world (with no money, power or army to bargain with) and demand the release of a million slaves. It's one thing to see a burning bush when you are alone in the wilderness, but

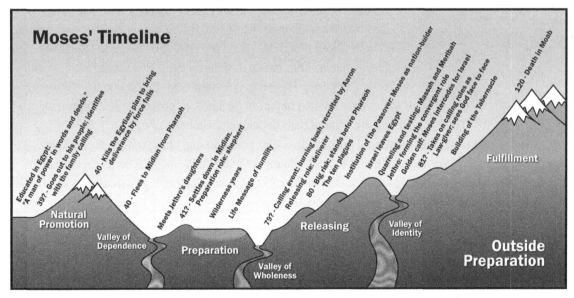

would God come through in the crucial moment, when his own life was on the line?

Keep in mind that Moses had been in this position once before. Forty years prior, he thought God would come through for him when he killed the Egyptian overseer. Clearly, he'd gotten out ahead of God and tried to make something happen in his own strength. Hopefully, this time would be different, but there was no way for Moses to be certain ahead of time that what God had promised would happen. Taking risks requires faith—and that is what God is looking for.

Dale worked for nine years in hospital administration during his Preparation stage, before leaving to follow his pastoral calling. "It was at the hospital that I learned to work with people, and especially with difficult people. That was what prepared me for pastoring, much more than seminary."

However, the actual transition turned out to involve a big risk. "That was a faith test," Dale recalls with a chuckle. "I thought we'd wait to have kids until we were out of school. I had resigned several months early to give the hospital time to find my replacement, and then three weeks later I found out Gwen was pregnant. I walked around in a daze for several weeks until it hit me one day—the God who called us to seminary knows what he is doing. So we decided to press ahead."

At the onset of the Releasing stage, God often asks us to trust him for a career change, financial provision or a geographic move. However, sometimes the challenge is internal. Tim felt he needed to end his tenure as a manager in the auto industry, but he struggled to pull the trigger. "Part of it was the money/security thing. But I was married to a surgeon, so the finances weren't a make or break issue."

He finally left that job, and six months later decided to move from doing corporate seminars on the side to a permanent position with a well-known consulting and training firm. "I felt called there, but I didn't feel equipped," he remembers. "Finally I found a senior guy I really respected, and asked him for advice. He talked to me a bit about how Jesus taught with stories and with authority, and then he said, 'It doesn't feel like you think you have the authority.'"

That conversation was a major turning point for Tim. As he grappled with God about feeling inadequate to stand up in front and show people how to run a business, he began to realize he *did* have that authority. Soon after, he took the job and eventually became one of the company's top-rated trainers.

> God does not allow us to enter our calling without risk.

An important calling principle is that *God will not allow you to enter your call without risk, with all your needs met.* Being self-sufficient completely undermines the kind of partnership God wants to create with you on your journey. He seems determined to protect you from thinking that you have enough money in the bank or professional expertise to launch out without daily dependence on him.

Over the years I've coached several businessmen who have told me, "I'm going to do this one big deal and I'll be set for life, and then I'll enter into my calling." Every one of those deals has fallen through. Walking in your calling will require you to risk, and to keep taking big risks as long as you wish to function in it. Being dependent on God is a good thing.

Apprenticeship to Your Calling

The Releasing stage is in effect an apprenticeship to your call. Some leaders function within their primary sphere of call but in a smaller role, others function in their calling role but in a smaller sphere of influence, and still others apprentice under a senior leader and learn the ropes from him or her. All three of those approaches provide room for you to grow into the fullness of your call.

King David's apprenticeship was the seven years he spent as king of Judah before he assumed control of the entire kingdom of Israel. He functioned in the same role (king), but in a smaller sphere (over one tribe instead of twelve). During those years he set up his capital at Jerusalem, learned skills needed to function in the kingly office, won the hearts of the people, organized a government, and led an army. Where untested Saul's intrusion into the priesthood led to his downfall, David's years of having to "touch not God's anointed" (even thought the man was trying to kill him) provided the character foundation that enabled him to respect the limits on his power.

Some leaders serve their apprenticeship under another leader—often the sponsor who recruited them into their Day of Release. While newly-saved Paul "kept increasing in strength and confounding the Jews who lived in Damascus by proving that this Jesus is the Christ" (Acts 9:22), his early preaching generated as much heat as light. When a plot to kill him came to light, the believers bundled him away to Jerusalem.

It was at that point that Paul's sponsor, Barnabas, came on the scene. Barnabas paved the way for Paul's acceptance among the Jerusalem Christians by introducing him to the top leadership. But when

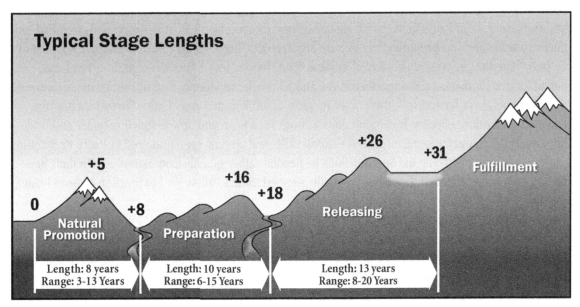

Paul's outspokenness stirred up a second plot to assassinate him, the community shipped him out of the country to Tarsus.

The next verse is one of my favorites in the New Testament: "So the church… had peace and was built up" (Acts 9:30; RSV). I love that! When Paul, who in his Natural Promotion period was "confounding the Jews" in his human abilities and stirring up trouble, finally left town, *then* the church had peace and was built up. I'm sure that was a bit of a comedown for Paul, to go from being the poster boy for conversion to being a nobody in Tarsus.

Paul served a long exile, going through his Preparation stage and presumably his Valley of

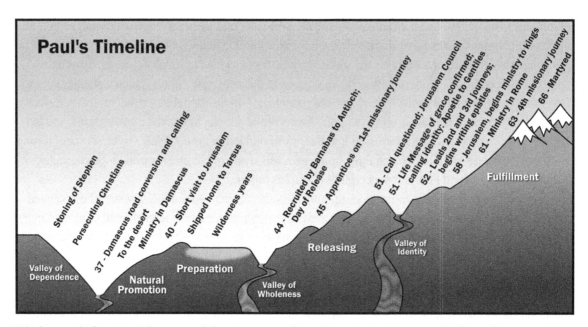

Paul's Timeline

Stoning of Stephen

Persecuting Christians

37 - Damascus road conversion and calling

To the desert

Ministry in Damascus

40 - Short visit to Jerusalem

Shipped home to Tarsus

Wilderness years

44 - Recruited by Barnabas to Antioch; Day of Release

45 - Apprentices on 1st missionary journey

51 - Call questioned: Jerusalem Council

51 - Life Message of grace confirmed; calling identity: Apostle to Gentiles

52 - Leads 2nd and 3rd journeys; begins writing epistles

58 - Jerusalem, begins ministry to kings

61 - Ministry in Rome

63 - 4th missionary journey

66 - Martyred

Fulfillment

Releasing

Valley of Identity

Valley of Dependence

Natural Promotion

Preparation

Valley of Wholeness

Wholeness, before Barnabas sensed the time was right and traveled to Tarsus to find him (Acts 11:25). Nothing is said about Paul's ministry during these Preparation years in Tarsus—apparently God had him under restraint and was preparing him outside his area of calling. But his return to Antioch, sponsored again by Barnabas, represents his Day of Release. Paul stepped into a larger role in his area of call, functioning as Barnabas's junior partner in the Antioch work. Apparently Paul was much more seasoned than years before in Jerusalem—there were no plots to kill him this time. Under Barnabas's tutelage, Paul learned healthy, effective leadership, how to work on a team and how to function under authority. Apparently the character foundations and General skills had already been mastered in Paul's Preparation stage, because he picked up the Specific Skills he needed rather quickly from Barnabas. On their first missionary journey together, Barnabas eventually stepped aside to allow Paul to function as team leader.

Leaving Your Spouse Behind

The challenge of how you relate to the calling of your spouse often comes to the surface in the Releasing stage. Married leaders travel on the calling journey with a partner, and having one partner lag behind the other on the journey can lead to significant problems. I've worked with several situations where God simply stopped the forward progress of one partner until the couple began to pay attention to the other spouse's destiny.

Two issues tend to get husbands and wives out of sync on their calling journey:

1. One of you is on the career track while the other is on the stay-at-home parent track;
2. The assumption that the wife's call is less important than or subsidiary to the husband's.

When child-rearing responsibilities begin to lessen, mothers (especially of the stay-at-home variety) tend to go through important transitions in their calling. For those who have seen themselves as primarily called to child-rearing, this is often a season of grieving and uncertainty. For those who have a strong sense of call outside the home, there is excitement about reentering the workplace combined with doubts about their abilities and questions about all the years they missed.

When a woman has been prepared outside her area of call, sponsors and supporters play an important role in her Releasing stage, helping her find a role that is commensurate with her stage on the calling journey. She has many years worth of character building and developing General skills, but may lack the credentials or confidence to find a role that will challenge her abilities. This is a key time for husbands to prioritize the needs of their spouse's calling, and become a sponsor and cheerleader for that call.

My wife is a hard-working, take-charge type whose primary call lies outside the home. She gave many years to child-rearing and home schooling to successfully win our kids' hearts, even though that wasn't always the most fulfilling thing for her. During that time her calling to helping leaders connect deeply with God was nurtured in secret, in her own devotional life (which is a little intimating when you have to live with it every day, I might add!) God did an amazing work in her during those Preparation years, using the kids, my issues and our financial situation to teach her to let go and trust God implicitly.

Because she has had so many responsibilities outside her area of call, she has some catching up to do on her journey. The place of most growth in her right now is getting in touch with her true desires. We've rearranged our business (my call) so she can work for a ministry in Alabama called Wellspring that helps leaders engage life from the heart. That has been a great opportunity. As she learns to stop assuming she should accommodate everyone else's needs and follows what God has placed in her heart, she's begun to feel a strong desire to live in a place of peace.

Our current home is definitely not that. We are country people who live in the city, at the end of a runway where roughly 1,000 fighter-jets roar over our house at a few hundred feet of altitude every day. Our business has grown to where our family room and dining room have both been converted into offices and the garage is stuffed with shelves of inventory. It wasn't the optimal situation for her call.

So when God released us to move, I basically said, "This move is about you and your call. I will move anywhere in the country you want to go. You choose what you want in a house—as long as I have an office, there is nothing else I can't live with. You can work as much for Wellspring as you feel called to, and if you want to host a retreat every month, go for it. If we need to make time for that in our lives, we'll hire bookkeepers or assistants or find a way to make it happen." So right now our house is up for sale, and we are planning to move 3000 miles across the country for the sake of her call.

My determination to promote her is rooted biblically in one thing: I don't want to get to heaven and find that I have failed at my primary task as a husband: "Husbands love your wives, as Christ loved the church and gave himself up for her." That's what being a husband is all about: laying down your needs and desires for the sake of the woman you are one flesh with. If I aggressively pursue my call and allow hers to languish, I've missed that mark. If I empower hundreds of others but fail to do so with Kathy, that's a pretty spectacular failure.

At a more personal level, I married her because she was a fitting partner for me: a peer. If we get separated on the road and one of us gets far ahead of the other, we cease to be peers and partners anymore. I want my wife to be a partner who can walk beside me on the journey, not one who is lost in the mist several stages back.

Unfortunately, many Christian men do not relate to their spouses as people whom Jesus has called and given their own special destiny. Instead, the wife is treated as an appendage to the husband's call, a personal assistant God has given the man to hold home, finances and family together behind the scenes while he pursues his personal calling. Instead of laying down our lives so our wives can fully obey Christ's call, we expect them to lay down their lives for *our* life mission. That attitude is a complete perversion of how Paul depicts a biblical husband's role.

Some spouses have a shared call that they must find and follow together. Others have more individual calls, both of which must be honored and supported within the marriage relationship. No matter which pattern fits your marriage, part of your marriage assignment is to help steward your spouse's calling so that both of you become who God created you to be.

The Temptation to Coast

Each stage has its own peculiar tests and temptations. When asked what the temptation was that might lead her off track in this stage, Jeannette quickly replied, "If there was one thing, it would be the temptation to coast. To not try to do any self-improvement career-wise, to stop learning and growing personally. My battle cry has been a line from the Terminator Salvation movie: "If we stay the course, we're all dead!"

David, a leader nearing the end of this stage, agreed. "That's definitely the temptation. The last year has been a coasting year for me. I was getting comfortable. I could have bought a house and settled down and done this for years. It wouldn't be evil, but it isn't necessarily God's best for me. He has been like a mother eagle, making the nest uncomfortable." Since I interviewed him, David has moved across the country and taken an interim pastorate in an ethnic church whose primary language he doesn't even speak. That's getting out of the nest!

The Releasing stage is a good place to be. You are doing satisfying work that often lets you operate out of your best strengths. You are more effective than you've ever been. You are seeing the rewards of all you've invested so far in your career and your personal growth, and it is good. The dream is still out there, but the years are rolling on, you have responsibilities and retirement to think of, and you could have a pretty nice life if you'd just stay put for another ten or 15 years.

Western culture has some peculiarities that feed into this temptation to "grow weary in well-doing" and stop short of Fulfillment. On one hand, as leaders move into their forties and fifties (often the time period when the Releasing stage is drawing to a close), they begin to feel a new urgency about their call. Time is running out. "I've only got so many years left, and I want to make the most of them," is a sentiment I often hear from leaders at this point in life. This urgency pushes us to make the leap into the Fulfillment stage and maximize our legacy.

But at the same time, the responsibilities of living in this world never cling to us so closely. Children are entering into college, and need money in bales. Our own parents are well on in years and may have serious health issues that demand our care. We start paying more attention to retirement, and realize that what we socked away isn't going to be nearly enough to maintain our lifestyle unless we are very aggressive about saving. But will following our call provide for those needs? Or will age discrimination make us unemployable if we leave the job we have now? And to top it off, we become grandparents, and experience a whole new tug to stay rooted close by our kids to spend time with the grandbabies.

The problem is compounded by the western concept of retirement. The American dream includes the idea that we will work hard and save all of our lives, and at 65 we will retire to a responsibility-free, financially-secure playtime that allows us to do whatever our hearts desire. We'll take the European vacation we always wanted, become snowbirds and winter in Florida, play golf every day and go see the grandkids in our RV whenever the whim strikes. If that's our image of the future, our financial lives will be encumbered from the day we enter the workforce by the assumption that we must save a nest egg of one or two million dollars to support it.

The Bible was written in a different age and in a different culture. However, it is still important to ask whether your concept of retirement is biblical, or if this is the financial course God is calling you to pursue. Moses led a productive life until the day he died, as did Peter, Paul, Samuel, Hezekiah, David, Eli, Elijah, etc. None of these leaders folded their tent and put their lives on the shelf just because they got older. In biblical times, seniors were treasured for their wisdom and became community leaders, advisors and consultants—that's where we get the office of "elder." Sometimes I wonder if the American vision of retirement is simply a stratagem of the enemy to take many of the years when we should be having the greatest impact and have us waste them in idle pursuits.

The closest Jesus seems to come to addressing this mindset is in Luke 12:

> *"And He told them a parable, saying, "The land of a rich man was very productive. And he began reasoning to himself, saying, 'What shall I do, since I have no place to store my crops?' Then he said, 'This is what I will do: I will tear down my barns and build larger ones, and there I will store all my grain and my goods. And I will say to my soul, "Soul, you have many goods laid up for many years to come; take your ease, eat, drink and be merry." But God said to him, 'You fool! This very night your soul is required of you; and now who will own what you have prepared?' So is the man who stores up treasure for himself, and is not rich toward God."*

I don't believe Jesus is saying no one should ever retire or save up for retirement. The parable is about attaining financial abundance, assuming it is yours to do with as you wish, and then keeping it all for yourself. The question is whether we have secured God's direction for what we intend to do.

Our culture says the wise, responsible thing is to store up goods for many years, and then retire to eat, drink and be merry. The problem comes when you assume that an American-style retirement is the goal, and arrange your finances around it without even asking if that is what God has for you. Have you asked, "Lord, what are you calling me to in my golden years? How do you want me to prepare for retirement?"

God has a unique plan for your life that fits your calling. If he is saying to prepare the finances to retire at 70, or 65, or even 62, then you have your marching orders. It may be that freedom from the need to work is exactly what's required to maximize your impact during those years. Or if God clearly says, "Don't worry about your retirement, I've got it well in hand," then arrange your life and your finances accordingly.

Which brings us to the point: what kind of lifestyle will allow you to be most faithful to your calling? Money and things can be an asset or a distraction, depending on what you are called to do. While you will certainly be declining physically in your latter years, spiritually you will be more imposing than ever. God has more for you as a senior than to just fade away.

Making the Most of the Releasing Stage

There are several keys to maximizing the Releasing stage. To enter it well, you will probably be required to take a big risk—to move, change careers, or step out financially in obedience to God. The start of this stage is a great time to step out in faith for your call.

False opportunities are especially likely for those who are in Outside Preparation. Just because an opportunity finally comes, that doesn't mean you are supposed to take it. The thing God has for you will not force you to ignore red flags or compromise your principles.

You will also need to be more focused about the roles you take on. You have enough life experience now to really understand your strengths and weaknesses, and therefore your roles need to be a much better fit for who you are. The funnel (see page 87) is much narrower than it was in your twenties, when you could do just about anything and still be growing.

This season is a time to make hay while the sun shines. Work hard, and enjoy your accomplishments. At the same time, maintaining a balanced life will save you a lot of pain in a few years. The upcoming Valley of Identity is a time where God helps you separate your identity from your work. If you allow work to consume your life, your Valley of Identity will probably involve God ripping you out of your career and sitting you down for an extended period to help you refocus. The more your work defines you, the harder that will be.

> ### Summary of Key Learnings
> - *God will not allow you to enter into your call without risk.*
> - *Leaving your spouse behind is a major pitfall in the Releasing stage.*
> - *Failing to examine cultural views of retirement can cause us to coast.*

There is a ready antidote, though. Sabbath-keeping is the discipline God created to protect us from getting our identity too tangled up in what we do. By taking a one-day fast from work (and thinking about work!) each week, we remove our hearts from the workplace and give them a reset. And, since we aren't working, we spend time with friends, play games, pursue hobbies and cultivate a life outside of the office. It sounds a little hokey, but taking a Sabbath every week really does help keep your identity fixed in Christ.

If you are married, this is a crucial time to sit down and take stock of each of your callings. To steward those assignments well, you'll need to know clearly what they are and that your future plans support both your callings. Without intentional planning, this is a point in life where spouses can easily grow apart on their calling journeys. If your wife is coming to the end of the child-rearing years, the two of you face an important transition in your marriage and your calling life.

Finally, take some time to get clear on what your Life Messages are (see the exercise on pg. 126).

After going through two valley seasons, you have enough life experience to identify them clearly. Without a concrete sense of the Message on your heart, you'll tend to get overly focused on your calling task and miss the deposit into others' hearts that task is meant to convey. *A Leader's Life Purpose Workbook* has a set of exercises for identifying Life Messages and then using them to create a calling statement.

Releasing Stage Reflection Questions

1. When was the event that kicked off this stage for you (usually the end of the Valley of Wholeness or the Day of Release)?

2. Was there a big risk that you took that moved you to a new level at this point?

3. What season of your life best fits the stage characteristics listed on page 140?

4. When did you begin to feel that the Releasing stage was coming to a close, the cloud was moving or that a new season was just ahead?

Bible Study Guide: The Releasing Stage

Look for characteristics of the Releasing stage in these two individuals' lives.

1. **Jesus.** His Releasing stage is represented by the days of his earthly ministry. Which of the stage characteristics in the box at right apply to Jesus' life? What big risk did he take right at the beginning of his ministry? Where was Jesus tempted to coast, and not enter into the fullness of his calling?

> **Releasing Stage Characteristics**
>
> - *Begins an average of 18 years after Lordship*
> - *Average length nine years*
> - *Time of expansion—increase of accomplishment and responsibility*
> - *Includes a Day of Release for those in Outside Preparation*
> - *Big risk required to move into it*
> - *Sense of apprenticeship to your calling*
> - *Building General and Specific skills*
> - *Temptation to coast later in stage*

3. **Paul**. His Releasing stage is from his recruitment by Barnabas to the Jerusalem council (Acts 13-14). Which of the stage characteristics do you see in Paul's life? How did Paul's apprenticeship to Barnabas flower over the years? What did Paul learn through it? Why did Barnabas allow Paul to lead later in the journey?

12: THE VALLEY OF IDENTITY

Jeff was a high-energy leader whose influence and ability had been steadily increasing. He had spent a decade in his Preparation stage as a counselor working with delinquent, suicidal adolescents from dysfunctional homes. "I hated it so many times," Jeff remembers. "It was tough work and my boss was very demanding. Due to insurance requirements, I often felt like more of a paperwork jockey than a therapist."

"Maintaining hope and compassion and creativity through it was a huge challenge. I learned to love past a lot of barriers—seeing people as people—and I got off the pedestal of professional clinical arrogance … I sought meaning in the suffering, and my advocacy for people was birthed out of that suffering."

During his Valley of Wholeness Jeff did a stint as clinical director for a therapeutic foster care agency under an insightful Christian boss. "God sent him into my life to learn grace," Jeff emphasizes. "I was self-righteous, judgmental and tough on people. I had grown up in a legalistic religious environment, and had become a Pharisee."

His new boss told him, "You are neurotic and you are sick; and God has ordained this season for you to relax and get well." So Jeff began supervising and training others instead of doing hands-on therapy. "I learned there to relax; that it didn't depend on my own efforts. I never worked less and saw more results. But God was saying, "Rest up, restore, it is not always going to be this way."

Jeff's mother happened to work at the same organization, and in a very unusual move, his boss assigned her as his secretary. "My parents had divorced when I was 14 after multiple separations," Jeff recounted. "[That time at work] was a gift to both of us. It was redeeming to work together as a team to help others… Family was her life, and the divorce had destroyed it."

After leaving the agency, Jeff moved into his Releasing stage. He spent three years building a ground-breaking lay counseling initiative involving 12 different ministries and several churches at one point. Three years later he and his wife were chosen by two community leaders to build a community covenant to better prepare, strengthen and restore marriages. His success in that endeavor snared him a job in the nation's capital, working to help other leaders create similar community partnerships. His career was in the midst of a meteoric rise.

At first, Jeff's natural drive and the intoxication of big opportunities and big successes overshadowed the signs that all was not well in his new job. As things continued to go downhill, "I finally began to see clearly that I wouldn't survive psychologically and emotionally in that position … I knew that I had to get out to save myself."

"I resigned that fall and went to work two weeks later for [a similar organization]. That lasted for eight months until I was fired. I wasn't getting the job done in terms of numbers that needed to be generated for a fledgling organization. So in one year I resigned one position because I couldn't hack the environment and expectations, and the next year was fired because I wasn't getting the job done. A few months later another organization picked me up for six months, then I was demoted and failed again. All my life I'd succeeded at everything I tried, then all of a sudden I couldn't succeed at anything."

Jeff's Valley of Identity was a difficult and confusing time where every door seemed to be closed.

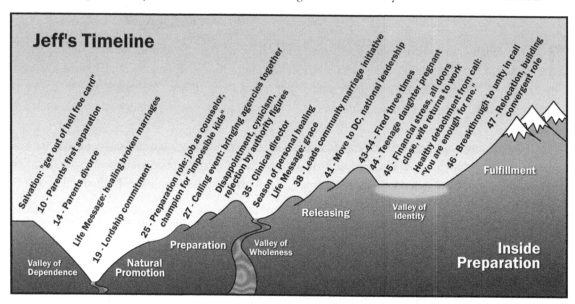

Finances became extremely tight. He and his wife were unable to sell their house to reduce expenses because the bottom had dropped out of the real estate market.

Then their teenage daughter became pregnant. That was a heavy blow to Jeff's identity and ego as a marriage and family counselor. Working through the situation with himself and God, then with his wife, daughter, her boyfriend and her boyfriend's family consumed his emotional reserves. Having a new baby at home forced yet another rearrangement of Jeff's life.

Through the pressure of events, deep changes began to take place in Jeff's inner being. "During that time, I learned how mega-maniacal I could be," Jeff emphasizes, "and that God will allow whatever it takes for you to depend wholly on him. I couldn't do anything. That was a whole-hearted departure from the past, when I brought things about by my charisma, gifts and manipulation. I saw how much I'd been operating on adrenaline intoxication and holding on to the reins."

"God would... take us to the pinnacle of hope one day and the depths of despair the next. One day we're in the Capitol building praying with the Senate chaplain, and the next day we'd have to cancel a class we were offering because no one signed up, even after being promoted heavily by [two leading training organizations]. If I didn't know better I'd think that someone was... watching all our prospective opportunities and coming along behind us to undo them."

"But our real conclusion is that he's not going to let anything work except exactly what He has planned. He is good and we are growing significantly through it all. He is enough when you are disappointed, disillusioned, discouraged and want to quit so badly that you can taste it; and he wants us so dead to the titillation of accomplishment that we can walk into any scenario and keep our equilibrium."

"If it isn't there, maybe it's time to sit for a while. I need to be able to take it or leave it [my calling]. Doing and accomplishing intoxicates me—or it has the potential to. But [I've come to the place where] he is enough for me even if this calling thing never works out. I don't want to lose this hanging out with God that I've found."

As suddenly as it began, after five years Jeff's Valley of Identity came to an end. The key event was his wife's decision to "go all in" with him in their call. Once the work of the heart was in place, everything broke loose all at once. They decided to make a move, and were offered free housing and office space. Donors came out of the woodwork to meet their financial needs. New opportunities didn't just pop up, but began to actually come through. They were able to rent out their house in a very poor market.

Jeff has been in my personal accountability group through much of this transition, and I've seen the suffering and redemption up-close-and-personal as we walked together through these struggles. Jeff is a much greater man for what he went through, and I look forward to seeing the fruit of what was birthed in this valley during his Fulfillment years.

Entering the Rest

While Jeff's story is more dramatic than most, it is a good illustration of many of the key characteristics of the third valley. While the first valley is about Dependence, and the second usually focuses on Wholeness, the third homes in on our Identity. In this valley, our being call is fully formed: we become the person we were born to be. Jeff states his being call as "to incarnate compassion and hope to broken relationships and broken dreams." The connection between this statement and his valley experience is obvious. God redeemed brokenness in both a key relationship with his daughter and with his most important dreams to put the finishing touches on Jeff's Life Message. Having become the man he was born to be, Jeff can now do the task he was born to do.

A second gift Jeff discovered in the Valley of Identity was freedom from being driven to accomplish and succeed. Notice how God accomplished that. Jeff had to leave a dream job to protect his sanity, then was fired from another great opportunity. Those circumstances helped sever the unhealthy connection between his identity and his work. In the process, Jeff found he could experience fullness without his work, and without even his calling. Being with Jesus alone became enough.

In the place of being a person who was driven to make it happen, Jeff became someone who could wait for God to make things happen. Instead of his confidence as a counselor being rooted in his own success as a father, he was maneuvered into a corner that forced him to put his confidence in God as a Father. No longer driven by the intoxication of doing, Jeff became a man who could be still and be at peace.

That freedom allows us to do the work of our call as a gift and an act of love to our creator, uncontaminated with striving to please him or to convince ourselves that our life is worthwhile. When the being work in our hearts is complete, we come to the place of rest. That identity shift is the central work of the Valley of Identity.

What an inexpressible gift God gives us, to patiently work with us over decades so we can truly give, freely love, fully trust. God doesn't do all this because he is pining away for us, needing to be loved. He has not set up the whole universe to get his own needs met. He has none. He does this because when we learn to love him truly, then we can share a real, mutual relationship. God does not need our love; he teaches us to love so that we can enter into love together with him.

> ## Valley of Identity Characteristics
> - *15-30 years into your Calling Journey*
> - *Averages four years long*
> - *Often triggered by ejection from long-time role, loss of influence and favor, or financial reverses*
> - *Stripping of identity in work, accomplishment or how others perceive us*
> - *Healthy detachment from call: you can live without it because Jesus alone is enough for you*
> - *Completion of being call/Life Message formation*
> - *A longer and more intense season for those in Inside Preparation; sometimes includes a wilderness time or dark night of the soul*
> - *Focus moves from doing to being*
> - *Finding success in the success of others instead of your own accomplishments*
> - *Taking on the mantle of your calling identity*
> - *Learning to present yourself as who you are*
> - *Standing alone in the decision to be who you are*

Valley of Identity Characteristics

This late-life transition was the most surprising discovery of my research into calling stages. It commonly begins 15 to 30 years into the calling journey, and lasts an average of four years. Leaders in their late forties to sixties seem to consistently go through an extended transitional period of major career change, wilderness processing, internal shifts in identity, and the need to once more take major risks for the sake of their calling.

As with Jeff, the Valley of Identity is frequently triggered by ejection from a long-time role that fits you well. Leaving your sphere of influence after the fruitful years of the Releasing stage is usually experienced as a great loss, particularly of identity. Jim, a senior pastor, recalls, "My whole career from 1972 on had been helping [the denomination] become what my local church was. This church was most like what I had wanted the church to be. So when it didn't work out and I left, it was like, 'This is what I have been working for all these years, and I can't do it.'"

"I reeeeally was demoralized—not suicidal or anything, but I was close to just leaving the pastorate altogether. I felt like a total failure—like I had really failed God. It certainly washed out of me some of my own human vision. It has thrown me back on the Lord. I was serving my vision instead of serving the Lord—they were so close together that it was hard to distinguish."

At that point I mentioned to Jim that one function of the Valley of Identity is God saving us from making our calling the object of our primary affection—a mistress that steals our first love from God.

"Well," Jim laughed, "When the mistress is gone, it gets pretty hard. That affair felt awfully good."

Loss of Favor and Financial Reverses

The onset of the Valley of Identity is often accompanied by a loss of favor and influence as well as financial reverses. In the middle of those painful times, the Great Redeemer does some of his best work.

Steve grew up with the wound of a father who never expressed love or approval to him. To fill the hole, Steve tried to earn the love he yearned for, measuring his success with metrics like the size of his business, souls won for Christ in missions and the length of his sailboat. Beginning with his Valley of Dependence, finding the true source of approval became a focus of God's dealings in his life and eventually a Life Message.

Upon entering his Releasing stage at 43, Steve added a home building company to his development business. It was another way to leverage his entrepreneurial gifts to advance the Kingdom. After a decade of explosive growth and expansion, that business went bankrupt in a financial downturn, and Steve entered into his Valley of Identity.

Steve's personal testimony seemed to evaporate along with the company he'd founded on biblical principles. He had to let go of the dozens of employees he'd been reaching out to, and was sued over a dozen times for millions of dollars. His sphere of influence shrank. In the middle of losing the financial security he had accumulated in 18 years of business, his home burned down, and he lost most of his personal belongings as well.

"I started the home building company as a marketplace ministry. It grew very quickly, but a couple of systemic mistakes I made blew it up," Steve admits. Meeting God in the midst of the difficult time that followed was crucial to refining his Life Message of finding God's approval and launching him into Fulfillment. What he learned in that season is constantly put to use today as he coaches other business leaders as an executive chair for Christian CEO's.

"I am helping others discover the difference between where God is calling them and where their personal pain is leading them," Steve explains. "Like me, they are driven to pursue success because of their wounds. Many of their business decisions flow out of that pain … I was trying to earn my father's approval by being successful as a businessman, and I was trying to earn my heavenly Father's approval by dedicating my business to him. I made lots of money and gave a lot to God to make it look good. Neither worked until I surrendered the "I." The bottom line on this was exchanging the currency of my approval from dollars to the success of others. I finally internalized the idea that when they succeed, I am a success."

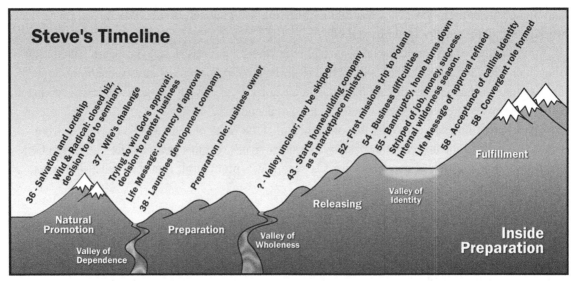

"It was a three to four year journey to accept who I am and quit fighting it. You lose your business, your house burns down, you lose everything financially—and then you realize that is just the externals. Now you still have the pride issues, the lust issues … you have the surrendering of all that to work through, too. That's humbling. Then I go to Poland to serve Central European business leaders and I discover that the Poles see me in a much different light than I ever saw myself. I am so loved in so many little ways. I'm still catching up to what God's best version of me really looks like."

God redeemed Steve's great loss of finances, possessions and favor, giving in its place the one thing in life Steve most wanted: to know his Father's approval instead of having to earn it. And in the process, he inherited a treasure that changes the lives of those around him, too. When God redeems something, we find we wouldn't trade the experience of loss and redemption for anything.

Stripped to the Essentials

Cynthia is currently in the midst of her Valley of Identity, and her experience of loss, isolation and movement from doing to being is similar. She and her husband had enjoyed deep relationships and success in ministry. However, it all came to an abrupt halt when political instability forced her family to leave the country they called home and move to a nearby nation. Brad and Cynthia were certain that the same type of ministry opportunities awaited them there. But soon those dreams died as well. As Cynthia faced one confusing and painful situation after another, she began to think that God must have a purpose in all of this adversity and lost opportunity.

"When we had to leave our country and all of our friends and co-workers there, it was devastating. We lost all our friends and relationships, our home and leadership status. During a training event we were participating in, I began to feel that God was calling me to lay down some of my remaining leadership roles to give more time to my family. It was confirmed by another leader who felt God prompting him to say, 'You have been a spiritual mother in Asia for many years, but God is calling you back to focus on your own flock for a season—on your own family.' I knew this was right, but it felt like another huge loss looming before me. God was speaking to me once again about finding my identity in

Him, not in what I did. I knew I had to give up these roles and positions I had worked very hard for. I wondered, would I ever be in that type of leadership again?"

"I'm still working through what that was all about... I know I had become addicted to ministry highs. The relationships in ministry were taking the place of my relationship with God. But now, all of that was being stripped away. God set us up to be alone—just us and him. At first, I was frustrated and angry. But slowly I realized that God had his agenda in it all. I had to go to another level of finding my significance in God—not success in ministry—and stop running after man's approval."

Cynthia's experience also highlights the Life Message formation that continues in the Valley of Identity. After walking through several major seasons of dealing with God in this area, finding her identity

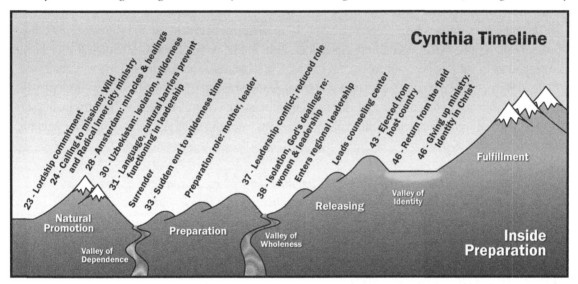

in Christ has become a Life Message and a focus of ministry for her. "It is still hard this time, but I am so much more peaceful and at rest in that. I'm OK not doing a million things right now."

As with Cynthia, the Valley of Identity tends to be longer and more intense for those in Inside Preparation. Where those in Outside Preparation wandered in the wilderness earlier in life (in Preparation), those in Inside Preparation are more likely to experience a wilderness season here in the Valley of Identity. That wilderness may include isolation, a decrease of favor and influence (often through unjust treatment by others), unclear direction for life, financial duress and nagging questions about the future.

Since by now we've been through several major transitions, we are more equipped to handle the questions and the uncertainty than in the first valley. But at the same time, the questions are more urgent. When I was single at 24, I struggled with being $500 in the hole. At 44, I found myself struggling with having a family and needing $50,000 to launch a business to provide for them. Later in life the stakes get quite a bit higher!

Healthy Detachment

Not everyone's Valley of Identity is as outwardly dramatic as Jeff or Cynthia's. Dale's was triggered by reading *Religion in America* by George Gallup Jr. Two decades later, he can still recite the key points from the book. "Barna's five characteristics of the American church were that it was religious, that there was a gap between belief and ethics, a lack of scriptural knowledge, that it was not making a real difference in society, and that it was superficial. I thought, 'My goodness, that's true!' I thought I would solve the problem in my own church. The next crisis was realizing that the paradigm of church I had been working from for 22 years could never solve this problem."

As Dale grappled with what church should be about, he began to think about what a disciple of Christ ought to look like. And that brought him to a third painful realization: "In 22 years of ministry at the same church I had never really made disciples." Dale's search took him on a sabbatical, led him to take the big risk of resigning his pastorate and eventually launched him into a trans-local church oversight role in his Fulfillment stage.

Through this stripping, God is creating a healthy detachment between you and your work or call. The goal is to get you to the place where you still desire it but know you are OK without it. If your identity is wrapped up in your call or your work, it is hard to live without it. And if you can't live without it, you will do anything to keep it. That's where a lot of tragic leadership failures come from—your identity is so bound to your role, you connive and cheat and manipulate and betray to keep it. By introducing some distance between your identity and your calling, God saves you from the tragedy of selling your soul for your role. Or as Jesus put it,

> *"If anyone wishes to come after me, he must deny himself, and take up his cross and follow me. For whoever wishes to save his life will lose it; but whoever loses his life for my sake will find it. For what will it profit a man if he gains the whole world and forfeits his soul?"* (Mt. 16:24-26)

Coming Out from Under the Tree

Sometimes, the painful moment God uses to launch us into Fulfillment is a conflict with or separation from the leader who we apprenticed under in the Releasing stage. For instance, as Paul was moving into Fulfillment he had a major conflict with his sponsor, Barnabas, over their leadership values. Paul was all about the mission. He didn't want to take someone along who had deserted them before. For Barnabas, raising up leaders like Mark *was* the mission, and believing in people who didn't deserve it (like Paul!) was his reason for living. Their disagreement became so heated that they parted ways. Paul may never have seen Barnabas again, although later in life he spoke very highly of him and even began working with Mark, the man the disagreement was all about (II Tim. 4:11).

In the book of Daniel, king Nebuchadnezzar is described as a tree "whose foliage was beautiful and its fruit abundant, and in which was food for all, under which the beasts of the field dwelt and in whose branches the birds of the sky lodged" (Dan. 4:12). That's a good picture of a healthy leader in Fulfillment. Other leaders grow up in the shade and sponsorship of a senior leader who finds success in the success of others. Leaders who are called to mid-level positions can find a lifetime role under that tree. Those called to top management or to lead a vision of their own must move out from under it to enter Fulfillment.

In a healthy situation, the senior leader makes room for these leaders and accepts them as peers as they move into Fulfillment. Sometimes, they even take over the sponsor's role, and he/she decreases so the new leader can increase. However, issues on both sides of the relationship can turn things sour. Since these younger leaders' destiny is always somewhat different than the senior leader's, coming into their own often means challenging the status quo—or directly challenging that leader.

For instance, the entrepreneur who founded Justin's organization was still going strong entering his eighties. While Bill had surrendered the CEO role, he remained on the board, and the top leaders in this team-based organization still deferred to him on the important questions. Not grasping what was going on, Bill continued to exert influence in a way that squelched innovative new products and systems, undermined his successor and kept the next generation from moving the organization forward. Several top VPs had already left, and others, seeing their decisions countermanded, were realizing their days were numbered. Hemorrhaging talent, the organization started to become less effective, and frustration within top- and mid-level management mounted.

After decades in the organization, Justin felt a great debt to the founder. Bill had been a sponsor, a role model and a strong supporter in difficult times. As Justin contemplated trying to get his mentor's attention on the issue, he was torn. *Will Bill hear my concerns and let go gracefully, or will challenging him destroy a life-long relationship? Is it even right to question his involvement in a company he started, that will be his legacy? And who am I to think I have a better idea of what to do?*

To enter his Fulfillment stage as a senior leader, at some point Justin must either face into the challenge of addressing his organization's issues or leave it. If he stays without dealing with what he sees, he is not being true to his calling as a leader, and has accepted a passive role as an underling. And for Bill, a failure to allow other leaders on his team to function as true peers and challenge him on that basis will lead to a great diminishing of his legacy.

Finding Success in the Success of Others

Another prominent theme in the Valley of Identity is moving from a focus on your own accomplishments to finding success in the success of others. Edward had taken over his family business in his early twenties, when it was in danger of going under, and built it into a successful trading firm with 50 employees. At the same time, he was growing spiritually, serving in his church, starting a family and giving generously. Life was good.

His Valley of Identity was triggered by a cancer diagnosis. He had beaten the odds and gone into remission once earlier in life, but now the beast was back. After an operation to remove a brain tumor, the doctors told him that he probably had about three years to live.

"My identity got completely stripped. I'm a good giver but not a good receiver, and I had come to see myself as a provider for others. This reversed my role... [I realized] my identity had gone bad. It was in what I was doing for other people in the guise of doing it for the Lord—it wasn't 100% in Christ like it should have been."

"I'm on disability, so I can't go in to work. But the company has actually done better this year than the year before. It is sweet to see God provide, but for the male ego in me, that is hard!"

"I had a problem: I did not delegate well at all. I had my hands in everything. I cheated the people who worked for me—I didn't have enough confidence in them so I didn't delegate enough, to the point where I inhibited their development in their abilities. When I got ill and they really stepped up, I really got upset because I felt like I had cheated them because of my own insecurities. We are so full of ourselves in life. You need events like this to pull yourself back and learn to not take yourself so seriously."

The Valley of Identity has pushed Edward to move from focusing on what he can achieve personally with his business to what his people can achieve.

Taking on the Mantle of Your Call

God is not stripping you of false identities for nothing. Removing misplaced identity makes room for you to take on the identity he has created you for: the mantle of your call. Wearing your calling identity means accepting that you *have now become* the person you were created to be. You are no longer being prepared; you are no longer looking forward to what you can become. You *are now* the person you need to be to do what you were born to do, and it is time to step into that role and fulfill your mission.

It would seem that after waiting twenty or thirty years for this moment that we would eagerly jump right in. But that underestimates the impact of this moment on our psyche.

For me, it came after a painful season where I had left an organization that I had helped found. Two thirds of my income went away, I effectively lost access to my life's work as a writer, and my favor and opportunities were significantly decreased. On the other hand, I felt like God had given me a plan to use my writing, speaking and internet skills to build a resource center for coaches.

The question was, how was I going to fund it? After years of working for low wages in ministry positions, my reserves were next to nothing. I had used up the computer equipment I had accumulated in a previous business venture—it was beyond obsolescence and needed to be replaced. I could count on some income from my existing endeavors, but I had a family and two kids to support, and since we were home schooling my wife couldn't work.

I set a deadline to create a business plan. That deadline came and went—as did my second deadline and my third—while I agonized over whether to borrow money, get investors, or set up a non-profit. Each of them had advantages and disadvantages. But choosing a business structure was just a smokescreen—an excuse to keep from having to pull the trigger.

A friend I'd met in one of my coach training programs traveled the country speaking to businesspeople on planning and prioritizing. He happened to be in town, so I buttonholed him and posed my dilemma, hoping I might get some advice. His answer: "Tony, I think you know in your heart what you are supposed to do." I wanted him to give me an answer, but he would only do what I'd taught him to do: coach me!

I left that meeting feeling a little frustrated, but also strangely buoyed by the idea that maybe God would give me a clear answer. At the stoplight in front of Wal-Mart on the way home, I heard something pretty definite from God: "Tony, if you don't believe in yourself enough to invest in yourself, you'll never do what you are capable of doing."

Immediately, I knew that borrowing my start-up capital was the answer. The other two options were just ways to spread out the risk by involving others. I only considered them because I was afraid I might not have what it would take to succeed. To go the partnership or non-profit route would be to shrink

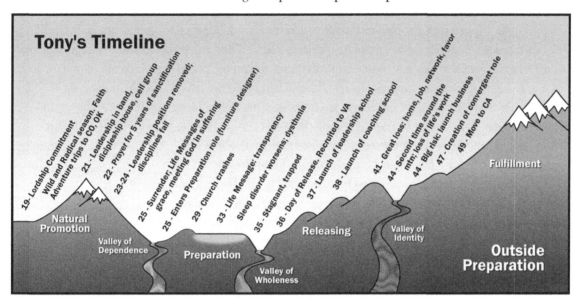

back out of fear, deny that I was who God said I was, and settle for safety instead of obedience.

That day I put on the full mantle of my call for the first time. I don't like debt, but taking out that loan was one of the best calling decisions I've ever made. The biggest financial wager I'd ever made was a bet on my own calling, and pulling it off gave me a confidence, a freedom in the assurance of God's provision and an authority in my calling that I couldn't have gotten any other way.

For Jane, an important part of taking on the mantle of her call was beginning to tell her life story. "[Up until then] I had thought that the definition of 'missionary to the corporate world' was to be a boss. I had finally been promoted to my highest level, but at the same time I was told that I had to stop talking about Jesus. 'Congratulations on your promotion, cut out the Jesus talk'—that was about all [my new boss] said to me in a five minute conversation. I remember floating across the campus celebrating on the way back to my building—the head guy of all programming knows that I talk about Jesus! Then I got to my office, and realized that, 'Oh crap, my career is over.'"

"Not long after that I shared what happened with a Christian friend at work. I wasn't going to stop talking about Jesus, so this friend said, 'Why don't you go into coaching?' I realized I could let go of the doing part—that I didn't have to be a boss to fulfill my call to be a missionary. I had attached the doing image to the call itself, and I had to let go of the container I put the call into."

"Up until then I had never really shared my story in public. This was the point when I first started sharing publicly that I was a missionary to the corporate world. Now I tell it every chance I get." For Jane, taking that step was a big part of taking on the mantle of her calling identity.

Standing Alone

The challenge of putting on that mantle is two-fold. First, it often comes at a low point in your life. You are in a difficult and unexpected Valley of Identity. Maybe you've been removed from your role, or suffered a big setback, and are wondering if the best times of life are already past. At that moment, when there seems to be no external evidence to support the idea that you have an even greater future ahead, God says, "Step up! You are the person I made you to be; now do what I have called you to do!"

Our circumstances put the weight of the decision squarely and solely on our own shoulders. In fact, many leaders report that they had to make this decision against the prevailing winds of opinion, or in a place of isolation. Only you can wear this mantle, and you alone will have to decide to put it on.

Consider Jesus. He began to come into the fullness of his calling identity as Savior of the world around the time of the Mount of Transfiguration. In Luke chapter nine, he talks to the disciples for the first time about the cross, converses with Moses and Elijah about his "departure," and sets his face to go for the final time to Jerusalem.

His second-in-command confronted him and tried to talk him out of it. His band of brothers couldn't even stay awake as he wrestled with God in Gethsemane about that decision. Then they ran out on him at the moment of truth. The mercy of God in letting us stand alone with him at this important moment is that the eventual doing of our call will require us to know that we know that we are called and that he is with us, without the benefit of any external evidence or confirmation. Jesus had to hang on the cross alone, with no support. The only way to reach the level of conviction he needed to stick it out was to decide alone that this was God's way.

> *The challenge of putting on the mantle of your calling identity often comes at a low point in life.*

The second reason it's so difficult to put on the mantle of our calling identity is the import of that choice. Up to this point, we are getting ready for our call. If we fail, it's all part of the learning process. If the thing we build blows up, we can always start again. But now that we're doing the thing we've prepared all our lives to do, there are no more false starts or second chances to fall back on. If we fail, we've failed at our life mission. It's one thing to step out in the Preparation or Releasing stage; quite another to take the big step of faith that leads into Fulfillment.

The Work is Done

Taking on the mantle of our calling identity completes our being call. We have become who we were created to be. The inward labor of accepting this new identity is made tangible in the Fulfillment stage. The hard work of being formation is largely done, and the actual doing of our call is simply working out the details of that inward reality.

That's a bit of a foreign concept, so let's look again at Jesus to explain. The work of accepting the mantle of his calling identity was completed at Gethsemane. Jesus' big risk—the one his calling identity demanded—was going to the cross. When Jesus wore that mantle and took the risk to die for us, the work of redemption was completed within his heart. Although the Gospel had yet to be preached throughout the physical world, in the spiritual realm the work was done.

That's what Jesus meant when he said, "It is finished." He didn't say, "I am finished," as if he was referring to his own mortal life. He couldn't be saying that the outward work of redemption and building his church was finished: he wasn't even resurrected yet! What *was* finished was his being call. In being obedient unto death, Jesus had fully become the man he was born to be. He had taken on the fullness of his calling identity. In his Fulfillment stage he simply sits at the right-hand of the Father, at rest, watching as what has already happened within his being is inevitably worked out in creation.

When something becomes real in the Spirit, it is only a matter of time before it becomes real in the physical universe. When Jesus died, his redemption became spiritually real. Everything in our Christian walk—experiencing his presence in prayer, becoming part of his body and even fulfilling our own God-given callings—is just the working out of what happened inside Jesus' heart as he took on the full mantle of his call and risked everything for us.

Here's what that means for you. When you take on the mantle of your calling identity and surrender to the risk it entails, *the spiritual work of your Fulfillment stage is already done.* You *are* the incarnation of Christ you were meant to be. Your being call is fulfilled, because it has become a reality inside you. The incarnation of Jesus has come fully alive in your Life Messages—you have literally *become* your call. And since everything you do is an expression of who you are, from now on you will express your calling as easily as breathing. The Fulfillment stage is simply a working out the details of what has already taken place inside your heart.

Presenting Yourself as Who You Really Are

One of the biggest battles we encounter in taking on our calling mantle is fought around the way we present ourselves to others. I've encountered my share of individuals who think more highly of themselves than they ought to think, but healthy leaders nearing Fulfillment are more prone to underestimating who they've become than to overestimating. The temptation is to shrink back into who we were, and present ourselves as less than who we are called to be. We usually do it in the name of humility, but it has more to do with a fear of risk and a lack of faith in the depth of God's work in us. The inability to present yourself as who you are is a huge obstacle to fulfilling your call. A series of coaching conversations with Lis provides a great example of this struggle.

After 25 years pioneering a mission work in Nepal, being jailed for the Gospel, building an organization of 2000 staff and launching a university, Lis and her husband took a much-needed sabbatical. "That time away and the coach training I got helped me to reflect on our ministry and where we were at," Lis declares. "We started to ask the question, 'Would we ever leave India?'"

While she was enjoying what she was doing, the work as a whole was stressful. The larger the organization grew, the more of her time was taken up with interpersonal conflicts and management chores. Neither was one of Lis's best strengths. Her husband was weary and feeling plateaued, so they finally decided to transition home. That move thrust Lis into her Valley of Identity.

After not living in the U.S. for 25 years, coming back was a big adjustment. "We had to give up everything—positions, roles, titles, and being in India." They had to form new relationships and relearn the culture, and living in a small town was not conducive to the transition.

That's when I began coaching her around her timeline. As she expressed her frustrations about the smallness of her situation and how people didn't understand who she was, I inquired, "When they ask you who you are, what do you tell them?" It quickly became clear she didn't know what to say. For instance, in church settings, Lis defaulted back to, "I'm a missionary." The problem was the opportunities that description produced were things like being on the deacon board of a small church, or an invitation to go sit with an older lady who needed companionship. After working to impact a nation, that kind of role didn't stir her at all. But she felt guilty about saying 'no,' because she didn't want to look like she was above doing the little things.

Lis was running up against an internal obstacle to presenting herself as who she really was. Planning the lady's afternoon tea is not a fitting assignment for someone who is used to organizing conferences with five thousand people in attendance. But if you tell people you "like to plan events" without providing a context for them to understand the scale you function in, teas may be what you'll get. When you say you are a missionary, the image in most people's minds is a couple off in Africa, working mostly

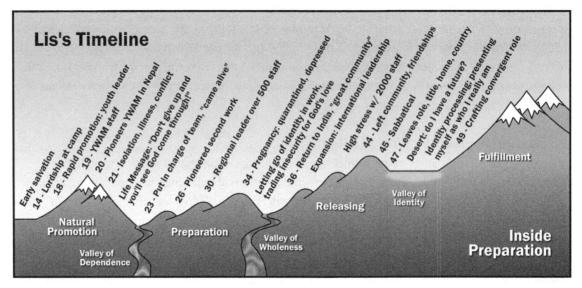

alone or in a small church, not a leader who travels and speaks internationally, has hundreds of staff who report to her and who has three hundred church plants in a single division of her enterprise. *If you are unable to present yourself as who you really are, the people you need to work with to fulfill your mission will never take you seriously.*

We began to brainstorm about alternate phrases. "I launch global initiatives" was a favorite. One of Lis's action steps was to take time on her own to write down who she was in ways that the different groups she worked with could understand (see the exercise at the end of this chapter). For instance, "I started and ran an NGO [non-governmental agency] with 2000 staff" was a phrase that gave business leaders a clear picture of Lis's abilities.

One issue behind how we present ourselves is our understanding of humility. For Lis, putting out such a clear picture of her impressive accomplishments seemed like boasting and self-promotion. Isn't it more humble to err on the side of modesty?

In short, no. True humility is being willing to be known for who you really are, good and bad. Presenting yourself as less than who you are usually comes out of a need to look good and get strokes for being so humble, out of fear that if you really say who you are you will be rejected, or the fear that you won't be able to do what you say you can do.

There are plenty of good examples of New Testament leaders who come right out and say who they are. Think of Jesus, stating, "I am the bread of life; no one comes to the Father except through me." Pretty bold statement of his identity, isn't it? Or Paul: "Am I not free? Am I not an apostle? Have I not seen Jesus our Lord? Are you not my work in the Lord?" Or again: "For I consider myself not in the least inferior to the most eminent apostles."

> *If you don't present yourself as who you really are, the people you need to work with to fulfill your mission will never take you seriously.*

The excuses you make to saying who you are will reveal your fears. Take time to meditate on who you are, bring those fears to the light, and let God speak to them.

It was a breakthrough for me when I began to tell people I was "One of the top Christian coach trainers in the world." I believed that to be a true statement at the time—I had helped found and was director of the largest Christian coaching school, trained over 1000 coaches and personally done around 75 multi-day coaching workshops.

At the same time, managing people is not a strength for me. I am too much of a perfectionist and I'm not good at following up with what I delegate. So that's part of my identity, too: I am not a great manager. It's healthy to be able to share both sides unselfconsciously.

Cultivate the ability to share all your strengths and your weaknesses without guilt or shame. If you are unable to say both, "I really excel at this," and "This is a weakness for me—most people do this better than I do," it's a signal that your identity is still somewhat grounded in how people perceive you.

Making the Most of the Stage

The Valley of Identity lays the foundation for your Fulfillment years. Only an increase in your ability to be in Christ—to find your identity rooted solely in him—can launch you into Fulfillment. At a time in life when you expected to be doing your best work, being ejected from your role, losing favor and influence or worrying about your financial future are scary things. But these are the circumstances needed to produce that in-Christ identity.

So first of all, relax! Let go. Trust that God will meet you as he always has before. If this is about finding your identity in Christ, then some other things will need to be stripped away, at least temporarily. So give them up gracefully. You almost certainly have a good portion of your identity tied up in work, or religion, or relationships—it's always something. But God's plan has already accounted for that, and the strategy to get you to where you need to be was well under way before you even realized there was a problem. Lay back into God—what you are going through is normal.

The temptation is to try to recover the productive life you had in the Releasing stage, or even to cover up the work that is needed in your heart with a flurry of fretful activity. Too many leaders who get ejected from a role at this point in life simply get busy finding the next job, without ever really asking God how he wants them to respond to their circumstances. Why are you so worried about what you will eat or wear? Life is more than putting food on the table. Why do you worry about providing for your retirement? Has God not provided for you for all these years, through thick and thin? There is no time in life like the Valley of Identity to seek first the Kingdom of God, and his agenda for you, and let him add all the other stuff in his time.

If you are ending a role or are parting ways with another leader, leaving well is an important task. When your fundamental perspective is that you've been wronged, it's hard not to leave a mess. If you believe God is in the transition, or even that it is a predictable part of God's plan to move you into the fullness of your call, it's easier to take it well.

A role transition in this valley is a great time to take a sabbatical. I'm talking three to six months, not a week between jobs. God has purposefully brought much of your doing to an

> ### Summary of Key Learnings
> - *In this Valley your being call and Life Message formation are completed.*
> - *Losing job or influence and being in a valley at this point in life is unexpected.*
> - *Misunderstanding humility is often an obstacle to your calling.*
> - *The key task is taking on the full mantle of your calling identity.*

end to carve out time in your life for you to think, reflect and to *be with him* in a more intense way. His primary objective for your call is to do it together. That's what the journey has been about from the start.

Will you alter your life pattern to lean into this time of inner formation, or will you fritter it away being anxious about your provision? If the only thing that can get you to stop and reflect is if God closes every other door in your face, he might just do that! God is the keeper of your calling, and he longs for the day when he can present it to you, when you are ready to grasp the full fire of your call while holding it loosely enough to keep from being burned.

Second, get clear on who God says you are, and practice aggressively presenting yourself that way. Odds are, you'll be challenged to take a stand on who you are called to be at a time when there is little support or evidence for it. Meet the challenge, and begin to talk about who you are as an act of faith, without worrying about whether you look humble or not. Your identity is in Christ, not in what anybody thinks of you. If he says you are a particular thing, then you are.

Entering Fulfillment will also call for another big risk. It may be launching out in a new financial venture, risking a certain kind of relationships, building a new organization or leaving behind a comfortable life for one that continues to stretch you. When you stop risking, you start coasting.

Valley of Identity Reflection Questions

1. What was my biggest late life (forties to sixties) transition? Was there a time in this period of life where much of what I was doing came to a close, or I wondered if there would be anything more for me in life?

2. What crisis occurred before my move into the Fulfillment of my calling?

3. Where in life did God bring me to the point that if my call never happened, he was enough?

4. How well does this season fit the Valley of Identity characteristics on page 158?

Exercise: Presenting Yourself as Who You Really Are

Write down who you really are. Don't gloss it up, and don't tone it down. Think of the various audiences you speak to—at church, at work, people you meet in the airport—and come up with a sentence or two that will accurately communicate who you are and what you are capable of.

- How does God see me? Who does he say I am?
- What has my life prepared me to be and do?
- Where am I great at something? What do I uniquely bring to the table?

Watch what is going on in yourself as you do the exercise. If you keep catching yourself skewing your description one way or the other, what is going on there?

Now, try saying the phrases you came up with out loud. How does that feel? If it makes you uncomfortable, why do you think that is happening? Where does the voice come from that resists saying who you really are? What does God have to say about those objections?

Bible Study Guide: The Valley of Identity

Use the questions below to explore how the Valley of Identity played out in the lives of these biblical leaders.

1. **Paul.** His Valley of Identity was most likely connected to the Jerusalem council, which involved a fundamental challenge to the Message of his life. Paul recorded some details of this experience in Acts 15 and Galatians 2. What step of obedience was required of Paul? How did he have to stand alone in his calling identity in this situation? In Galatians 2, what phrase did Paul use to present himself as who he really was?

2. **Abraham**. Without more information on Abraham's inner world, it is difficult to determine whether his Valley of Identity was around the birth of Isaac and the casting out of Ishmael, or the sacrifice of Isaac. What clues do you see that would lead you to choose one over the other? Since Abraham's call was family-related, God often dealt with him through family conflicts. What family conflicts do you see in Abraham's story? What was God doing in Abraham through them to form his Life Message?

> **Valley of Identity Characteristics**
> - *15-30 years into your Calling Journey*
> - *Averages four years long*
> - *Often triggered by ejection from long-time role, loss of influence and favor, or financial reverses*
> - *Stripping of identity in work, accomplishment or how others perceive us*
> - *Healthy detachment from call: you can live without it because Jesus alone is enough for you*
> - *Completion of being call/Life Message formation*
> - *A longer and more intense season for those in Inside Preparation; sometimes includes a wilderness time or dark night of the soul*
> - *Focus moves from doing to being*
> - *Finding success in the success of others instead of your own accomplishments*
> - *Taking on the mantle of your calling identity*
> - *Learning to present yourself as who you are*
> - *Standing alone in the decision to be who you are*

13: FULFILLMENT

Margaret's movement toward the Fulfillment stage took her first through the Valley of Identity. In her early sixties her husband Bryan developed a very rare disease where his lungs gradually lost their capacity to absorb oxygen. The disease progressed until the only life-saving option was a lung transplant. So Margaret retired early from a satisfying teaching career, put all her future plans on hold and moved half-way across the country to wait for the transplant.

Organ transplants can be an emotional roller coaster. You wait, for months on end, constantly available for a call that never seems to come. The process of moving to the top of the waiting list and then finding a donor match can take months, and all the while your loved one is declining in strength. It was an exhilarating day six months later when a donor was found. Margaret and her husband rushed to the hospital and the operation began almost immediately. From a flurry of hope and activity, came the hours of waiting, alone, where one's darkest fears surface. Then—success! The operation went well. What a wonderful word to hear.

But Bryan's condition did not improve. He remained in a coma day after day. Then his body twice began to reject the organ—a process where one's own immune system, though suppressed with powerful drugs, still manages to decide that the new organ is a foreign body and begins to attack it. With her husband on life support with virtually no prospect of recovery, Margaret made the difficult decision to pull the plug. On Christmas day, her husband, and my dad, died.

She came home for the holidays at 63 with a body instead of a life partner. Her home was rented out, so we all gathered for Christmas at a house loaned to us by a friend. Many of Mom's hopes died with Bryan. They had dreamed of traveling or serving in a foreign country together, and of enjoying their grandchildren. If any of that was still going to happen, it wouldn't happen together. Margaret prayed a lot, and cried a lot; and eventually, moved forward with life out of the deep strength that was in her.

When asked how that time shaped her, she talks about the change of emphasis in her spiritual life. "That took me into a being stage and not just doing," she recalls. "I've always been so busy with what's at hand. I learned to slow down and be able to listen."

"I did a lot of journaling, reading and spent much more time being quiet. That has been a tremendous blessing. Just being able to sit quietly and listen to what God has for the day is affirming and eye-opening. The spiritual side of my life has grown tremendously in the last 15 years... My life would never have been the way it is if Bryan had lived. I never would have had these opportunities—maybe some of them, but not all of them."

"It's made a qualitative difference in how I lead," she adds. "Now I am expecting surprises from God and rolling with the punches. I'm more at peace with my place in the world—that it doesn't have

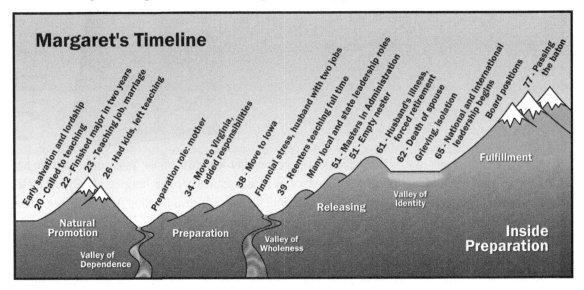

to conform to all my expectations... I learned that suffering and death are a part of life... and that God could use that kind of experience to open all kinds of new doors."

Opening doors is exactly what happened. Margaret had functioned as a stay-at-home mom for a decade, then an elementary teacher for two decades more. She had been a lay leader in her local church, become president of the local teachers association and served on the hospital board. Most of her leadership to that point had been within her church and profession in a small farming community.

All that began to change about a year after Bryan's death, when she was 64. Margaret joined the library board, the board of the local university, and co-chaired a committee that raised funds to build a new central elementary school. She was named citizen of the year in her town at age 69.

Her sphere of influence began to expand far beyond the community. She became a leader in a women's political organization working at both the local and state level. Traveling as a denominational representative took her to Ireland, the West Bank, Israel, Jamaica, and to Kenya (four times). She took a two-year appointment to preside over her district in the denomination, and later became an officer of the denomination's national board. Among many committee appointments, she oversaw the planning of a conference for the Americas. She also headed up their international women's society for several years, and won the Eisenhower distinguished service award for her years of work for an international service organization.

Coming to a place of clarity around her call helped Margaret choose which opportunities to pursue. Using her leadership and organizational gifts to communicate her Message of servant leadership is at the core of all her involvements. Margaret has become a team-building, consensus-style leader instead of a directive one.

Multi-cultural or cross cultural endeavors also tap one of her Life Messages. Margaret grew up in a highly-conservative, insular Amish/Mennonite community where plain clothes and horse-and-buggies were a common sight. Her calling journey moved her from farming communities to university towns to international experiences. Now, she talks quite a bit about learning as much from those she ministers to as they learn from her.

Margaret's Fulfillment years of greatest impact and widest influence were from 64 to 78. She was rapidly recruited and promoted into places of larger influence, mostly in roles that involved strategic decision making rather than ground-level implementation. And she functioned out of a new place of being, joy and inner tranquility.

God certainly did not take her husband away to make her more productive. However, he did take that great loss and redeem it, turning it into a source of great good. Margaret's pain was the stimulus that drew her to a deep place with God, where her own transformation launched her into a much larger field of service than ever before.

Characteristics and Convergent Roles

This stage is the most difficult one to write about, because I am just entering that part of my own journey. The last stage is also the hardest one to find good stories. Everyone in a later stage is also a good example of all the earlier ones, but only the people who have made it all the way through the journey have Fulfillment stories. Consequently, this chapter only covers the beginning of the stage. Leaders continue to go through struggles and transitions during Fulfillment, but I have not attempted to map them.

However, some qualities of the Fulfillment stage are very clear. Beginning after the Valley of Identity (or a short interlude after it for those in Outside Preparation), this season is most commonly

Fulfillment Stage Characteristics

- *Enter by taking a big risk*
- *Rapid promotion—favor and open doors to larger influence*
- *Development of a Convergent Role that brings your best skills and strengths to bear to convey Life Messages*
- *May move from organizational to personal influence (coaching, mentoring, writing, or empowering)*
- *Role may offer fewer responsibilities but larger influence*
- *Formation in Valley of Identity is the basis for expanded impact*
- *Clarity about both doing and being calls*
- *Working with God instead of for him*
- *Urgency to make the most of the years left and leave a legacy; thinking beyond your life span*
- *The joy and peace of a life well-lived*

entered 25 to 40 years after the Calling Journey begins. (Stop and contemplate that for a few moments: it takes several *decades* to get you ready for your calling!) In this stage, we function out of the best of our doing and being calls. It's a place of inner satisfaction, productive work and rest.

A key task for those entering it is the development of a convergent role that allows our best strengths and abilities to be used as a channel for our Life Messages. I'm indebted to J. Robert Clinton for the concept of the convergent role. For most of our lives, we function in roles that only let us use our best strengths in a limited way. Fulfillment, however, demands that our role be redesigned to allow us to use our best natural gifts and abilities to serve our calling the majority of the time.

For instance, one mature senior pastor I worked with had his best strengths in relationships and communication. Preaching, team-building, mentoring and visioning were right in his sweet spot. However, hiring and firing, making daily operational decisions and policy-making were also in his job description—and those were definitely not his best. He hated to see anyone get hurt, so disciplining staff or letting anyone go was an excruciating process. It sucked away his time and energy, and he still often did it poorly in the end. When it came to day-to-day decision making, his love of exploring options led him to keep reopening decisions that had been made, to the great frustration of his staff. It wasn't until he built a core team of equals with a mature, experienced strategist and an effective implementer that he was able to extricate himself from his weaker areas and focus in on using his best strengths the majority of the time.

> *A Convergent Role lets you function in your calling using your best strengths the majority of the time.*

In Margaret's case, early retirement (which she had not contemplated before) was what enabled her to move into a convergent role. Freed of her daily teaching tasks, and financially independent due to her and her husband's pensions, she moved from being able to serve a small, local audience within the boundaries of her job expectations to being able to take on large, unpaid roles that involved extensive travel. The fundamental vehicle for her Life Message switched from classroom teaching to organizational leadership, and her Life Message of service both directed what roles she took on and was powerfully channeled through what she was able to do.

The process of converting your role into something that really fits you is a challenging task that usually takes several years. Leaders at this stage often invest significant time in clarifying their calling and understanding their innate design in order to take this step. Personality and strength inventories, calling clarification tools, Preparation and Revelation inventories and more are all part of this journey. Without a deep understanding of who you are, it is difficult to move into a convergent role.

Messages and Your Being Call

The laser focus on imparting your Life Messages is the salient characteristic of your Fulfillment role. Just functioning in your best strengths isn't enough. Those strengths must be leveraged toward the impartation of the Christ in you: your Message. It is easy to get focused on the joy of flowing in your strengths, without adequately considering what those strengths are meant to channel.

Here's an example. My central Life Message is about meeting God in adversity and suffering and being transformed. I am also a highly skilled leadership coach. If I chose to function in the sweet spot of my skills, I could be coaching leaders in many practical areas like building teams, growing their churches or creating effective small groups.

However, being skilled at team building and having the opportunity to do it isn't enough for me to say, "Yes," to an opportunity. To tap into my Message, it also needs to involve inner transformation—which happens most readily in the place of adversity. If, for example, a ministry leader has failed at his assignment because he was unable to build a team, and begins to realize he can't delegate because he is unable to trust others, that coaching situation hits the bull's eye where my skills and my Message intersect. When I am coaching leaders through failure and painful transition, that's where my best skills most effectively impart my Life Messages.

Over and over, these conversations go to my places of power: being comfortable in the place of brokenness, God works all things for good, transparency is trusting Jesus as your healer, the fellowship of his sufferings leads to the power of his resurrection. When I go beyond just functioning in my coaching skills and they become a conduit for my Life Messages, I have a deep impact almost every time. The whole calling journey revolves around learning to operate simultaneously in the full measure of both your doing and being calls.

Risks and Rewards

Moving into this stage requires another big risk on the part of the leader. For Margaret, the risk was to believe in her own call enough to move beyond her comfort zone of local service into a much larger sphere. In Joseph's case, the big risk was relational. He had to decide whether to open his heart again to the brothers who had betrayed him, and rejoin the family call. Jesus' big risk was going to the cross. For Moses, it was leading a whole city's-worth of people into the desert with no idea where to go or how to keep them all alive. Moses had no inkling beforehand that a pillar of cloud would show up to guide them, or that he would bring water out of solid rocks or that no one's clothes would wear out. He simply had to take the risk of trusting that the God who brought them out of Egypt had a plan for their provision in the desert.

Remember, the objective of this journey is not just for you to accomplish a task—it is for you and Jesus to do it *together*. If all he wanted was to get something done, he could have used the skills you had way back in the Natural Promotion stage. You are on a journey *together*, Jesus invading your vocational world and making it into a fellowship time with him. Your call enables you to carpool to work

> *Calling is Jesus invading your vocational world and making it into a fellowship time with him.*

with Jesus in the same way that you sit down together for your devotional times. Because the focus is already shifting from doing to being, you will embrace this shared journey much more readily than you would have only a few years before.

Advancement and Influence

Another frequent characteristic of this stage is rapid advancement. It's like that heady time of Natural Promotion back before the Valley of Dependence—doors are opening and God's favor is all over you—except this time, you have the character to back up your natural ability. Margaret saw many new doors open that took her beyond her local sphere and really stretched her abilities during these years. For her, this season saw the flowering of her leadership gifts to exert organizational influence in a way that was not possible in the culture she grew up in.

However, advancement is not always what we think it is. *What increases is the impact of our Message on others,* not necessarily our position, status or outward accomplishments. For some, positional authority and leadership responsibilities will grow during this time as a vehicle for more impact. Moses, David and Joseph are all examples of leaders in Outside Preparation who took on large roles in their Fulfillment stage.

However, others who are just as faithful find that their largest outward roles and responsibilities come in the Releasing stage. On entering Fulfillment, they leave positions of broad responsibility and take outwardly smaller roles to focus on replicating their Message in others. Barnabas is a good biblical example of this pattern. He seemed to love stepping back to allow others to flourish. We know little of his own teaching and leadership, but what a legacy he left through sponsoring Paul!

> *In Fulfillment, some leaders move from exerting organizational influence to leaving a legacy through relational influence.*

For some leaders, the primary channel of influence in Fulfillment is relational. Coaching, mentoring, networking, sponsoring and empowering become the focus instead of organizational leadership. The shift begins with a change God fosters during the Valley of Identity, when we are freed from our need to accomplish great things for God and begin finding our greatest success in the success of others.

For example, a friend of mine recently left a prominent national leadership position with a large church association, and took a position as an associate pastor (not even as senior pastor!) in a local church. Yet he seemed very content with his choice. "Climbing the ladder just has no appeal for me anymore," he asserts. However, he believes his current position gives him a tremendous amount of favor and freedom to build a ministry model that works for a new generation. What seems like a demotion may actually become the vehicle that keeps him relevant and passes on his legacy to another generation of leaders. This ability to think beyond your lifetime is another salient characteristic of the Fulfillment stage.

Gary is a prominent leader who exemplifies the movement from focusing on his own organizational leadership position to being a mentor of the next generation. Now in his seventies, his life-well-lived, academic credentials and body of published work allow him to write his own ticket. Instead of using that to find more places on stage or to feather his own bed, these days Gary puts much of his effort into encouraging and mentoring younger leaders one-on-one.

For instance, in addition to part time teaching at several graduate schools, he spends time on campus simply being available to meet with whoever (students or faculty) wants to draw on him. Gary has taken initiative to be available but the schools see value in this role. "It's what I do best," he explained enthusiastically. "The schools seem to like it. The students and faculty fill the slots quickly. And I think this is leadership far beyond any talks I give or things I write."

Jane left the large organizational role she filled in her Releasing stage for what seemed at the time like a smaller sphere—only to find she was exerting a greater influence than in her previous role. When she began to bump up against restrictions on her ability to talk about Jesus in the workplace, Jane left her position as a Fortune 50 project manager to become VP of a spin-off company. "The mission was to create a coaching culture there," she recalls. "But I was only there a year. I decided that this was not 'it'—the company was too small. So I left my corporate position, that part of my life came to an end and I started my own business."

Jane lost the favor and influence that went with her role when she went out on her own, ushering in her Valley of Identity. "I had a couple years of retooling where I didn't make any money. I thought, 'gosh, I'm working really, really hard for nothing!'"

After about two years, things suddenly broke loose. "I got some publicity, and started signing up clients left and right. I was choking out my coaching rate to them, wondering if anyone would pay it," Jane laughs. Her focus was on coaching senior executives. But then something interesting began to happen.

"An organization asked me to teach a group of pastors how to coach. I was wondering how I was going to deal with those inquiries given my calling as a missionary to the corporate world. Then I realized that all missionaries go on furlough! They spend time in churches telling fellow believers what they are doing. So why don't I go on furlough, and tell the church about what I do?"

"That became my furlough work. It will never amount to over 25% of my work time, but when I put it in their language, pastors understood the furlough concept and were able to respect my boundaries. Churches are not my mission field, but I have a responsibility to educate the church and recruit more missionaries to the corporate world. One pastor said, 'I realized all my members are missionaries to the business world, and I need to treat them that way.' So now they have a commissioning service every year for their business missionaries. That's one of the prouder accomplishments of my life."

Learning how to present herself as who she really is in both these arenas helped keep Jane focused. "I learned to say 'no' based on my calling, and people could understand that."

When we are talking about calling, it is important to not lose sight of what is eternal and what isn't. Organizations, books, media attention, fame, great accomplishments, moving mountains—none of that will last forever. The only things from earth that make it to heaven are Jesus and his people. Therefore, the only outcome of your work that really makes an eternal difference is the impact you have for Jesus *on* people. That is why we so often see a shift from organizational to relational influence in Fulfillment: our true legacy is counted in the people we pour ourselves into.

Working with God

In the chapter on the Valley of Identity, we talked about the rest and peace that comes when we become who we were born to be and stop needing accomplishments to make our life seem complete. This joyful rest enables us to work *with* God and not *for* him in Fulfillment.

In the first stages of the calling journey, we tend to see ourselves as working for God to get his work done. And for a few years God blesses this beginning. Then he takes us through several Valleys that set us free from the tyranny of work, by learning that we can live without it and fixing our identity in him instead of in what we do. In the Fulfillment stage we've come full circle, working with great productivity together *with* Jesus, out of the shared life we've built in years of journeying together. The consummation we experience in the Fulfillment stage is the fruit of a lifetime investment in that friendship with Jesus. More and more, we hear God saying, "Well done, good and faithful servant! You were faithful with a few things; I will put you in charge of many things. Enter into the joy of your master!"

That's not just a nice phrase. There is a wonder and gratitude that overflows from inside when you realize you've made it to this point in life. Through everything that you've experienced, the Great Redeemer has been faithful. Amidst all your own fears, failings, and the faults you are so intimately acquainted with, you have succeeded at the most important thing in life: you have stewarded the life you've been given well.

Fulfillment is about being full. You have been filled by Jesus' incarnation in your life, so you can overflow for others. It's a pretty good feeling!

Failures and Temptations

Getting to this stage of the journey doesn't mean success is assured. We've all heard the stories of the leaders who have failed spectacularly later in their careers. Interestingly, those who crash and burn often do so because they have failed to meet God in one of the Valleys. For instance, the Valley of Wholeness is designed to deal with unhealthy drives and lingering wounds in your life. When a

> ### Symptoms of Misplaced Identity
> *Here are some characteristics senior leaders with misplaced identities seem to share:*
>
> - *If this leader died, the organization would flounder.*
> - *Resources flow in toward the leader's projects, not out. Anything (i.e. someone else's call) that does not directly support the leader's personal vision is resource-starved.*
> - *The organization only invests in developing leaders who will stay and help that organization's vision.*
> - *The organization has a higher than average burnout rate and staff turnover as people are used up and discarded.*
> - *People who leave are viewed as having made a mistake instead of being sent.*
> - *The senior leader has no real peers within the organization, and no functioning peer accountability.*
> - *The leader's life is imbalanced, and this is replicated in the staff—too much work and too little family time.*
> - *Those who challenge these flaws are ostracized.*

leader undergoes a moral failure, damaging divorce or burnout later in life, it can often be traced back to not going there in the Valley of Wholeness. Somehow, the lesson was missed, and the consequent lack of relational and personal wholeness undermines the leader's call to the point of collapse. Haggard, Swaggart, Baker and others are names that are familiar to all, as the weaknesses they refused to deal with in private have been brought to the harsh, unyielding glare of the media spotlight.

Another major source of late-life leadership breakdowns seems to be the failure to meet God in the Valley of Identity. The purpose of this time is to create a healthy detachment from our call—so if it never happens, God is enough. Leaders who never come to that place of detachment are wedded to their call in such a way that if they were ever removed from it they would lose their identity. Life without the vision is incomprehensible. When leaders stay too long, manipulate or dominate others to succeed, fail to develop successors or compromise their character to hang onto their position, the lack of that detachment may be the culprit.

The distinguishing mark of a leader with misplaced identity is selfishness. When identity is not fully grounded in Christ, it always comes back to self. Leaders who have not walked through the desert and discovered that Jesus alone is enough for them will be driven to hog the limelight, compare themselves to others and find their identity in success. Often, their organization becomes simply a tool that the leader uses to accomplish his or her personal vision, without regard to the callings God has placed on the lives of the people in it. God is deeply grieved when we use people like that.

Jim Collins has done a good job of describing some of the qualities of a healthy senior leader in his classic business book, *Good to Great*. Studying companies that became and stayed great, he found that one of the most important qualities of their top executives was humility. The leaders with the greatest lasting impact were not the charismatic superstars or those of public acclaim, but the ones who shunned the limelight, shared the credit and were more committed to the mission than to their own part in it.

One of the great temptations at this stage of life is that the farther along in the journey you are, the more likely the people around you are to be enablers of your failings. A year or so ago I got an object lesson in how this works. I run a web site service, and we had experienced a catastrophic failure on one of our servers. Unfortunately, the server company we hired had committed the giant no-no of putting the back-ups on the same computer as the actual web sites. So when that hard drive went to computer heaven, everyone's sites disappeared and we had no backups. Sixty peoples' web sites and e-mail were down, and the angry calls started coming in.

My partner was heading up the tech side, and after a few days she called me and said, "Tony, I just can't deal with these calls anymore." People were justifiably frustrated by our poor service, and they were taking it out on her. To lighten her load, I took her list of 30 upset customers and started calling.

I admit I had a bit of a knot in my stomach as I made that first call. But it was nothing like I expected. "Oh, Tony—I'm so glad you called!" Or, "Are you the author of that book?" Or even, "Is this *the* Tony Stoltzfus?" Everyone was so nice and respectful, happy to talk to me and ready to

---

How Well Do You Know Your Call?
Leaders in the Fulfillment stage who have a clear sense of call should be able to answer these questions:

- *If someone asked you right now what your calling is, could you rattle it off in a phrase or sentence from memory?*
- *Name the key Life Messages that make up your being call.*
- *What are three of your key leadership values?*
- *What are the top strengths and weaknesses of your personality type?*
- *What percentage of your time are you using your best strengths and abilities to channel your Life Message?*
- *What one role or task must you complete before you die?*

Bonus Challenge: Can you answer these questions for your spouse?

cut me some slack, because I was *somebody*.

That was one of my first brushes with the peril of fame: if people think you are somebody, they will let you get away with just about anything! If you are well-known and your identity is still in your accomplishments or in how people see you, you'll find no shortage of people willing to put *their* identity in knowing you. Soon they'll have given you enough rope to hang yourself.

Making the Most of the Fulfillment Stage

There are several keys to making the most of the Fulfillment stage. The first is an in-depth knowledge of who you are and a clear understanding of your call. It is not enough at this stage to have a strengths or personality assessment in a drawer somewhere, without understanding what the letters mean. It isn't enough to have a basic idea of your call but not be able to rattle it off on a moment's notice. Without thoroughly knowing yourself, you won't be very successful at crafting a convergent role that fits you. And without a very clear grasp on your call, you'll waste significant time and energy trying to sort through all the opportunities that come your way to find the ones you should be accepting.

The questions in the box on the previous page will give you some feedback on how well you understand yourself and your call. If you aren't satisfied with your answers, the companion book, *A Leader's Life Purpose Workbook,* includes a full suite of self-study exercises that will help you clarify these areas. Finding a professional coach is a great option as well—these individuals are trained in life purpose discovery and have the tools to help you nail down who you are and what your life mission is.

Second, use what you've learned about yourself to take a thorough look at your role. What fits you and what doesn't? By this point in their careers, most leaders have at least some freedom to adjust their role to fit their call. What should you say 'no' to, and where should you be saying 'yes'? What things that are not in your sweet spot can you delegate? Where do you need to put a team in place to complement you? And where can the way you do the mission be redesigned to rely more on

> ### Summary of Key Learnings
> - *In Fulfillment, influence may increase through a decrease in responsibilities.*
> - *Failure to meet God on character issues earlier in life can derail your Fulfillment.*
> - *The whole calling journey is designed to bring you to this place of greatest impact.*

your strengths and less on your weak areas? Creating a convergent role will make a big difference in the impact of your legacy-leaving years, so it deserves your attention.

Third, you must know your Life Messages. These are your places of power and greatest impact. It isn't just functioning in your best skills that leads to Fulfillment, but the channeling of your Life Messages through those abilities.

Finally, continue to take risks. You will not enter your Fulfillment stage without significant risk. The risk may be simply believing in your own call enough to take on the mantle of your calling identity. Or God may arrange things so that you must stand alone in a big relational, financial or career risk, and say, "I am called and I can do this." At this crucial moment, to say, "It is too close to retirement to take that kind of financial risk," or "Life is pretty good now—I'm not sure I want to take that chance" is shrinking back from what you've prepared for your whole life. God is with you! There is no time in life like this stage to step out and see his provision.

Fulfillment Stage Reflection Questions

1. When in life did you craft or enter into a convergent role that fit your best skills and maximized your ability to communicate your Life Messages?

2. Was there a season where your greatest impact took place after a wrenching late-life (forties to sixties) transition?

3. Where do you sense you moved from working on your own call to finding your legacy in promoting the callings of others?

4. How well does this phase of your life match the characteristics list on page 170.

Bible Study: The Fulfillment Stage

1. **David's Fulfillment.** This stage began for David when his apprenticeship ended and he became king of Israel (II Sam. 3-5). Which of the stage characteristics listed below seem to fit this period of David's life? What risk did he take to enter into Fulfillment? How did his convergent role as king fit both his skills and strengths and his Life Message?

2. **David's Failure.** (II Sam. 11-12 and Ps. 51) What brokenness in David's family relationships that he failed to deal with earlier in life contributed to his later moral failure with Bathsheba? How did God work to redeem even this failing and use it to strengthen David's Life Message of being a "man after God's own heart?"

3. **Jesus.** Following a short interlude after his resurrection where he appeared on earth, Jesus' ascension marks the beginning of his Fulfillment stage. What was the big risk he took to enter Fulfillment? Which of the stage characteristics fit this transition?

   Things get a little tricky here because when Jesus ascended he stepped outside of time, but what is he doing during his Fulfillment stage? What is his convergent role?

> **Fulfillment Stage Characteristics**
> - *Enter by taking a big risk*
> - *Rapid promotion—favor and open doors to larger influence*
> - *Development of a Convergent Role that brings your best skills and strengths to bear to convey Life Messages*
> - *May move from organizational to personal influence—coaching, mentoring, writing, or empowering*
> - *Role may offer fewer responsibilities but larger influence*
> - *Formation in Valley of Identity is basis for expanded impact*
> - *Clarity about both doing and being calls*
> - *Working with God instead of for him*
> - *Urgency to make the most of the years left and leave a legacy; thinking beyond your life span*
> - *The joy and peace of a life well-lived*

14: COACHING THE CALLING JOURNEY

Calling timelines are a powerful tool for those who coach and mentor other leaders. Since perspective is the key to traveling well, having a model of the stages and transitions we go through is invaluable.

I was on the phone yesterday with a young pastor in a self-described "leadership funk." He was not accomplishing what he hoped to, and felt bogged down, guilty and frustrated about his lack of progress. His church was stuck in neutral and the excitement he'd felt at the beginning of his tenure was waning fast. He called to see if I had any quick insights that would get him out of the hole he was in and back on track with his calling.

Given that description of the problem, it might be natural for a life coach to explore how he could better align his life with his values, reconfigure his role to fit his strengths, or take practical steps to begin fully functioning again in his pastoral calling. However, this kind of approach makes two critical assumptions:

1. Feeling productive and significant confirms that we are on track; feeling frustrated and stuck means something is wrong;

2. Everyone should be functioning in their calling now (regardless of their age or life stage).

After studying timelines, what do you think about the validity of these common assumptions?

The first would likely be true much of the time during the three stages. However, in the valleys in between, feeling the way he does is normal. If you understand calling timelines, his frustration doesn't necessarily indicate something is wrong. God is leveraging adversity to shape him for his call.

If I coach a person who is in a valley to pursue accomplishment and productivity, I may actually be encouraging him or her to resist what God is doing! When it comes to life purpose, *the approach to take is dependent on the stage the coachee is in.*

The second assumption (everyone should be functioning in their calling now) seems to me to be almost universal in coaching. We assume that if you don't know your call you should find it—now—and that if your roles are not aligned with your call, now is the time to change. In other words, we picture the ideal calling timeline as a smooth, uninterrupted, rapid climb to our destiny. If a person is stagnant or seems to be going down and not up, we assume there is a problem.

Our timeline research upsets these assumptions. In fact, you won't step into the fullness of your call without several decades of refining—and several major dips and disappointments along the way are part of the program. So to coach as if functioning in your destiny role now is the objective—regardless of the person's calling stage—often won't work and may even be counterproductive.

Coaching the Process

So how did I respond to this young pastor? Since this was the first time we'd met, one of my first questions involved determining his calling stage: "How old are you?" Just knowing that he was thirty gave me some strong hints on what might be helpful to ask. At that age, it is a virtual certainty that he's not in the Fulfillment or Releasing stages. So, for example, asking him how he could construct a convergent role that fits his best strengths (a task for Fulfillment) is not likely to yield the solution to his dilemma.

Once we find out when he made Jesus Lord (in his teens), the most probable stages at that age are the Valley of Dependence and Preparation. In those years, a key objective is building the foundational character and disciplines to support one's calling. In other words, it's mostly about your own growth. So I tried reframing the situation using some "What if" questions that focused on God's work in his heart. "What if God is in the fact that you aren't accomplishing much right now? What if God *is* answering your prayers to change your church, but the road to changing it begins by changing you? You mentioned your leaders' "reticence to step out." If God were going to first work the ability in you to step out without fear, so you could teach it to them, how do you think he would do it?" When he began thinking of his situation in terms of personal growth instead of merely getting tasks done, he quickly discovered how to start moving forward again.

If I had operated out of the fulfill-your-destiny-now model common in coaching, he couldn't have made that happen if he tried. Instead, I worked to identify and coach him around the stage in the calling journey he was in. I call that "coaching the process"—coaching in a way that fits the person's age and stage in life.

Years ago I learned to change my coaching style to fit a coachee's personality type. For instance, with hard-charging high 'D's on the DISC, I am more direct and to the point, while with 'P's on the Myers-Briggs who like to keep all their options open, we spend extra time making sure we've developed committed action steps that actually get done. Speaking the language of their personality type removes communication barriers and helps the person make better progress. The calling timeline taught me to make the same kind of adjustments based on where the person was at on the calling journey.

If you only get one insight from this chapter, make it this: *coach leaders toward the calling*

> *Coach leaders toward the calling **process**, not the convergent role.*

process, not the convergent role. Instead of assuming the solution lies in being in the perfect *role*, a more effective approach is to help the person lean into God's agenda for this *stage*.

What Stage Are You In?

The first step of coaching the process is identifying the stage the person is in[18]. While one way to identify an individual's calling stage is to take him or her through the entire process in this book, sometimes you simply want to address the stage the person is in right now. The two basic questions for identifying the current stage are:

1. How many years has it been since you made Jesus Lord?
2. Are you in an extended season of adversity, loss or transition, or a productive time of effective work?

The first question gives you a sense of how far into the calling journey the person is. The second query indicates whether this is an upward stage or a valley time. You will probably know the answer to the second question already, based on what your coachee has been sharing with you. In fact, the best clue that introducing the timeline would be helpful is when the story you are hearing starts to match up with the characteristics of a stage or valley.

For instance, if a person made Jesus Lord six years ago, and has suddenly experienced great disappointment, confusion and disorientation, the most likely stage is the Valley of Dependence. Or, if the person is 17 years into the calling journey and has finally taken on a wonderful position in his/her area of call after years in a boring job, this may be the Day of Release. Once you have a good guess as to the season the person is in, run through the stage characteristics and ask whether that description fits. The timeline brings a powerful perspective: that this experience is a normal part of God's master plan.

Coaching Natural Promotion

Each stage has tasks to be accomplished, and each demands different things from the coach. Coaching the calling journey process is not putting your agenda on the person. On the contrary—it is letting go of your assumption that everyone ought to be functioning in their calling now. Instead, look for the unique thing God is doing in each person's life and align your coaching with it.

For instance, "Whatever your hand finds to do, do it with all your might" is the operative phrase for people in the Natural Promotion stage. Celebrate the energy and sense of call young people have (it's great to be radical and all-in when you are young). Help them find ways to channel that energy, without being too worried about how it fits into the long term plan or whether they are doing things exactly "right."

This stage is designed to build faith in God's power, so God will often call people to step out in unusual or seemingly-unwise ways. Let go of your need to protect your coachees from consequences you think you foresee and allow them to try new things. Who knows—God may do the impossible! God's plan accounts for all of this, and he is well able to teach them wisdom and discernment in his time!

An important task in this stage is recording the calling insights the person has, so they aren't lost

---

18 A "Cheat Sheet" with the characteristics of all the stages and valleys is included in Appendix B.

in later years (see the *Building an Altar* exercise on page 61). The Revelation Journal (page 120 in *A Leader's Life Purpose Workbook*) is another excellent exercise for recording the perceptions of this stage.

Creating a personal timeline is most helpful for leaders in their late twenties and up—at 18, there isn't much life experience to put on the map! Due to their lack of life experience, leaders in Natural Promotion tend to think they are farther along in the timeline than their maturity justifies. So I don't usually introduce the timeline until the person is at least in the Valley of Dependence. An unrealistic self-concept is common before the big crash of the first valley: before you've experienced real failure, God's release into mighty acts of faith and power seems just around the corner.

If you do introduce the timeline here, studying the calling development of a biblical character is a better way for those in this stage to grasp it than to try to fit their own lives into the framework. Abraham and Joseph make good studies—enough of their life stories are included that you can find the stages, but the accounts aren't overly long. Studying David or Moses is a much more ambitious project!

Coaching in the Valley of Dependence

Leaders entering the Valley of Dependence often come to a coach desperate for perspective. At this point in the timeline, it is likely that life is difficult, dreams are dying and God is stripping us of false beliefs about life. Most are operating under the assumption that this is not what the Christian life is supposed to look like, and strive to get back to the way things were in the Natural Promotion stage. However, God's redemptive purpose is poles apart: for us to understand the limitations of our natural abilities. Our failure can bring us one of the greatest gifts in life: letting go of confidence in the false self. So how do we coach these leaders?

The first step is to go back to the basic coaching value of believing in people. I am going to believe in this person and their relationship with God. I will believe that they haven't thrown their life away—that what is happening to them has purpose, and that God is in it. I will believe that this adversity holds the seeds of a great victory for them—that it may even contain the key that will unlock their destiny.

When God is dealing with us in the Valley of Dependence, sometimes the most painful injustice comes from well-meaning advice-givers who misrepresent the heart of God. Like Job's friends, our human tendency is to believe that adversity or suffering means something is wrong. From there, it is only a small step to assuming that our suffering is a result of our failings and that God sent it as punishment. When we bring "help" from that perspective, we have totally misrepresented God's heart. Yes, sin has consequences, but God's entire strategy for dealing with the human race is about saving and redeeming.

> *Perspective is the most important need in the Valley of Dependence.*

When young leaders have flown too close to the sun, lost their wings and crashed, understanding God's heart in all this is the key issue. Failure catches us by surprise because in our youthful exuberance we didn't believe we could fail, so our minds start searching for a scapegoat. Human nature is to find someone to blame—usually ourselves or God. The coach's job is to help these leaders find God's perspective on their situation. That means relating to them as someone who loves, not one who blames or shames or punishes. A key purpose of suffering is to move us beyond simplistic, "if you do well, will you not be approved?" thinking to discover that God loves us no matter what we do.

A coach's belief in the person and in God's work in his or her life can help break this cycle of guilt and blame. When we assume God is at work in what we are experiencing, then blaming becomes irrelevant. Our faith in the sovereignty of God and our knowledge of the calling timeline offers another perspective: that this is the normal way God builds leaders, and that he loves us in everything. Everybody goes through this valley season. Often the greatest gift I have to give as a coach is simply saying, "That sounds normal to me."

And I can go even further. The really spectacular crashes are often a reliable indicator of a large-sphere calling. Generally, the more talented and strong-willed you are, the bigger a mess you'll make in the process of learning to lean on God! When leaders who have blown it are encouraged, championed and gain perspective on the larger purposes of God, that's when growth is maximized. Unwavering love and acceptance in the midst of failure accurately represent God's heart for his people, and can be a wonderfully healing experience.

Coaching Preparation and the Valley of Wholeness

Leaders in the Preparation and Releasing stages are more likely to look for performance coaching to build skills and increase effectiveness. Creating a practical plan to acquire the abilities and experience one's calling requires is a big task in this stage. The Five Fingers exercise (page 94) is a great way to flesh out what General skills are needed and start working on them, even when the exact details of the call are still fuzzy.

Those in Outside Preparation often come to coaching late in this stage, frustrated with the trajectory of their lives. Just showing them a picture of where they are at on the timeline can be revolutionary. Seeing the timelines of biblical leaders is also quite helpful—David and Joseph are great examples many can identify with. Near the end of the stage, the leader in Outside Preparation is often asked to lay down the call, sometimes by saying "no" to false opportunities that involve compromise, or by having God withhold opportunities until the leader reaches a place of contentment. When it is darkest before the dawn (a dawn that the coachee cannot see coming), the timeline's perspective can be a lifesaver.

This point in life is often when people first start doing serious work on discovering their life purpose. By now, they have enough life experience to make some major conclusions about who they are and what roles fit best. Steps like creating value statements and internalizing their personality type will be a great help to the leader over the next decade or two. Because this valley is a key time of Life Message development, it can also be a good time to do some Life Message discovery.

The Five Fingers exercise (page 94) can be quite helpful for those in Preparation. For example, Lisa's desire is to be an influencer, evangelist and discipler in the political sphere. Because she sees herself doing that through a career in politics, her key competencies might include evangelism skills, networking skills, a track record and resume that will get her hired into the right kind of roles, and policy knowledge and experience. Key character areas to work on might include life balance, boundaries, humility, and faith.

Those competencies may not be a perfect fit for her real destiny role 20 years down the road, but they are a great starting point. Now Lisa can choose the roles, responsibilities and training opportunities she takes on based on how they will develop what is needed for her calling role. For instance, she might take a certain job for a few years just because she needs it on her resume; or she might take a less demanding position for a time to focus on evangelism training. The Five Fingers exercise provides a general-enough picture of what you'll need in the future that you don't have to obsess over getting all the details right, but it's specific enough to get you out of your recliner and put you to work on your destiny.

Since of the three valleys the second has the least direct connection to one's calling, coaching will tend to focus around personal issues. A vital issue is healing from past wounds. I am continually amazed at the number of senior leaders I coach who have never even thought of pursuing emotional healing for critical incidents in their lives. Every Christian needs to meet Jesus as the healer of their deepest pain. There is no special exemption for leaders. If in a coaching relationship you uncover a pattern of rejection from a father, abuse, alcoholism, or even basic dysfunctional parenting, feel around in that area a bit. If it still hurts when you touch it, or the person's present behavior is still affected by those experiences, that's a place to challenge the person to pursue healing. You might say:

- How have you pursued inner healing in this area? What help have you gotten?
- To cope with this, do you discipline yourself a while and it goes away, or does it feel like something you will have to exercise discipline around for the rest of your life? (If basic discipline doesn't work, that means there is an underlying issue.)
- If you stopped coping with this and set out to really eliminate its effects from your life in the next 90 days, what would you do?
- If someone came to you with this issue, how would you advise him or her to deal with it?

Coaching the Releasing Stage

The beginning of this stage is an exciting adventure for leaders in Outside Preparation, when their Day of Release launches them into their calling sphere and they are recognized and powerfully affirmed by key people.

However, after seeing so many doors close over the years, it can be hard to step out into the new. Leaders often overstay their Preparation Roles because they are afraid the new thing won't pan out. Recently, I worked with a leader who was facing the challenge of taking this next big risk. He dilly-dallied, tried to dip his toe in while still clinging to the security of the old, and got less and less motivated about his job as the cloud moved farther and farther away.

One day he called me up and said, "I got fired today." We spent about half an hour processing what had happened. One of the key techniques I used was reframing the conversation from 'something bad happened' to 'what is God doing?' It wasn't long until he admitted, "Yeah, God fired me. I was too much of a chicken to leave on my own, even though I knew it was time, so he finally stepped in and did it for me!"

Any time a leader is nearing a major transition, there are clear signs that it is approaching (see the box on the facing page). Try reframing the adversity the person is experiencing as transitional signals—sometimes that can lead to a huge perspective change and a breakthrough in getting moving.

Usually, a person in Outside Preparation is recruited into the Releasing stage. Coaching can also be an important help in recognizing the right opportunities and profiling what kind of leader would make the best mentor. Leaders may struggle at this point to stay true to their values instead of leaping after the first open door they see. If you as a coach know your coachee's heart, you may be the voice that calls them back to their true identity and keeps them from selling their birthright for a bowl of pottage.

Another important task of this stage is translating General skills into Specific ones. Those in Outside Preparation have mastered the fundamentals, but still need help knowing how they apply in this new sphere of influence. Confidence is often a big issue: I can remember many times as a coach where I've championed a person in this stage by saying, "You may not see it, but you are just as qualified as any of these other people to be here. Be confident in who you are! The character work in your life is done—all you need is to translate the skills you learned in your last role over to this arena. You *are* ready for this!"

> ### Signs of Impending Transition
> *Since transitions tend to come upon us unawares, it is helpful for life coaches to know the early warning signs. Here is how leaders describe their inner world when transition is at the doorstep:*
>
> - *General restlessness or boredom sets in.*
> - *What was once satisfying is no longer. "Is this all there is?"*
> - *Feeling frustrated, stuck or that your world is too small.*
> - *A loss of energy or desire.*
> - *A longing for time away.*
> - *Disorientation, confusion or uncertainty about what's happening inside.*
> - *Questioning yourself at a fundamental level.*
> - *A lack of direction—the future is cloudy.*
>
> *And a few outward indicators to look for:*
>
> - *Productive doing is significantly reduced.*
> - *A major change in circumstances.*
> - *Something important to you comes to an end, dies or is taken away.*
> - *Being removed from a major role.*

The *Five Fingers* exercise (page 94) can be employed in this stage as well to create a plan for building the key competencies required for one's calling. Or it can be used to assess our readiness for transitioning into Fulfillment. To be ready for your convergent role, I am looking for high competency in at least three, and preferably four or all five of the top competencies you identified. It is extremely difficult to fully function in your call while you are still learning the major skills it requires.

Pete's story is a good example of the impact of these competencies. He is a 36-year-old entrepreneur leading an innovative business professional services business that he founded. While the idea behind his core product is brilliant and he has an excellent team, Pete's organization is only growing slowly. Two of Pete's five key General skills are managing people and keeping many balls in the air at the same time. He still has a lot of growing to do in both areas. Successfully leading in areas where our competency is low consumes much more energy than do the things we've mastered and do effortlessly. Consequently, much of Pete's focus is on keeping those two areas functioning as he grows into his role. His situation is exacerbated somewhat because as a high "C" perfectionist personality on the DISC, everything must be done to Pete's high standards.

The growth limitation for Pete's organization is the two general skills he has yet to master and the amount of energy he expends on them. As his confidence and skills increase, it will free up the energy and focus needed to take the company to the next level. Functioning in the fullness of your call requires effortless competence in your key skill areas.

Coaching the Valley of Identity

This valley is most challenging to those in Inside Preparation. After a whole career in their calling arena, they may be forced out of a long-term role in the prime of life. Perspective on the calling journey and the knowledge that this is normal can pay big dividends here.

The most common area of processing in this valley is a misplaced identity. When our identity becomes too entangled with a role or calling, heart surgery is required to separate the two. This is the kind of deep-rooted bondage that "only comes out through prayer and fasting." But in this case, the fast is not from food, but from work itself. For many of us, only a time of complete detachment from work can bring the freedom we need to enter Fulfillment. But when the job is removed, the corresponding loss of identity makes us feel bad about ourselves, get discouraged and wonder who we are. The intensity of those feelings provides the energy we need to take our broken hearts before God.

Since the core issue is putting our identity in Christ, reframing our sense of loss in terms of identity and inner growth can be an effective coaching technique.

A frequent topic of discussion in this valley is sabbaticals, unpaid leave or lengthier transition times. When coachees try to break the fast prematurely and avoid God's processing by immediately going out and finding another job, some are blocked at every turn until they are forced to sit, while others find a job but just come back to the same crossroads when that role, too, is yanked away a year or two later. Being able to discuss why this is happening is an important gift the timeline can bring.

Many leaders make an important career transition in this valley, sometimes by coming out from under the tree of a senior leader and going out on their own. A big risk is required—making a sizeable bet on their readiness and ability to do what they are called to do. Your belief in the person is a vital support. Talking through the cost of not risking ("Imagine you are looking back on this moment at 80 years of age, and you had chosen **not** to take this risk. How would you feel then about your choice?") is a great technique for helping a leader decide if the risk is worth it.

Another important task of this valley is assuming the full mantle of one's calling identity. Last week I sat down with a leader who wanted help finding a job. He had a lifetime of experience, a full toolkit of skills, a call to spiritual formation (I was helping him get started on a book on that topic), and mature, seasoned character. He had also had some painful leadership battles in the past. His business in a cyclical industry had dried up due to an economic downturn, and he had only worked sporadically over the past two years.

As we talked, I began to pick up on some things that made me very curious. Although he was a hard worker and enough of a go-getter to be a successful project manager, he had not created a resume for the new direction he wanted to move toward. His dream was to work in spiritual formation, but he had done nothing to pursue a job in that arena. While his large church was great at empowering people, and desperately needed help in his area of expertise, he had never approached them about a job or let them know he was available.

He was a dead ringer for the Valley of Identity: 60 years old, ejected from a long-time role, in a difficult late-life wilderness season, wrestling with identity questions and having trouble presenting himself as who he really is. I observed the things I had seen and then said, "What makes me curious is that over here, in the project-management world, you are aggressive and determined and confident, but when it comes to your call and what God has made you for, you seem like a shrinking violet. What's going on there?" We had a good conversation about real humility, presenting himself as who he really is and believing in his own calling, and now he is on the move, taking practical steps to push himself forward in his calling.

These kinds of obstacles around humility and self-promotion are common. A favorite exercise of mine is to have coachees actually write out who they are and read it to me (see page 157), or write out how they will present themselves to different groups and then try out those lines. Voicing your identity is awkward at first, but your confidence in your calling grows tremendously once you start doing it.

Coaching Fulfillment

Two main issues come to the fore in the first years of the Fulfillment stage: coming to full clarity about one's calling and crafting a convergent role around it. This is a place where leaders are motivated to fill the holes in understanding who they are. Many leaders enter this stage of life without a definitive grasp of their strengths, passions, personality type and the like, so the coaching process often involves mining these areas for insight. These tools are familiar to most life coaches.

The insights from this process are put to use immediately in reconfiguring the leader's role to fit his or her Life Messages and design. Leaders at this stage usually have a fair amount of say in their own job descriptions, so changes that make a real difference are possible. All the practical coaching tools about best-fit roles work here—building teams that complement you, the 80/20 rule, removing energy drains, finding your sweet spot and working in it, etc. This is the place where coaching the person to find a role that really fits works best.

In any valley, what God does in you prepares you for what you will do in your next stage. An interesting implication of this truth is that patterns in the way God processes a person predict their future ministry. For instance, one businesswoman I interviewed for this book recounted three significant incidents where God used her in supernatural healing—all at times when she was angry at God!

That's a very unique pattern! I pointed out what those three incidents had in common and then offered a tentative statement about this person's call: "Given that God has taken you to this place repeatedly, I would guess that your call might involve impacting others in similar situations. God might use you to catalyze acts of faith or the supernatural in desperate situations or when people feel distant from God. How does that strike you?"

To use this technique you assume God strategically directs the character growth process, and that he plans to use the places he processes as foundations of one's call. So as a coach, you simply extrapolate into the future how God might make use of a person based on how they are being formed now. When I make this kind of coaching observation, I always allow coachees to decide whether or not it applies to their lives. It is their job to decide what things mean—I simply offer a potential insight and ask them to evaluate it.

Brian, a top-notch young leader I am coaching, was on staff in one church that split and two others where the senior pastors had moral failures, all by the time he was 27. That pattern seems significant. We might conclude that he will end up working with broken churches or broken leaders, or that God will use it to give him a special heart to care for the flock when a leader falls. The key to understanding how this will play out is homing in on *what God did in the leader's heart* during what happened.

> **Predictive Processing**
> *Here's how to use processing patterns to identify aspects of a person's call:*
>
> 1. *Identify a pattern in how God is processing the person over time and point it out to the coachee.*
> 2. *Extrapolate that pattern into the future as a statement about the person's call.*
> 3. *Ask the coachee to decide what it means.*

In Brian's case, God's dealings were around putting his trust in a system, a formula, a person or an institution (the church) instead of in Christ. Therefore, my observation would be that God will place Brian in situations where people are wounded by the system, where he will help them move beyond trust in what can be shaken to real trust in God. It probably won't turn out exactly like we foresee, but Brian's life story seems designed to develop him into a person who could do just that, and God is the author of that story.

The impact of these observations is less about getting the details exactly right than it is helping the person tune into a new point of view. That perspective moves us away from thinking that life just happens to us and we have to endure it, and toward believing, "God is in this—what is he doing?" This is the "called according to his purposes" perspective mentioned in Romans 8:28. When we engage life like someone who is called, where God is in everything, purposefully preparing us, *then* everything that happens to us ends up working out for good.

In Conclusion

Hopefully, this book has lifted back a corner of the great mystery of God's concourse with you. There is so much to discover about him just from looking at your own story! However, an even more amazing picture emerges when you become aware of God's hand in the calling journey of others. Because God has a unique Message he wants to communicate about who he is through each life, every life story you look at opens up a new dimension of his identity.

Now that you understand your own timeline, I want to encourage you to take the next step and learn to discover God's revelation in the journeys of others. Want to know more of God? He is there, in the people around you, revealing himself through their life stories. The timeline is like a translator that can unlock the story-language of God's dealings with each person.

So take a friend and walk him or her through the timeline. There is probably much more of God there than either of you know!

Appendix A: Glossary

Apprenticeship to Your Call: During the Releasing stage, leaders (particularly those in Outside Preparation) often apprentice under a senior leader, or in a limited version of their final convergent role.

Audience: The people or groups you are called to impact or serve.

Being Call: The part of Jesus you uniquely incarnate to your Audience. Also, all your individual Life Messages rolled together. Sometimes your being call is simply referred to as your "Message." Also see *Calling* and *Doing Call*.

Big Risk: A large step of faith based on the belief that you are called and that God is with you, which you must take at the beginning of the Releasing and Fulfillment stages.

Building an Altar: Creating a tangible reminder of what God has revealed to you about your call. This practice is based on what Abraham did after he first arrived in the Promised Land.

Calling: An external commission from God for others. See also *Doing Call* and *Being Call*.

Calling Event: A specific experience where God reveals a major piece of your life call.

Calling Journey: The well-defined path of stages and valleys leaders travel on the way to fulfilling their call.

Calling Statement: A written-out version of your call. The format used in this book is "your Message for your Audience through a Task/Role to create an Impact."

Coming Out from Under the Tree: The point when God calls you to leave the sphere of influence of a leader who has sponsored and empowered you and strike out on your own (See Daniel 4:10-12).

Convergent Role: A role in your Fulfillment stage that utilizes your best strengths a large part of the time to effectively convey your Life Message to your Audience. Based on concepts from J. Robert Clinton's *The Making of a Leader.*

Darkest Before the Dawn: For those in Outside Preparation, the last few years of the Preparation stage when you deal with the strongest feelings of stagnation and abandonment.

Day of Release: The sudden moment after the Valley of Wholeness when the leader in Outside Preparation is promoted into his or her calling sphere.

Descent: Another word for a valley. The downward-trending part of a calling stage.

Descent Before Lordship: The variant timeline pattern where the Valley of Dependence comes *before* Natural Promotion and not after. This most often occurs when an individual grows up in a Christian environment, runs from the Lord for a number of years (the valley), and then makes Jesus Lord at the low point of the valley.

Desert: See *Wilderness.*

Destiny: The future God has purposed for you. Here, it is used synonymously with "Calling."

Doing Call: What you are called to accomplish in life. Your life mission or life task, which channels your being call to your Audience. See also *Calling* and *Being Call.*

Faith Adventures: Faith-building experiences in the Natural Promotion stage where God directs you to go far out on a limb for him and you experience his provision.

False Opportunities: Near the end of the Preparation stage, opportunities for those in Outside Preparation to move into their arena of call, but which compromise that call. Also, a signal that the Day of Release is near. See also *Recruiting.*

Four Elements of Call (Message>Audience>Impact>Task): A framework for creating a Calling Statement that references both your Being Call (the Message) and your Doing Call (the Task).

Fulfillment Stage: The culmination of the calling journey, where the leader's being and doing calls function in partnership for maximum impact.

Impact: The reason for the call—how your life is meant to touch others. See also the *Four Elements of Call.*

Interlude: A short period after a valley before the leader moves into the next stage. Most common after the Valley of Identity for leaders in Outside Preparation.

Life Message: An individual, incarnational theme God works into your being, often during one of the valleys. Put together, the sum of your individual Life Messages is your Being Call.

Lordship: The one-time decision to put Jesus in charge of your decisions and your future. Sometimes it is experienced as part of a salvation experience, and sometimes a separate decision.

Mantle of Your Calling Identity: Taking on the mantle is accepting who God says you are in the fullness of your call. It involves both reorienting your self-concept and Presenting Yourself as Who You Really Are.

Natural Promotion Stage: The first stage on the timeline, where God's grace flows through your natural character (or lack thereof) and abilities to give you a taste of your call.

Preparation Stage: The season between the Valley of Dependence and the Valley of Wholeness which focuses on acquiring skills and experience to prepare you for your call.

Preparation, Inside: Going through the Preparation stage in a job within your calling area.

Preparation, Outside: Going through the Preparation stage in a vocation outside your calling area.

Presenting Yourself as Who You Really Are: A task in the Valley of Identity where you learn to introduce yourself as your calling identity.

Recruiting: The process late in the Preparation stage where leaders in Outside Preparation are sponsored or brought into their calling arena by another leader. See also *False Opportunities.*

Releasing Stage: The season of outward advancement between the Valley of Wholeness and the Valley of Identity where the leader builds Specific Skills needed to accomplish the call.

Season of Healing: A brief time (usually a year or less) God sometimes grants at the beginning of Preparation where things go well and the leader recovers after a difficult Valley of Dependence.

Shaping Event: An experience that provides the extra-ordinary stimulus needed to cause you to rethink your identity. Shaping Events are the seedbed of Life Messages.

Skills, General: Fundamental life competencies (like time management or emotional intelligence) that can apply to any role.

Skills, Specific: General Skills that are adapted to a certain, specific role. An important Releasing stage task for those in Outside Preparation is converting General Skills to Specific Skills in their calling arena.

Task: One's doing call. It describes the mission or role used to channel one's Being Call.

Timeline: A map of one's Calling Journey with each transition assigned a certain year or age.

Trigger Event: An experience (often negative) that catapults you into one of the three valleys.

Valley of Dependence: The first major season of adversity God leverages to shape your Life Messages. It focuses on building reliance on him instead of your raw gifts and natural abilities.

Valley of Wholeness: A second season of adversity between Preparation and Releasing that God uses to shape your character.

Valley of Identity: A third, late-life transition where the leader wrestles with identity, moving from doing to being and surrendering the call.

Wilderness: An extended season where God removes or reduces productive doing from your life to make room for internal formation. Synonymous with Desert.

Appendix B: Stage Characteristics Cheat Sheet

Natural Promotion Characteristics

- Begins immediately after Lordship commitment
- Usually one to nine years long (longest if Lordship commitment is made at an early age)
- Confirmation of call or Calling Events
- Rapid promotion based on natural ability
- Faith Adventures and being wild and radical for God
- A sense that God can do anything
- A taste of functioning in our call
- Self-sufficiency, hubris or ignoring counsel may lead one into the Valley of Dependence

Valley of Dependence Characteristics

- Focus: Dependence
- Averages two and a half years in length
- A negative trigger event often leads us into the valley
- Our character flaw (i.e. arrogance or self-sufficiency) may contribute to the crash
- Difficult time of failure or adversity
- Formation of key Life Messages
- Life not meeting expectations causes doubt, fear of missing it, feeling lost, anger at God or cynicism
- "Kicking against the pricks"—we fight against entering the valley
- We ask God to get us out of our circumstances and he explicitly refuses
- Isolation or rejection by friend or authority figure

Preparation Stage Characteristics

- Normally six to fifteen years long
- Usually starts three to eight years after Lordship commitment
- Onset may be marked by Season of Healing or entry into Preparation Role
- The leader gains experience and skills needed for his/her destiny role
- A focus on growing in ability to take responsibility and lead
- Sense of getting ready for God's future
- Living in tension—I have a call but am not yet released to it
- May be prepared inside or outside area of calling (see page 84)

Valley of Wholeness Characteristics

- Focuses on Wholeness
- One to three years long
- Often triggered by family or relational issues, life balance, unrefined gifts or hidden sins
- The Valley most likely to be entered voluntarily (by asking for help instead of being forced to get it)
- Deepening of Life Messages first formed in the Valley of Dependence
- Less prominent or sometimes skipped by those in the Inside Preparation pattern
- Those in Outside Preparation usually have a Day of Release connected with this valley

Characteristics of the Day of Release

- Darkest before the Dawn
- False Opportunities to compromise your call
- Being recruited into your calling sphere
- Major transition from a vocation outside your area of call to one inside it
- Abrupt promotion to a much larger sphere
- Often includes geographical move
- Functioning as an apprentice to your calling, often under a more senior mentor or leader
- Must take a big risk to believe in your call

Releasing Stage Characteristics

- Begins an average of 18 years after Lordship
- Average length nine years
- Time of expansion—an increase in accomplishment and responsibility
- Includes a Day of Release for those in Outside Preparation
- Big risk required to move into it
- Sense of apprenticeship to your calling
- Building General and Specific skills
- Temptation to coast later in stage

Valley of Identity Characteristics

- 15 to 30 years into your Calling Journey
- Averages four years long
- Often triggered by ejection from long-time role, loss of influence and favor, or financial reverses
- Stripping of identity in work, accomplishment or how others perceive you
- Healthy detachment from call: you can live without it, because Jesus alone is enough for you
- Completion of being call/Life Message formation
- A longer and more intense season for those in Inside Preparation; sometimes includes a wilderness time or dark night of the soul
- Focus moves from doing to being
- Finding success in the success of others instead of your own accomplishments
- Taking on the mantle of your calling identity
- Learning to present yourself as who you are
- Standing alone in the decision to be who you are

Fulfillment Stage Characteristics

- Enter by taking a big risk
- Rapid promotion—favor and open doors to larger influence
- Development of a Convergent Role that brings your best skills and strengths to bear to convey your Life Messages
- May move from organizational to personal influence (coaching, mentoring, writing, or empowering)
- Role may offer fewer responsibilities but larger influence
- Formation in the Valley of Identity is the basis for expanded impact
- Clarity about both doing and being calls
- Working with God instead of for him
- Urgency to make the most of the years left and leave a legacy. Thinking beyond your life span
- The joy and inner peace of a life well-lived

Appendix C: Calling Resources

On-line Timeline Builder Tool
A free, on-line tool for building your timeline is available at www.TheCallingJourney.com. Designed for use in conjunction with the book or as a stand-alone tool, the Timeline Builder will walk you through the process of creating and printing a color version of your timeline.

Companion Books
This book is part of a three-volume set that covers life purpose discovery, calling timelines and coaching others to find and follow their purpose. All three books are available from www.Coach22.com

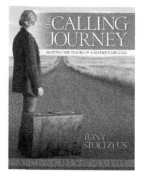

The Calling Journey
You are on a journey with God toward your destiny, and he has a different method of forming you at each step along the way. Understand the stages of calling development and learn how to create a calling timeline that shows how God is growing you into your destiny with *The Calling Journey*.

A Leader's Life Purpose Workbook
The more you know about your calling, the more you'll get out of your calling timeline. This in-depth life purpose workbook offers dozens of self-discovery exercises on topics like personality type, strengths, values, passions, what energizes you, your influence style, creating a convergent role and more.

Christian Life Coaching Handbook
This reference guide teaches the coaching skills needed to help others find and follow their destinies. Build around the same exercises in *A Leader's Life Purpose Workbook*, the handbook adds sample coaching dialogues, examples, application how-tos and an in-depth look at the techniques of life coaching.

Workshop Outlines
Workshop outlines and PowerPoint presentations for offering a workshop on the Calling Journey and helping others create their timelines are available through www.Coach22.com

Life Coaching Bookstore
Coach22.com offers a wide variety of books on life coaching, coaching skills and calling discovery, including many exclusive products by Tony Stoltzfus.

Made in the USA
Monee, IL
28 January 2023

26453861R00105